THE
INTRIGUE

Elizabeth Connell

LONDON, 1814

ISBN 978-1-09831-646-4 eBook 978-1-09831-647-1

Dedication, To:

Albert Chesley Brown, my big brother

Chapters

CHAPTER 1

The Wedding That Wasn't

He appreciated his surroundings. The magnificent church was a feast for the eyes; steeped in history, and redolent with incense. The morning sun shone through exquisite stained-glass windows; Corinthian columns outlined the side ones, repeated by the larger columns supporting the huge, barrel-vaulted ceiling. Enchanted by the splendor, Darrell found himself thinking about marriage as he waited for his cousin's wedding to begin. His desire to marry Anne Delford ended in failure. Perhaps he had learned a bit about love since then.

A near-death in Dublin last year resulted in a change of how he looked at life. Being more introspective, he realized how selfishness ruled him for years. Now he wanted to be useful—wanted to serve his country. With the war still going on in Europe, there were many opportunities to make a difference. Perhaps after it was over, he might find someone to marry.

Weddings are usually the backbone of a family, thought Darrell.

He listened to the vicar's sonorous words of the wedding ceremony, "If any of you know just cause or impediment why these persons should not be joined together in Holy Matrimony, come forward now."

As usual, a pregnant pause gave everyone the opportunity to respond. Silence held them spellbound until the huge doors opened with great violence and a man ran in, shouting, "Stop the wedding!"

The soldier ran up the aisle much distressed; blond hair disheveled, eyes wild with anguish. "This bride is betrothed to me!"

"That is not true!" shouted the startled bridegroom.

The vicar, overwhelmed by this unnatural scene, saw the man come face-to-face with the groom; anger radiating from him.

"You stole her from me while I was away fighting a war, you scoundrel," he spat out; hands clenched at his sides.

"That's not so, Miss Beckworthy accepted my proposal!"

Lord Hector Beckworthy rose to his feet from the front row, but before he could speak, fists began to fly. Tall and slim, Humphrey Beales did not compare favorably to this soldier with his muscular physique. In a moment, it appeared he was getting the worst of the fight. Deciding it should be stopped, Darrell stepped between the angry men, receiving blows before he separated the fighters by grasping each by the shoulder.

"That's enough, gentlemen. This is not the place for your quarrel."

The groom glowered at Darrell, as though he wanted to punch him too, blood running down his face. Lord Beckworthy approached to protect his daughter as she stood back from the fray, staring in shock.

"This discussion will move to the chapel," he said as he motioned them to follow him. The congregation sat silently until the combatants left the nave, then murmurs and exclamations arose. The mother of the bride sank into tears of humiliation.

When the group removed, he was unsure whether he should go, but hoped his uncle could handle the fracas. Concerned for Bernice, he wondered what this was about, since it seemed most unusual.

Vicar Lambert came back to the nave. "The gentlemen wish for your presence, Mr. Coletrane, come with me please."

As he entered the room, he perceived three angry men and a sobbing bride.

Lord Beckworthy spoke first. "Well, nephew, as usual you acted without thinking. How could you cause embarrassment to Humphrey?"

Surprise gleamed in Darrell's eyes, but he kept his composure.

"An intervention appeared to be the best course to quell such a public display of emotion, sir."

Still holding his handkerchief to his bleeding nose, the groom glared at him.

"Thank you, but I can handle myself. Now it appears otherwise after your arrogant interference. Name your seconds, Mr. Coletrane."

The expressive right eyebrow rose as he held Humphrey's angry gaze.

"No! My cousin only tried to help," said Bernice, turning to her father.

This change of events made his lordship realize the subject of the quarrel was being overshadowed by the proposed duel; the fact that the wedding was interrupted was more urgent.

"This is not the time or place for this. The issue is the conflicting claims for my daughter's hand. The whole family can feel humiliation after this unfortunate scene."

He looked at the two young men as he spoke; "Now, Mr.?? By god, I don't even know your name!"

"My name is Captain Mark Littleton, at your service, sir."

"Well, I want to know the substance of your claim. Mr. Beales, you will refrain from interruption."

All eyes turned to the soldier, whose face revealed righteous indignation at the manner of this request, but he knew he must bare his soul to have any hope of keeping his beloved.

"Your Lordship, I courted your daughter during her come-out Season."

The would-be bride was overcome; head bowed in shame.

"When I received my orders to return to Spain, we entered an understanding that she would wait for me, then we would marry—with your permission, my Lord."

Pain and hope were revealed in his eyes. No encouragement could be seen from either his lordship or Miss Beckworthy, and Humphrey glared again but kept quiet as ordered.

Growing uncomfortable, Darrell felt like a voyeur in this intimate confrontation. Clearing his throat, he said, "I fear I am *de trop*, sir. This conversation would be better in private."

"Yes, I will take my family home. These two gentlemen may call on me this evening. My daughter is too distraught to talk now."

After bowing, Darrell turned briskly and walked out of the room. The guests lingered, probably waiting for news; but he could not presume to speak, so returned to his seat.

Soon, Beckworthy approached the vicar; who announced the postponement of the wedding; thanking everyone for coming. The family retired to the chapel.

When Sir Giles Coltrane greeted his son, he said, "What a to-do! Did you quell another bout of fisticuffs?"

Eyes holding a devilish gleam, he said, "No, Father, once was enough. The groom called me out!"

"For saving his skin? What is his claim?"

"Apparently, I humiliated him."

"Saved him from a beating is my guess. Now, how is the problem of two grooms to be resolved?"

As he helped his father out to his coach, he said, "There is to be a meeting with Beckworthy this evening. I'm sorry for Bernice, she is overwhelmed; but will need to face the situation to decide which one she wants to marry."

The wedding breakfast was cancelled, so Darrell took his father to White's for luncheon, where they greeted several acquaintances. Over luncheon, their conversation came to Darrell's position at the Home Office.

"How is Lord Carter treating you, son?"

"Since I am one of the newest, I get simple tasks, but he always treats me with the utmost civility when we meet; probably from his respect for you, sir."

"Pleased to hear it; are you satisfied?"

Sitting for a moment before answering, he said, "Well, Father, I have not yet had a duty that was worthwhile—making appointments, running errands, glorified clerical work, I'd say."

"It's a beginning for you. Can't start at the top, you know."

Nodding his head, he hid his amusement. *A sermon, by Jove!*

As they started to leave, a greeting made him turn to see who had spoken.

"Chad!" Extending his hand, they shook with a strong grip.

"Haven't seen you in ages." A big smile showed his pleasure.

"This is my father, Sir Giles Coletrane. Father, this is Chad Peterman, a school fellow."

When Chad saw that he was leaning heavily on his cane, he said, "Darrell, would you be available for dinner this evening?"

They made plans quickly before they left; Father was in pain, and he must get him home.

A hackney coach took him to Harley Street, since he seldom walked in the city anymore after the lesson he learned in Dublin. The landlady took him upstairs to Chad's plain rooms, then the manservant received Darrell's hat and cane, and took him to the parlor. Entering the room with a broad smile on his face, they soon began to reminisce over old times.

"Do you remember Dawson from Oxford? Saw him in Portugal last year, now a Colonel in the Hussars; military life suits him."

"When were you there?"

"Been there on-and-off for several years."

"Oh, I hadn't heard that. What regiment are you with?"

Leaning forward, he said in a soft voice, "Special Services." After giving a moment to take it in, he added, "I am attached to the Foreign Office, doing undercover work."

As he revealed this, Darrell thought, *why is he disclosing this to me?*

"Takes all kinds of service to win a war," said Darrell.

With a grin on his face, he said, "Information is crucial." After a short pause, he added, "I heard you are at the Home Office now."

"Yes, I'm still learning about the government; struggling to find something useful."

The servant announced, "Dinner is served, sir,"

During the meal, they talked of sports and women.

"So, you've never married?"

Slowly he replied, "No, but I came close once—the other man won the lady. How about you?"

"Well, I prefer to wait until this war is over before I wed."

"Actually, I thought at my cousin's wedding this morning that I look forward to having one of my own at St. George's in the future—such a magnificent church. But you're right; not the time to start a new marriage."

Later, as they lingered over their Port, they reminisced some more about schooldays and their youth.

"That was a long time ago. Some of my crazy larks are best not recalled."

"Right you are! Remember the time . . . No, I won't embarrass you. I was glad to meet your father, although he did appear fatigued."

"Yes, a rather a long day for him, since he suffers with the gout."

"This fracas at St. George's this morning—you stopped a fight I hear. Good show!"

Laughing, he said, "Saved him a beating, but he showed no gratitude—called me out for humiliating him!"

"That seems harsh, what was his reason?"

So, Darrell explained the dual grooms and the boxing match, adding a little spice to make it comical.

Then he said, "I'm curious about what your Service is, Chad."

Studying him as they talked, Chad had made a decision.

"Have to tell you, I seldom speak about my work with anyone but my confederates, but I know I can trust you." He filled their glasses again, and settled for the story.

"It covers a broad territory; has brought rewards, and been dangerous—gathering facts to assist the army and navy to help them make decisions and maybe win battles. One of the most common espionage jobs in Europe is finding out each other's plans. Must infiltrate the enemies' operations to obtain valuable intelligence, and sometimes false information is passed. It takes a cool head to accomplish these things and I think you would be good at it."

While Chad explained, Darrell was turning it over in his mind.

"Since I am just learning about the procedures of the government, I can't see doing this type of work without the why, where and when background."

"True, it helps to understand it, but it is not necessary, believe me. My first operations were quite simple and there was a network for support. You are needed, Darrell."

Although Chad was not a striking-looking man, he had a friendly demeanor, with blond hair falling over his forehead; eyes gray, his nose and mouth average. About medium height, he moved with ease rather than with Darrell's athletic grace. *He could become lost in a crowd*, Darrell thought.

"First, I must take some time to determine whether I will pursue this further."

"Understood, and I'm sorry to drop it all on you, but it was the perfect opportunity. Perhaps we should meet again in a week?"

"Yes, thanks."

The morning after the cancelled wedding, Beckworthy paid a call on Sir Giles and Darrell. The butler showed him into the library where Giles was going through his mail.

"Good morning, I hope I find you well."

"Yes, thank you. What brings you out so early?"

A look of pain crossed his face. "Where is that young lad of yours? Owe him an apology."

When Darrell came in, they exchanged greetings. It was evident he was dressed for riding and was about to leave the house, and Hector couldn't help but admire his nephew's *savoir-faire*.

"Came to apologize to you, Darrell," he said in his pompous manner. "Said some things I shouldn't have yesterday in the heat of the moment."

"Thank you, sir, but I was not offended at such a tense time. How is my cousin?"

"Sadly, Bernice is not doing well since she was embarrassed by those two young whippersnappers; met last evening but did not resolve the matter, so I called a halt to either one marrying her under the circumstances, and I have ordered that there be no contact with her for a month. Time is what she needs to reflect on this horrific event and how it can be resolved."

Raising his eyebrows upon hearing the result of the fracas, Giles said, "You know your own daughter best, but this is rather harsh for a young woman who was almost married yesterday."

Hector looked pained. "Perhaps Bernice will suffer harm to her reputation but there should be a protracted period of consideration. Don't want to ruin her chances for her future, but neither do I want to see two suitors fighting over her. Humphrey has a nasty temper and it is impossible to have a discussion with him, since he disregards the feelings of others."

Having a devilish look in his eyes again, Darrell said, "Well, Uncle, I don't know either man well, but I must say that the Captain showed courage. Think he would make a good show of himself at Gentleman Jackson's boxing salon. In reality, he was protecting his rights to the bride he had assumed would be his."

"There will be a loser in the end. Let's hope Humphrey will try to be sensitive of the Captain's position and be fair. She may lose both!"

After several days, Darrell realized the idea Chad had expressed held his interest. Work at the Home Office was mostly clerical, like research and setting up meetings for the under-secretary. Reviewing the potential, he determined it would take time, maybe years, before he could rise to any meaningful level where he would be in on the decision-making. If he desired to make a difference for his country, he would have to be patient.

The need for reforms in England kept rearing its head, but the government leadership tried to quash it and continue with the current system. The danger of suppressing so much of the population when many people suffered did not seem to worry them. When he learned about the outrageous conditions under which a large portion of people lived, Darrell wished he could do something. The slums in the cities kept growing and the cost of bread rising. Sometimes he went to the worst areas, purchased meat pies from the vendors and gave them to the children on the streets.

The war in America dragged on and seemed senseless; taking many lives and causing damage. Why had Britain gotten into it? Already fighting on the Peninsula, the army was spread too thin.

The country needed every advantage possible. Should it mean doing some spying . . . By the end of the week, Darrell became more convinced that he might be helpful, so decided to talk with his father before going to Chad.

"Well, son, I never expected this."

"Sorry, Father, but I've given it a lot of thought and realize I may be of more use there than in the Home Office. The war on the continent must be stopped. If I can be a small part of it, I will do so. I'll meet with my friend again, to review the options."

"The frustration you feel is understandable—they move like snails at the Home Office. Find out all you can from this fellow before you commit yourself."

"Yes, sir." Father would wish him well but had just gotten used to having him home after his year in Ireland.

The meeting with Chad was drawn out and covered many topics, explaining operations he had been involved in and the results. Many times, facts were found that tipped the scales for the British. Then they reviewed the details: how Darrell would be transferred to the Intelligence Division of the Foreign Office, how he would be trained, and how he must keep it all secret.

"Agents must always be on the lookout for anything unusual; something which may be a clue to a plot by the enemy, even here in London. Then it becomes a way of life; your senses stay alert and you always watch what you say and do."

The rest of the evening was spent talking about some of Chad's experiences, with details of how missions had been carried out. The questions Darrell asked indicated his keen mind, just like he was at Oxford. Chad had no qualms bringing him into this difficult business. He admired Darrell's maturity, considering his reputation in the past as a rogue.

He stood at the top of the wide stairs; surveying the crowded ballroom with a slight smile on his handsome face, the dark curly hair set off his amazing deep blue eyes, which gleamed as he raised his right eyebrow. His elegant attire was worn with a stylish flair—the exquisite black coat and pantaloons relieved by a splash of color on his embroidered waistcoat and the sparkling white of his cravat, tied into the Mathematical fall. He portrayed a gentleman of the *Ton* who knew what he wanted; at six-and-thirty he had the self-confidence to take on anything.

A hand fell on his shoulder.

"What do you think?" said a deep voice. "Shall we go in?"

Turning slightly, he looked into the dark eyes of Lord William Smithson. Controlling his surprise, he deepened his smile.

"Yes, it is the usual squeeze."

"More pretty girls to meet," he said as they walked down the steps. The Castlereagh Ball always drew a crowd.

The two gentlemen were soon surrounded by friends and acquaintances and became separated. Darrell wondered why he had been approached and a foreboding flashed through him—he did not trust the man.

"Shall we show them how the Quadrille should be danced, Lady Strangford?"

Delighted; she said "Of course, Mr. Coletrane."

Dancing with her was a joy; tall and willowy, she had the face of an angel, but the look in her eyes suggested otherwise. The flashing dark eyes held a mystery, such as sultry nights and possibilities, but he took care not to encourage her. He relaxed into the dance, knowing his work would soon take him abroad, and he must keep a clear head.

Since Smithson favored the debutantes, he danced with several. *What happened to the chaperons or did the title overcome their sense?* Darrell thought.

Later that night, he enjoyed a brandy in his father's library. In a reflective mood, he looked back over his life as he often did now, and his thoughts turned to Dublin and his friend Colin Brownlow; whose family had contributed so much to his recuperation from his injuries. Staying in their home, experiencing their spiritual devotion and kindness had started him on his road to redemption.

Remaining friends of the Beverlys, after his letter of apology and their forgiveness, he realized he had not been worthy of Anne; and Joseph had been the perfect match for her. *Someday*, he thought, *I will meet the woman meant for me.*

Having received an assignment in Paris, they got details and their cover names. False papers provided the characteristics of their persona. Since Darrell moved well in society, he would be a visiting diplomat and Chad would investigate some leads in the underworld. This mission was a simple plan to get information from Napoleon's minions who were involved with preparations for the next battle; including procurement of supplies.

The two men sailed on a Navy frigate, and met a confederate in Calais who took them to Paris. As a diplomat, Darrell stayed in a classy hotel and went to public places where diplomats and officers gathered; presenting himself as worldly and sophisticated. A French gentleman, Monsieur DuPries, was his contact.

After a superior dinner, they sat over their wine. He scanned the room, and saw a party being seated near their table. His eyes remained for a moment on the beautiful woman facing him. Her companion was trying to entertain her, and she softened her demur countenance with a laugh, lighting up her whole face—it was amazing. Turning back to Monsieur, he watched the lady surreptitiously, especially her interesting green eyes.

After more drinks in the lounge, DuPries made up to two women who obviously would join them; so, he played along with the charade, but as he sat talking with his designated date, the mystery woman entered the room. Eyes met—one pair green and one blue. She reacted; raising her eyebrows for a moment, stunning him, then both looked away, but the memory lingered.

DuPries acted like a lady's man, easily charming the fair madams into dancing. Soon they adjourned to the Frenchman's rooms. The more he drank, the more DuPries's tongue loosened and Darrell obtained the facts he wanted. After some time with the woman, he pretended to fall asleep, then he extricated himself and left the room.

The next day, he went to a tavern frequented by officers. By careful listening, he heard a petty disagreement between two sergeants of a regiment preparing for a battle. The argument heated up, and they revealed much of what he needed.

That night he met Chad at the designated place; a quiet café in the River District. The scheme was that he would improve his dress while Darrell became more casual; wearing a drab coat to look bland. Pomade slicked his curly hair back from his brow, and he squinted so his blue eyes were less noticeable.

Comparing their reports, they decided they had what they needed. The battle would be at Laon, a town east of Paris. When they left the café alone, Darrell checked for anyone following him, then took a round-about route; using several hackneys and hansom cabs and shedding the coat before he got back to his hotel.

Back in London, after giving their report at the Foreign Office, Chad invited his partner to his rooms.

"Since we had no chance to discuss our mission, I thought it important to meet privately."

"I appreciate that, let's review everything to help me understand how it went."

"Overall, you did very well."

Settling back in his chair, he said, "We turned in valuable information that may save some lives. But I want to discuss our meeting at Café Canard; we were lucky to get away without being discovered."

Looking surprised at this statement, Darrell said, "I thought it went well. Explain it to me please."

"The conversation was too emotional and showed that we were pleased about something. Some heads turned our way, perhaps hearing a word or two which raised interest. We must not draw attention to ourselves, it might lead to speculation."

"Sorry, I didn't realize how much my feelings were noticeable. Yes, I was excited by our success—must practice a dead-pan demeanor, must I?"

"The main objective is to always *stay in character* of the person you are representing. That must be maintained until the mission is over, and we are removed from the scene. Must admit I got carried away myself in this instance."

"Well, that makes me feel a little better, but it is a good object lesson for me and I trust it will help me to adjust to this unnatural world."

Clapping him on the back, Chad said, "I'm sure you will do fine."

Leaving Chad's rooms, he thought of what had happened. Then he realized he must become himself again, now that he was back in London. Hailing a hansom cab, he returned to Broom Street, and repeated: *I must always remain aware of my behavior in my different roles.*

Going on a solo mission, Chad had specific orders to get information on the situation in Paris, since the Allies were getting close. Not liking the set-up, Darrell remembered that his friend had years of experience, but it still gave him an uneasy feeling.

When he did not return by the time expected, they thought he was gathering more intelligence, and realized it must be a distressing place to be now. The French still won some battles, but the opposing armies had far greater numbers. The Allies may enter the city any time and the people felt nervous.

Finally, word was received at the Foreign Office that Chad had been captured and was in prison, charged with spying. In the same communiqué, the French alluded to the British arrest of a Frenchman on the same charge. The Comte de Maitree was being held in London, and they offered to trade Archie Fraser for him.

Darrell learned about this offer, and volunteered to go on the mission. Since Lord Castlereagh was in Europe negotiating a peace proposal, Peabody interviewed him.

"Are you sure that you have enough experience to do this? These prisoner exchange meetings are difficult."

"Whatever it takes, sir, I will not fail Chad."

"All right, but take Clint Warden with you. A team is needed. Luckily, we have a bargaining tool in the Comte. Perhaps they will be reasonable."

A date was set for the meeting. Trying to be patient was hard, for who knew what Chad was going through? And now a new agent would be with him.

CHAPTER 2

Prisoner Exchange

The carriages traveled long and hard to make the appointed meeting place. Rain still fell and the cold penetrated. Darrell pointed out to Clint that they should practice their cover names; Webber and Croft, before they arrive. One of the men looked angrily out of the window as they reached the house, which appeared to be abandoned, so they approached with extreme caution.

Exiting the carriage, their woolen capes flapped in the wind as they strode to the door; looking around as they climbed the steps. The door was not locked. Their eyes met, and a questioning look was exchanged, then a pistol appeared in Darrell's hand.

The door opened and a short man with a wide girth greeted them.

"Right on time, Monsieurs," the man said.

"Is everyone else here?" asked Clint.

"Only M. Bonnall and the prisoner. The others should be here soon. Where is yours?"

"He is in place, under guard."

"Good, I am Brune."

Stepping back, he motioned for the two men to enter and took them across the hall to a library, where a fire burned in the hearth. The newcomers walked over to it with hands outstretched to the warmth. The short man presented a glass of brandy to each. A large table took up considerable space in the room, surrounded by six chairs. The long thick draperies at the window were shabby, and the room worn. They heard a thump upstairs and wondered who was up there—could it be Chad?

The sound of a carriage indicated the arrival of the others, so Brune hurried to welcome them and brought them into the library.

The man who entered first looked pinched from the cold, surveying the waiting men as he led his companion to the fireplace.

"Thank you for coming, Mr. Webber," he said as he bowed, "I am Monsieur Perey."

Webber nodded his acknowledgement, "This is Mr. Croft, my associate."

Then he introduced M. Ponce, his assistant, as well as M. Brune, the short man.

The door opened and another man entered. "Hello, Bonnall."

The fire still held their attention, and he put on another log; then offered brandy to the new arrivals.

When they surveyed the situation, it was obvious they were outnumbered in a strange house and their safety depended upon their captive; waiting in another coach under guard a way down the lane, hidden in a copse of trees.

An older man, Perey had black hair graying at the temples, giving him a distinguished air, with dark eyes and thick brows plus a short beard; he was of average height.

Ponce had red hair, bushy brown eyebrows over sharp blue eyes and a nose which looked like it was broken at least once, and he looked like he could hold his own in a fight.

The stature of M. Brune may be to his disadvantage, but his stern features indicated a no-nonsense attitude. At middle-age he had grown rather fat.

Next was Bonnall, the wild card in the group. Dressed as a gentleman, his manner revealed his edginess; with brown hair worn in the latest style and dark eyes that made his face look sardonic.

After everyone finished their brandy, Brune indicated they should be seated. The Englishmen chose chairs that stood near the door at an angle, so they would see anyone coming or going.

A tall, handsome man in his mid-thirties, with deep blue eyes and a well-trimmed beard; Webber had a muscular build.

Partner Croft was younger, with blond good looks and light blue eyes which twinkled when he smiled. Shorter than Webber and slighter, he didn't miss a nuance of the interaction of the four men, who were uneasy in this meeting with the British. Even M. Perey seemed stressed.

Continuing to play the host, Brune watched while attaché cases were opened to reveal papers. As people settled, Webber took the time to plan his strategy. The mission was urgent and must succeed.

Impatient to get on with it, Bonnall turned to glare at Webber in challenge, their eyes locked, and Webber's held until the other man looked away. A slight twitch at the corner of his mouth told Croft his partner was satisfied with the outcome of the staring match. Ponce reviewed his documents, and turned to M. Perey, who nodded.

"Let's begin this meeting with a review of our positions," he said. "Would you present first, Mr. Webber?"

He coughed, shifted in his chair and raised his eyes from his papers. *This must be handled carefully,* thought Darrell.

In a deep, clear voice, showing respect for now, he stated, "Thank you gentlemen. The two people we are considering here deserve our utmost efforts. Your country has a British citizen in your custody, and we have a French one in ours—both accused of spying. For the moment, we will concentrate on these facts so that we can resolve the issue cleanly and fairly."

Making a slight nod to Ponce, he settled back in his chair.

Sitting forward in anticipation, Perey began in a sonorous voice. "What you stated is true, Mr. Webber, but there is much more to it. Your man, Mr.

Fraser, was arrested in the act of spying against France. This is a grave offense. The penalty is death."

The menace in his voice was unmistakable as he glared from Webber to Croft, having drawn out the last word, leaving it hanging in the tense air of the room. Ponce glanced at Perey to see if he was finished before nodding to Webber to continue.

In a voice showing disbelief, Webber said, "Monsieurs, that fact is offset by that of the Comte de Maitree being caught trying to sabotage Britain's interests right in London! Also, the fact he had sought asylum from the French Terror in London and had been granted it, shows disrespect to his hosts." Pausing for a moment as though gathering his thoughts, he took his time.

Suddenly, he spoke again, causing several of those present to start in surprise. Now he had their full attention.

"Since we have been charged with this mission, we must act in haste to restore our two prisoners to their own sovereign states." In a hard voice, Webber continued. "We can draw this meeting out for days, but there would be no benefit to anyone in doing that." Eyes set on Perey, he dared him to interrupt. "Let us agree to complete this exchange, receive our respective prisoners with decorum, and be on our way."

A commotion arose, with mutterings and a few curses from Bonnall. Chairs scraped against the floor, but Webber sat at ease, awaiting the next salvo.

Leaning toward his two minions, Perey kept a lid on Bonnall's rage and finally reached an agreement with them, or overrode them. Perhaps he remembered his precious Comte was cooling his heels in the coach down the road and would not appreciate any delay.

"Correct, Mr. Webber, we could go around and around with accusations and rebuffs, but the result will be the same. Let's get it done."

"Thank you, Monsieur."

He rose from his chair and made a bow.

A quick discussion settled the procedure for the exchange. A lantern was taken out into the yard and Croft signaled the waiting coach to come in while Webber stayed in the hall so he would be ready to receive Archie when they brought him down. The prisoner was moved to the head of the stairs, but being dark up there, Darrell could not get a look at him. Then he turned his head as the Comte was being led into the house by the two guards. The sneer on his face was aggravating. They held him in place.

"All right, bring your prisoner down now."

Perey motioned to the men holding Fraser, and they moved the injured man down the stairs, half carrying him.

With difficulty, Darrell controlled his desire to go up those stairs; for he wanted to run to Chad, to free him from the rough handling. Now he realized why they agreed to move along; because it would not suit their purposes to deliver a dead prisoner.

The Comte was also brought forward, with not a mark on him.

A brief exchange of words completed the hand-over, and they moved to the fireplace. Then Darrell went to Chad, who was barely conscious. The coach was still at the door, so Darrell scooped him up and carried him out while Clint gathered their papers from the table, hardly able to contain his emotions. *The bastards, they've tortured the poor fellow almost to death.*

The most important thing was getting away from here as soon as possible, for the safety of them all.

Administering to Chad with brandy from his flask, he tried to make him as comfortable as possible on the seat with thick robes around him. Clint and the guards took the other coach, and they all moved off. There was no talking because he slipped into unconsciousness, which was a blessing since the road was rough.

After a couple hours of travel, they reached Eibeu and entered the Renard Inn. Worried about him, they asked if there was a doctor nearby, but there was not. The wounds on his face were treated by cleaning the cuts and bruises before applying basilicum powder. Bandages were fashioned from one of Darrell's shirts.

After that he laid on a bed for a few hours, while food was ordered, plus extra bread, cheese and ale for their travel tomorrow.

"This chicken stew is excellent." Clint scraped his bowl. "Too bad he couldn't eat some."

"The guards have treated him horribly and who knows when he last ate anything."

"Makes me wish we had roughed up the precious Comte on the way, but we're gentlemen, not barbarians."

"Well, at least we have our principles. Best get some sleep, Clint, we have a half-day of travel before we reach the coast. Let's hope our ship will be on time."

After sleeping some that night, Chad seemed a little stronger in the morning.

"Are you able to eat anything, or take any liquids?"

The face was a swollen mass of cuts and bruises. One eye would not open, but his other held a twinkle for Darrell. He could only drink some ale, and he didn't try to talk through his mangled lips.

Lunch was eaten without a stop and the sway of the coach kept putting Chad to sleep.

"Thinking about Chad's condition, it will take a long period of rest and healing for him to recover, and I believe London will not do. So, I will ask my father if I can take him to Banford Grange for a while. A nurse can be hired to care for his wounds."

"Good decision, Darrell, since he won't want anyone to see him this way. Perhaps we should take him directly to Broom Street when we disembark."

Near La Havre, they started scanning the harbor for ships.

The crossing was rough, and the frigate's doctor simply looked Chad over and gave some pain medicine. "You did all that can be done for now. The beating was severe."

"Yes, the French took their vengeance with their savagery."

When they reached London, they proceeded to Broom Street straightaway and Darrell went in first to greet his father.

"Glad you've come back!"

"Yes, sir, we brought an injured man with us, it is Chad. Can he stay here for a few days?"

Looking surprised at first, his face crinkled into a smile. "Of course, son; are his injuries serious?"

"Yes, he had a tough time of it and may become feverish. His captors did their worst and it shows on his face. I do not want his landlady to see him; so, brought him here."

"Very sensible."

"Let's bring him in then. Will the blue room be all right?"

"Yes, I'll ask Jenkins to have it prepared."

"Thank you, Father." Darrell grasped his arm in gratitude. Not being demonstrative men, they rarely embraced, but he instinctively showed his deep feelings.

A cold wind whipped along the street as he carried him into the house. While the servants prepared the room, they placed him by the fire in the library.

"Father, this is Clint Warden, whose help has been invaluable."

His head rolled back on the tall chair and Chad appeared to be sleeping, but more likely unconscious. A footman was sent to fetch his manservant; the message only indicated an injury. Another went for the doctor.

Shuddering at Chad's appearance, Wilkes asked, "What happened to him? What are his injuries?"

Taking him over to the window to talk, Darrell said, "Must keep this quiet, you understand. Having been imprisoned in France for some time and tortured, he could not tell us anything, and he was often unconscious during our long journey from Rouen, but he can only take liquids—didn't want food, so we did not remove his clothing and only checked his facial injuries. A doctor has been summoned, and should be here soon. A room is being prepared for him."

Being an old soldier, Wilkes's stoicism was obvious.

"After the room is ready, I will carry him up," said Darrell.

"Oh, no sir, I will care for my master. I brought some supplies for him in case his baggage did not survive his journey, and he will feel better just getting out of those clothes and into a loose nightshirt."

Some of his clothes had to be cut away, revealing more injuries, and Darrell's anger boiled over.

"How could they be so cruel?"

Doctor Drake arrived and Darrell stayed only long enough to give a brief overview of how he got his injuries.

"A dangerous thing, to be in France," he said.

A thorough examination revealed even more injuries than the face. Ribs were cracked, one broken; the right leg mauled; but the most distressing was the evidence of repeated kicks to his abdomen.

"If there is internal bleeding from damage to the organs, he cannot be saved."

Standing by, stony-faced as he heard the dire news, Wilkes's anger seethed inside him.

"That's all I can do for him until morning. Here are some medicaments to relieve the pain. The ribs are wrapped, but he will still suffer until they are healed."

"Thank you, Doctor, I feared grave injuries, but not as many as you have found. It is not necessary to caution you, but it would be best no one hears that he was in France."

"Of course, Mr. Coletrane."

"So glad you are here to nurse him, Wilkes. Your devotion is evident and you must ask for anything you need. Also, we will hire someone to spell you."

"Oh, no, I will do it myself. Beg your pardon, but I can tend him best."

"Surely you are right, but you cannot go without rest, so we will prepare a room for you."

"Would prefer a pallet in this room, sir, as I could not rest away from him."

Back in the library, Darrell relayed the shocking news to his father and Clint.

"Sadly, his life is still in danger as his internal injuries are life-threatening. Only time will tell."

Turning to his father, he said, "Thank you, Father, for accepting him into your home. Diligent care is needed and Wilkes will do his best, but he will need a nurse to help him. Do you have someone who can be discreet?"

"Yes, I employed Mrs. Ustus at times when my gout acted up; and I'm sure she can be trusted."

Looking thoughtful for a moment, he said, "I think we must consider our servants as they know everything that goes on and are often guilty of gossip with others on this street. Perhaps we should develop a story about his injuries. What do you think?" and he turned to both young men.

Minds busy, Darrell and Clint locked gazes.

"A fall from his horse would not explain his battered face."

"No, you are right." Clint's brow furrowed.

They sat quietly for some time, each trying to come up with a plausible explanation.

Then his father said, "My servants do not know he was in France unless the doctor let it slip, so we'll consider how he might be injured here in England. Perhaps it happened away from London. Where are his people from? Or where might he have traveled?"

Turning it over in his mind, Darrell realized the servants were not stupid—they would hear of an altercation of his friend. But how would they hear of it since he and his father always remained discreet now that he had gone into espionage? No, they must think of something unusual that happened outside of London.

"Since we arrived in a well-traveled coach and four, I had been on a journey; where from? The servants probably heard from the butler of the grave condition of the young man, and also know of the footmen's messages to fetch the valet and the doctor. Maybe it happened in the south, at a coastal location—perhaps a severe attack by a gang of sailors at the port or in an Inn? The beating had taken place some days or weeks ago, and why did I not stop it, or have been injured myself?"

As he voiced his thoughts, his father had an idea.

"How about a trip you three made to Dover, and you two went to visit some old friends and left Chad at the inn. That night, a group of toughs took offense during a discussion of smuggling and when they got verbally abusive, the landlord requested they all take it outside. The young man could not quell the quarrel and was beaten by the drunken men. When Darrell and Clint returned late that night, they found him in his room in poor condition. The landlord insisted he had no knowledge of who the toughs were, so they could not be sought for punishment. But the injuries appeared to be so bad they called in a doctor; who merely treated his face and said he needed rest before traveling."

"After several days, they bundled him into a coach and headed for London, where they determined he should go to Broom Street instead of his rooms."

The story impressed Darrell and Clint.

"That is a rational explanation, Father, and I think it covers all our concerns."

"Yes, quite perceptive, sir."

It would be dropped around and soon would be accepted as truth.

A report must be made at the Foreign Office, so they went to see Lord Peabody; where they told him of the exchange.

"So sorry to learn of Chad's condition, but it is not unusual for the French to torture their prisoners, like spies," he said.

"But it seems to me, your lordship, that an extreme amount of savagery was used against Chad in this case; almost like a vendetta."

"What are you saying? Do you have some knowledge you did not divulge?"

Before replying, he must remember that he didn't know much about Lord Peabody or others in the department, like Smithson.

"How much do we know of the people here? Might someone here be resentful? Even worse, might we have a double agent in our midst? Were there any other incidents similar, or unusual?" Wanting to go further, he must be prudent; *don't give away too much*, he thought.

"That's preposterous, Mr. Coletrane!"

As Clint followed this interchange, he thought, *What Darrell said might be true.*

"Yes, I agree, your lordship, but our type of business could lead to unscrupulous behavior, don't you think?"

Lord Peabody grimaced. "I'll have you know, I fully trust in all our agents, even the women. They are all loyal Englishmen. Why, Lady K is one of our best! We get reliable information from them all, not meaning some are better than others."

"Any captured in what appears to be a trap and severely tortured?" said Darrell, trying to keep his anger and disgust under control.

Lord Peabody appeared distressed. "Don't recall such an occurrence in recent times. For several years during the Terror, anyone suspected of spying would soon be executed. Joseph Fouché was ruthless."

"Yes, he still is, your lordship," said Clint; trying to take attention off Darrell. "And still runs an efficient spy network throughout France."

"Perhaps Chad got careless and blew his cover," said Lord Peabody.

"Even though I am new to this operation, he had years of experience and was thorough and careful, so I cannot imagine he slipped up."

He agreed, but his feathers had been ruffled by Darrell's suggestions. Is *there a double agent?*

Improvement was slow, and Chad's ribs and abdomen continued to give him excruciating pain. Lying motionless helped, but one must shift positions sometimes, and he still could not sit up.

Disturbing dreams of the torture he had undergone were still vivid. The savage, cruel faces of his captors appeared in them. Somewhere at the margins of his mind, he thought he had seen Lord Smithson, but must be mistaken. Why would he be with the French?

Darrell refrained from asking questions about his experience since he didn't think Chad could withstand reliving it, but he was anxious to find out how he was trapped and who he saw.

CHAPTER 3

Mesmerizing Green Eyes

Sitting by himself eating lunch at White's, he saw an old friend, Jones.

"Well, it's ages since I've seen you, Darrell. How are you?"

"Fine, thank you."

"Just the man I need. My party for the Opera tonight is short because Harry cancelled. Would you be able to attend?"

"Yes, I would be happy to. Have not been to one for some years. What is playing?"

Giving him details, Jones included where to meet him in front of the theatre.

That night, he made introductions and Darrell gave his arm to his date, Sandra Webster.

Once seated in Jones's box, he sat back and looked around. As he scanned the boxes opposite, his eyes locked with the green eyes he saw in Paris, and time stood still; no sound, no movement reached his senses and her face looked flushed before she broke the connection, lowering her head in a sort of nod. Breathless, he couldn't make a move. *So, she must be English,* he thought.

"Are you all right, Darrell?" asked Jones.

"Yes, certainly. Thought there was someone I knew, but I was mistaken and who is the lead singer tonight?" He checked his program before looking at the stage.

The next day he received a note from the Foreign Office. After a meeting with Peabody about a mission, he was reviewing his check-list, when he crashed into a body—grabbing her with both arms to keep her from falling.

"So sorry. Looking at papers instead of where I was going," he said, and looked down into the greenest eyes he'd ever seen.

"Yes, me too," she murmured, looking up into the bluest eyes on earth.

"Perhaps it's time for an introduction; Darrell Coletrane, at your service."

Reaching out her hand, she said, "I am Lady Kerrigan." They stood in stunned silence for a moment, before he said," My pleasure; I am glad to finally know your name."

That beautiful face lit up as she smiled at him. "Now it seems we have something in common," and she gestured to the hallway.

Hesitating a moment, he worried about how much he could say.

"Would you care for some refreshment? There is a sweet shop down the street."

"No, I don't usually meet with strangers in a public place, sir," she said with a mischievous look.

"A pity. Perhaps next time we meet, and I hope there will be a next time."

Courteous farewells, and they were gone, an opportunity missed. *But may be for the best,* he thought and remembered Peabody saying, "Lady K." *So that's her.*

A new mission was given to them, this time in London. There was a strong suspicion of more spies among the émigré community.

Assuming deep disguises, Clint dressed as a servant named Paul Jenson, cut his blond hair and dyed it dark brown, and affected a limp in his left leg. Finding difficulty in changing his appearance enough without altering his debonair gentleman persona, Darrell used a beard and shorter hair; as well as his squint and eye glasses to disguise his blue eyes, and used the name Horace Devine.

So, he would need to mix with the *haute ton* on this mission. By attending routs and gambling salons, he might pick up some gossip. He recalled that some émigrés had been friends of Comte de Maitree, who was now in France. His French accent sounded genuine so people accepted him in the group at the Soirée.

"Oh, Ma Chéri," a handsome matron cried, "Pleased to meet you. Have you been in London long?"

With a chivalrous bow, he said, "My pleasure, Madame; and I am fortunate in my many visits to this fair city; not comparable to Paris, of course! But it offered refuge to me when needed."

Those squinting blue eyes observed her swelling bosom at the mention of Paris, and he wondered if she felt pain of absence. He led her to a settee in an alcove, and they talked intimately; eager to impress him with her knowledge of London's émigré community. She disclosed many tidbits of information, including the arrest of the Comte de Maitree and his return to France.

"A sacrilege, as he was only doing his duty to Napoleon!"

"Ah, Madame, but clumsily, to be caught."

He gave her an opportunity to tell him more.

"Yes, he is too arrogant in his approach. Now, it is a different story with Monsieur Martineau, who is always on guard and preserves his anonymity with the English gentlemen. They think he loves them, but he uses them for his own ends—finding out their secrets." She smiled broadly as though it was a great joke.

"Mon dieu!" said Darrell. "How clever! How does he do it?"

Eyes glittered as though she held a treasure inside and wanted to share, she said, "He consorts with the ladies with well-placed husbands! You would be surprised what a lady will divulge under the allure of the bed."

"Oh, how naughty!" declared Darrell. "That is too much! Surely they must be stupid or else he is such a remarkable lover that they are not aware of their mistakes."

"Yes, it is a joke on the Stoic English and their pride! Let me point him out to your attention when he comes."

"Is he expected tonight, Madame?"

Acting as though in eagerness for a rare treat, he raised his eyebrows.

"Oui, I believe there is a lady here whom he wishes to meet."

"I will look forward to it."

Now he had a name and soon an introduction, so he would ask Clint to check on the morrow. For now, he would size up the scoundrel.

Having chatted with several people, he looked at Madame Bignoir leading a tall gentleman toward him, and noticed his unmistakably continental flair, with a swarthy complexion, black hair and eyes, and boredom on his face.

"See, Monsieur Devine, he came!"

The man seemed surprised as he made his bow.

Turning to her, he frowned, "So this is your find! To what do I owe the pleasure?"

She looked put out and perhaps embarrassed.

"But you are always seeking new acquaintances. Are you so anxious to meet Mademoiselle Claude that you cannot spare a moment?"

Relenting, he took her hand to his lips.

"Non, I assure you I am grateful."

The man spoke in fluent French as though still in Paris, but Darrell bore up under the scrutiny.

"Oh, do not let me keep you, Monsieur, we may have other opportunities to converse."

Martineau raised his eyebrows and gave a shrug. "Perhaps, au revoir."

So, his cover had been blown! What tipped him off? Or was he indeed bent on meeting the intriguing lady? So, he kept an eye on Martineau just long enough to see which woman he approached, then left the room.

Going over the incident on his way home, Darrell tried to perceive what he did wrong. Was it possible that Martineau also knew him as Coletrane? Did they meet before? Maybe in France? Or had someone put him on his guard against an English spy? Was there a cuckoo in the nest? He was aware of such a possibility since Chad's arrest. Perhaps they should check on Smithson, since he had a vengeful nature, and hated Darrell since schooldays.

Changing his disguise again, just in case; he realized it was harder to be undercover near home. Once he was finished with this mission, he would take Chad to the Grange to rest in the country for a while.

A message was sent to Clint, requesting his attendance at Broom Street, then he visited his friend, who was just finishing his breakfast of porridge and tea.

"How are you feeling this morning?"

A slight nod was the best he could do.

"Hope that means that the pain is less than yesterday." So, he nodded his head again, grimacing.

Gently laying a hand on his arm, he asked, "Do you mind if I talk with you?"

He raised his hand as he settled back down, and Darrell indicated that the nurse should leave the room.

"Had an unusual experience last night." Then he briefly told what transpired with Martineau and Bignoir, dwelling on the rejection.

"Did anything like that ever happen to you?"

A slight shake of his head was the answer.

"Either I did not wear a sufficient disguise or someone warned him about me."

"War...ning," mumbled Chad.

"Yes, I realize I will have to change again or avoid this fellow, and I wonder if someone in our department is too closely connected in the émigré community. Were you suspicious that something wasn't right before you were arrested?"

Nodding his head, his good eye opened wider.

"Wish you were able to talk, Chad. Could you write?"

When he raised his hand a little, it pained him, so he shook his head.

"All right, I will set Clint on it and see what he can discover. In the meantime, I will avoid contact with them all."

When Clint arrived, Darrell took him to the mews, and drove out of the city in his curricle before conversing. The streets were so crowded with carriages, carts, and vendors that one had to watch every step; the constant noise made it impossible to carry on a private conversation.

After they reached a quiet country lane, Darrell told Clint what occurred last evening.

"This Martineau must have been warned about you."

"Perhaps my disguise was not good enough, but he just blew me off and walked away."

"Does this tie in with what you told Lord Peabody about a possible double agent?"

"That could explain a lot."

"Then we must be extra careful as it would be a dangerous situation."

"I am becoming more inclined to think it is, and I think we should proceed as though it is, and try to discover who. Perhaps we should set a snare of our own since Chad is not well enough to talk about his experience yet, and is still in tremendous pain, poor fellow."

By the time they returned to Broom Street, they had discussed possible ways to trap a traitor.

Clint immersed himself into the émigré community to try to get a clue, and picked up some names and locations as he sat in different pubs and inns around the area. The 'working man' disguise made him almost invisible. When he overheard a man at the Coach House Inn in south London grumbling about having to travel to Bath with Lord Ainsworth, and his friend laughed at him, making him angry; he paid attention.

"This is not funny, Kurt! I must leave Bertha behind and who knows what trouble she will get into."

"I'll take care of her for you," said his buddy, snickering.

"Stay away from her if you know what's good for you."

"What does he have to go to Bath for?"

"Oh, some Frenchman invited him to a house party."

Leaning closer to Kurt he said, "Maybe there's foreign intrigue to be done, since he has some Frenchie friends, that he's thick with."

When they left the inn, Clint followed the valet, making discreet inquiries from a servant to determine which was Lord Ainsworth's house. After changing his clothes, he went to Darrell's home.

"This could be important," he said. "The valet's talk of Frenchmen made it seem it was a common occurrence."

"Yes, we will go to Bath and pick up the trail. Can you get a look at Ainsworth?"

"Of course, if I hang around Clarges Street."

"If there is a house party, I must go as myself to get an invitation."

"But if Martineau is present, what will you do?"

"Overplay my own persona—look like an absurd fop. That way, he will not be on guard. Have had experience at that, you know."

A devilish expression changed his face as he spoke, and Clint; who had not known him in his wild days, was surprised at this side of his personality.

There were rumors of dissipation in years past, and they still came up at times; but he did not believe them, perhaps he should!

"Will I be your servant again?"

"Yes, a fop needs a valet. And you will be able to mingle below stairs with the other valets also, which could be beneficial."

Both men prepared to be absent from London for some weeks, and Darrell made a report to Lord Peabody, hoping that it would remain a secret. Of course, if someone else from the department was in Bath, they would recognize him; but it was a chance he would have to take.

CHAPTER 4

The House Party

After arriving at Bath, Darrell took an apartment at the White Hart Inn on Stauls Street, so they would be in the center of activity. The Pump Room, where people gathered to see and be seen every morning, and the Assembly Rooms were nearby.

The first morning, he signed the Guest Book; now everyone will know he is here. He scanned the room and saw several people he knew and soon had a group around him, asking questions, like: "Where have you been, abroad?"

Lady Gantre came up to him, as brazen as ever.

"Well, Coletrane, what a pleasant surprise! Did you just arrive?"

Performing a creditable bow, he took her hand, touching her gloved fingers with his lips. "Delighted to meet you again."

"Too kind. Are you staying in Bath or are you on your way to Brighton?"

Hiding his annoyance at her directness, he kept the smile in place as he said, "My dear, if I knew my intentions, I would share them. However, I try to live my life without plans; so boring!"

"Always the opportunist. Are you following a woman as you often used to?"

The gaiety seemed strained, and he wondered what she was up to, as it appeared that she intentionally pressured him.

He placed her hand on his arm as he turned away from the group, and said, "Let us take a stroll, dear lady," as cheerfully as possible. "We can seek a tête-á-tête, if you would allow."

As they strolled down the length of the room, they avoided the crowd around the man serving the famous waters.

"Surely your ladyship is not here to take the waters."

"No, Mr. Coletrane, I am visiting my niece, Sarah Renwick."

"How delightful! But I do not recall meeting her."

"Not surprising, since she resides in the north. Her father died recently and her brother brought her to Bath for a visit."

"Oh, then, perhaps I will meet her."

Looking sharply at him, she said, "I should protect her from a rake such as you, Mr. Coletrane, since she is an innocent who lives a cloistered life in the country."

As Darrell's expressive eyebrow rose, he replied in a hurt voice, "MOI? How could you be so cruel, Madame?"

At that, she laughed—a deep, spontaneous guffaw.

"Oh, you are priceless, Mr. Coletrane. How can you in good conscience affect such innocence?"

He placed his hand to his heart and inclined his head.

"Maybe she would be better to avoid my acquaintance, my lady, and I may find her too young in any event."

Deepening his voice, he added, "Perhaps I enjoy the more mature over the young ingénues."

Her eyes widened in response to his veiled invitation.

"Really, sir, you are still as audacious as ever, so I will keep you away from Sarah."

Then she removed her hand and stepped back to protect herself; and raised her gaze to perceive a friend.

"I must leave you now, Marie is here."

Relieved, he did not intend to be ensnared to distract him from his mission, so he left and crossed the street to his hotel. It was such a beautiful day and the sun was shining brightly on the Cathedral. How he longed to go inside for some reflective solitude, but refrained as he had a job to do.

The bags and trunks were unpacked and Clint had arranged everything neatly in Darrell's rooms; his valet's disguise as Baxter was complete. His clothes were a shade under the quality a gentleman would wear, and his hair was still brown and trimmed short.

Travelers of modest means frequented the White Hart. The York House enjoyed the patronage of the high sticklers, and he did not expect to see many of his acquaintance here—so was surprised to meet Wally Finchly on the stairs.

"Is that you, old boy?"

Blinking as though to clear his vision, his mind busy on his plans, he did not notice his old friend.

"By George," said Darrell, offering his hand. " Have not seen you in an age." And they exchanged proper greetings.

"Must get together, as I'm sure we both had many adventures since last we met."

"Say, it would be my pleasure to invite you to dinner this evening. Are you traveling alone?"

"Yes, I am."

"Then I can entertain you in my rooms; would seven o'clock be convenient?"

After completing their arrangements, they went their separate ways. Again, Darrell looked longingly at the Bath Cathedral as he emerged from the Inn. *Just for a few minutes,* he thought. He entered at the big double doors, and his breath caught in his throat, *magnificent!"*

A group of visitors stood to one side near the back. A few words spoken in French attracted his attention, but he was not able to come closer without being obvious, so went up the aisle to take in the splendor of the Sanctuary. In turning to see the ceiling and the windows, he recognized two of the faces—he had seen them at the émigré party in London.

If there is an important meeting here in Bath; they must be making plans.

The valet answered the door and showed Wally inside to a well-appointed room with comfortable sofas by the fireplace, carved walnut chairs by a round table, and striped green wallpaper. A chest by the window displayed bottles and glasses. Then Darrell came from the bed chamber to greet him.

"Looking well, my friend. What brings you to Bath? Not the most genteel of society."

"Well, London can be a bit too hot at times, so I like to rusticate once in a while."

Wally grinned. "Still up to your old tricks, are you, and who is she this time?"

After he poured drinks for them, he indicated one of the sofas, and sat on the other, where they studied each other. Darrell noticed a look of stress on his face. He still had a playful look in his gray eyes, and his hair was as dark as ever, but he definitely showed the passing years.

"Well, it is not a lady this time; just running too hard for too long. Now, tell me all your news," so he settled back into the cushions and sipped his wine.

Twisting his glass in his hands, he said, " Lost my wife last year."

"So sorry, where you married long?"

"Yes, for ten years. She was Theresa Hodges from Bristol, a lovely girl. Had to be a saint to marry a Navy man, with so many long separations. Have two children, a boy and a girl. Thank God for them; my mother took them under her wing."

After Wally shook off the melancholy, he smiled. "When will you do it? Not getting any younger, you know." Darrell stirred in his seat; felt a pang in his heart, and pushed it aside again. *Not the time or place to recall that,* he thought. "Can't think of it until this war is over."

"Which shouldn't be too long now, I think Bonaparte is on the run."

The knock on the door signified the arrival of dinner and Baxter directed the servers as they set up the table.

"Which wine would you prefer, sir?"

"The Chablis please."

Moving to the table, Wally said, "This looks promising—I could eat an ox."

"Bon Appetit," said Darrell.

During their long meal, they reminisced over schooldays, recalling the boys of their House and the rigors of those days at Harrow.

"What ever happened to . . ." was heard often.

"Remember that bully who caused so much trouble?"

"There were several bullies, Wally," laughed Darrell, "believe I was thought to be one myself at times."

"No, I'm thinking of the one who was so cruel. Started with an S."

"Oh, do you mean William Smithson? Yes, he assumed his title right after Oxford, but his father didn't leave him any money, so he went to India to make his fortune."

"I still recall his chastising those poor young boys at Harrow—already tearful from being away from home for the first time. I wonder what happened to him to make him so spiteful and cruel?"

"I heard that he was ignored by his parents and raised by servants. He must have been a lonely little boy, and lashed out," said Darrell

Since dinner was finished, Baxter rang for the staff to clear as Darrell served Port by the fire.

Talk went back to the war, and he told of some great battles he was in, including Trafalgar.

"Been pretty lucky; never had a ship shot out from under me like many of my friends. A nasty business and the loss of life is staggering."

Then Wally recounted the fracas in 1796 when they chased the French to Bantry Bay, where they proposed to help the Irish have their own little revolution.

"This Nor' Wester came up from the Atlantic before they reached Cork, and the troop carriers couldn't land. Some broke up along the cliffs; others foundered in the Straight or were harassed by our ships and driven back to France. A couple years later, they tried again up north, but it was not successful."

"Spent last year in Ireland," said Darrell, "and I've heard many hair-raising tales of the uprisings, like the one in 1798. On top of that, there's the whole fight for Catholic Emancipation. The Irish are a fighting lot and keep trying; have to admire them. Made some good friends there, like the Brownlows. Lord Brownlow is fighting that issue in Parliament. This fellow, Daniel O'Connell, is their leader and it will happen. Did you know, when the measure had passed in 1801, the King vetoed it; was adamantly against it? That and America were his key issues in those days."

How refreshing it was to talk with someone who understood it all, so Darrell relaxed and touched on subjects that interested him. He felt he could trust Wally, and he assumed it was mutual, but he was obliged to stop short of telling of his spy work—couldn't betray his colleagues. Would like to discuss his suspicions about Smithson, but could not.

About to leave, Wally said, "I say! How about I get an invitation for you to the House Party I'm to attend? The host was a Navy man until a serious leg injury put him ashore. Estate is in Westbury just south of Bath. Are you available for a couple weeks?"

"And who is the host?"

"Lord Jasper Betterton's house; a friendly chap. I would enjoy your company; might get in some good riding and hunting. What do you say?"

Since Wally's face was a study of anticipation, how could he refuse? Especially since it was the very House Party he needed to attend.

"Of course, and we'll have lots more to talk about. Thank you for asking."

CHAPTER 5

It was another glorious day. The countryside began to show signs of the coming spring, with green dressing the rolling hills.

The coachman slowed for the village of Westbury; his team prancing along in unison and their hooves creating a clamor as they struck the cobbles. The showy black horses carried a display of fancy harness brass which glinted in the sun. People turned their heads in case royalty had come into their midst, but when no crest graced the doors of the coach, some of them lost interest; but many waved anyway. The tall, handsome gentleman opened his window to wave and smile at them.

Word had spread in Westbury about the House Party, so this must be one of the guests. Several children dashed across the village green to get a better view, shrieking and waving as they came.

Clint grinned, "Perhaps you should *really* make their day by stopping and strutting about in your exquisite raiment. Were you rotund, I believe they would take you for Prinny."

The chuckles spread and soon Darrell felt the lightheartedness of the moment.

"Here's an opportunity to simply enjoy the pleasure of notoriety."

Then they arrived at Allen Court, a handsome gray stone home nestled in the low hills, giving the illusion of protection—like a haven. But they both knew that danger lurked; a conspiracy by people trying to harm England.

The gravel drive swept in an arc by the house where the coachman drew to a stop in front of the door. Grooms came running to hold the horses while the passengers disembarked and the plethora of baggage and trunks had to be unloaded by footmen. *A grand arrival,* he thought, *an excellent beginning.*

A couple came to greet him as the butler read his name.

"Lord and Lady Betterton," Darrell said after his impressive bow, "I am grateful to be so warmly welcomed to your home. Finchly assured me all would be well."

"Very happy to welcome you, sir, since we are short a man—to balance the numbers!"

She stumbled in embarrassment, and saw the expressive eyebrow rise over the intensely blue eyes; so, she laughed, and he treated her to his sweetest smile.

"My Lady, I am delighted to help!"

Walking with them up the stairs to a large drawing room crowded with people, he noticed Finchly, who broke off a conversation to come to greet him.

"I had begun to despair of you; any trouble?"

"No, no, had a delightful ride through the countryside and the charming village of Westbury. Some of us must make the grand entrance, you know."

"Yes, some of us are grand gentlemen, while some of us are simple folk."

A slap on the back replaced the punch to the shoulder Wally would have preferred, but Darrell's exquisite apparel kept him from doing it.

As he was introduced to many of the guests, he used his "foppish" mode; making an ass of himself where necessary, to make them think him absurd, not a threat. Things looked as they should be, but Darrell felt the undercurrents running through the room and made an effort to remember names.

Seeing some old friends and meeting new people, Wally was enjoying himself now that he was out of mourning for his wife and ready to get back into society, and he was grateful to have his old friend Darrell, who shone in any social gathering, with his suave manners and handsome face.

There was surprise, however, at his current behavior; over-the-top jollification and seeming to be a bit dense, because he was certain his wits were sharp.

When they met again among the milling throng, he said, "I'm planning an excursion in the morning, to view some old ruins to the south. Do you want to join us?"

As he eyed his friend, Darrell realized this was going to be difficult; noting he was confused by his behavior. He didn't like using Wally this way, but must keep his mind on his job.

"An early ride? Believe I'll need my beauty sleep, because I like to take a day of quiet to recover from a trip."

"You, Darrell? Since when?"

"Learned the hard way it is better to care for myself than to always be on the strut. Oh, I enjoy it, but try to spread it out more. Perhaps the next morning will be more convenient for me. Can we go together then?"

"Yes, that will be fine. There are some challenging hills to explore."

Since he was valet, Clint had set up Darrell's room, and was bursting to talk about his findings below stairs.

"The valets of Effington and Samuelson fought for their precedence, but it seemed like they had already crossed paths, and Tanner's man is a sneaky sort with shifty eyes and I will keep an eye on him."

"Yes, I took Tanner to be untrustworthy also and I think he is looking for a rich wife. Have not seen Ainsworth yet; the one whose valet complained of coming?"

"No, I have not seen Jake."

Darrell was seated between Mrs. Fleur and Mrs. Monroe at dinner.

"Mrs. Fleur, I understand you live in London. It is refreshing to get some country air, is it not?"

Her smile did not reach her dark eyes.

"Yes, Mr. Coletrane, it is good to get out of the city for a while."

"Do you enjoy the Season, Mrs. Fleur?"

"Oh, yes, so many entertainments. Do not you also, Mr. Coletrane?"

"Yes, I do, with so many pretty girls enjoying their first appearance."

Making a show of giving her a brilliant smile to see how she would respond; he was not disappointed.

"Oh, Mr. Coletrane! Have you not been caught in parson's mousetrap?"

Gazing at her with a mischievous glint, he said, "No, no, Madame, not yet. There is much to enjoy before entering into a lifelong commitment."

Her attention was taken by her neighbor, so he took a moment to survey the other guests. A lively conversation was in progress between Lady Gantre and M. Pelletier, while her nephew, William, was neglected on her other side.

So, Darrell turned to the lady on his right; who had just finished talking with Lord Effington.

"Now, Mrs. Monroe, I have not had an opportunity to converse with you. Are you enjoying the party?"

As he took a sip of his wine; his blue eyes met hers over the rim of his glass.

She was taken back for a moment, but soon recovered enough to take up her own.

"Yes, sir, I am so far."

The strange gleam in her eyes looked like speculation. *So, the lady wants to play,* he thought, *perfect.*

"And I'll wager you are good at finding enjoyment. Do you like dancing?"

"Yes, I do and I love this new dance, the waltz. I wonder if they do it in the wilds of Wiltshire."

"Possibly, since it is near Bath, but I think the old tabbies may take offense."

He flashed a smile at her, causing an evident intake of breath, and she controlled her hand from covering her generous bosom in time. The faint blush looked quite becoming.

Lord Effington again commanded her attention, and she turned away from the charming, handsome gentleman; hoping to get to know him better.

Staying alert for other's conversations, he caught a snatch or two. At the foot of the table, Lady Betterton conversed gaily with young Harold Tanner and staidly with Lord Samuelson on her other side, and Darrell admired her fortitude. In addition, she kept an eye on her two young daughters further down the long table, where they had young Edward Monroe between them and the three were enjoying the humorous story he was telling.

Soon, Lady Betterton rose from her chair to take the ladies to the drawing room, and port wine was brought in for the gentlemen. The conversation began with a discussion of the war, in which Napoleon and his Grande Armee were being challenged by the Allies.

"Received a letter from a friend in the Austrian Army, which is part of the Alliance, and they are pushing him hard toward Paris. Expect it will soon be over," said Captain Finchly.

"That is an optimistic view," said Samuelson, "but I am not so sanguine. The little emperor is just playing his games as usual."

Their host spoke up.

"So, we must commend the Navy in controlling the seas. If we still had a threat from the French fleet, our chances would be much lower."

Sitting back, Darrell played with his wine glass; watching under hooded eyes the reaction of the Frenchmen. Pelletier's face was thunderous and Fornier's wasn't much better. But he was surprised at Monroe's expression. Granted, the seas and the navy would be of interest to a man in shipping, but this was something deep and Darrell was unable to put a name to it as Monroe struggled to control himself, holding back comment.

Young Tyler took the opportunity during the lull to say, "I know Britain fought valiantly on the Peninsula for some years, but really, the kudos have to go to the Navy, as it ruled the seas and thereby kept the fighting confined to the continent."

Heads nodded, but not all; Pelletier and Tanner refrained, keeping their eyes downcast.

Next, Effington made a pompous little speech, in which he extolled all Britain for its noble behavior during the long war; a patriotic speech that gave the glory to the Peerage of the Realm. How the Peers won their glory, he did not say—it brought embarrassed frowns to some men, but no one refuted it.

The Port decanters passed around the table again.

After a pause, young Edward Monroe said, "Did any of you attend the races last week? A rollicking good time. A long-shot took the big race, bringing joy to a few lucky fellows, and you never saw such a spectacle. Shady Boy was superb and out-raced all the favorites."

As he stopped for breath, Lord Effington said, "Can't abide these races. And the gambling! Many a fortune is carelessly lost."

Weatherbee said, "The boys must enjoy some sport. Would rather have them there than the cockfights, I must say."

A heated discussion about all types of entertainment brought the session to a close. The gentlemen joined the ladies in the Drawing Room for cards and music.

Since Clint would be waiting for him, Darrell did not stay late. He relayed disturbances which took place at the servant's dinner table where Pelletier's valet started a row with Monroe's about loyalty. Each held a strong view on what was owed to their masters but stopped at suspicious behavior.

"Just let me say this," said Wendel, "I won't take the blame for what a master does. A man must obey but should not pay for his actions."

"Are you saying they are doing evil deeds?" asked Claude with a challenge in his eyes.

"No, but the issue still stands. *If* they did any wrongdoing, we should not take responsibility, that's all I say."

"His face turned a deep red as anger made him tremble."

"So, some valets are worried. That might mean they learned something unsavory about their masters," said Darrell.

Then he told his observances of the evening, and agreed on who was the most suspicious; but they knew it was still early days.

"It is almost certain Pelletier and Lady Gantre are involved; could even be the leaders, and Tanner acts suspiciously but is probably only trying for a rich wife. The Renwicks do not appear to be involved in their aunt's intrigue. The thought of finding a husband for the girl may not be a stretch, although she is young. Would be better to introduce her to the *ton* during the coming season. Perhaps this house party is to prepare her. Since William is a reticent fellow, he doesn't seem to be making an effort socially. Is he just shy or is there another agenda?

Betterton is not too suspicious, although he is friendly with the French. However, he may just be doing his duty as the host. I would be interested to learn if any of them suggested this house party.

The families who have their children in attendance are friends already and there is some history there, except the Renwicks, who came from the north. Wonder what Gantre's motive was for bringing them here? It appears William is a young man suffering under an aunt's pretensions. Does he realize her involvement with the French, since she doesn't hide her friendships?"

"Since most of the young men don't keep a valet of their own, I am at a disadvantage where they are concerned," said Clint.

Darrell added, "Also, there's the mysterious Marie Fornier, a close friend of Ladies Betterton and Gantre; what is their history? Lord Betterton used to be in the navy, is the connection through him somehow? So many questions, Clint. By the way, I must make a late appearance at breakfast in the morning."

As he lay in his bed, Darrell couldn't keep the images of the guests from his mind. The Samuelsons and Tanner had been neighbors of Lady Betterton in Bristol, so it is an acquaintance of long-standing. The irony is, they are as different as can be; the Samuelsons feel their status fully. As a Viscount, his is the highest title of the guests. Even his valet vies for attention below stairs.

The Timberleighs are apparently friends with them as well. Their daughter Diana is a beauty at nineteen and an accomplished horsewoman who brought her personal mount and groom. She had her first Season last year, but is not betrothed. An independent streak may be keeping her from coming under the rule of a husband, since it is clear she has subjugated her father. Tanner appears to be hanging around; but she has not become friends with him.

Although Baron Effington and his wife do not appear to be a threat, their consequence is their favorite topic. Lady Effington is a remote relation of Jasper Betterton; hence their inclusion as guests. Never hurts to invite someone of their status to raise the social level of the party, since Lady Betterton is not high in the instep. The fact that they traveled from the north to support distant relatives is admirable, but is there another agenda?

The Weatherbee family is an enigma. There is no evident connection with any of the guests. Where did they come from? Was he also in the navy at one time? Perhaps their son might be a former school friend of one of the young men? Time to get acquainted with them to solve the puzzle.

Finally, he pulled his bed covers into a more comfortable arrangement after an hour of tossing, and went to sleep.

Darrell did not come into the breakfast room until it was almost too late; wanting to appear a self-centered, arrogant gentleman who ruined several cravats before being satisfied. There he encountered five guests plus Lady Betterton, sitting around the table, talking.

"Good Morning!" said Darrell with an exaggerated smile and slight bow. "Trust I am not too late to partake of breakfast."

"Gracious me Mr. Coletrane, not at all, please join us."

A chair was vacant between Pelletier and Archibald Monroe, so he served himself from the buffet and came to claim it. As he sat down, a footman appeared, offering tea or coffee.

The Monsieur acknowledged him and returned to his conversation with Priscilla Gantre.

"Hope Peter recovered from his mistake."

"As do I, perhaps he learned a valuable lesson."

At that point, Darrell raised his expressive eyebrow as he looked at the Frenchman and said with an evil twinkle in his eyes, "Monsieur, what can have perpetrated such concern?"

Placing his right hand over his heart, he displayed just enough amusement to infer irreverence.

"Playing off your tricks so early?" asked the lady, "even before you breakfasted?"

Inclining his head to her, he said, "As you see, dear madam, I never miss an opportunity. But Monsieur, am I not to be privileged to learn all about this?"

A deep frown emphasized his cold dark eyes as he tried to stare Darrell down with no success, since he resembled a hound on a scent.

A flash of anger swept across Pelletier's face.

"Yes, Mr. Coletrane, Peter is my nephew who fell into a trap set by a charming, dangerous lady, and will be lucky to escape matrimony."

Busy re-arranging his food into a more artistic arrangement, Darrell appeared to be lost in thought. When he was satisfied, he sipped his coffee before replying.

"Getting married to the wrong bride is a great concern. Perhaps he can come away unscathed."

The gentleman turned back to him, and it was obvious he could not figure him out.

Just then, Gantre jumped into the fray—probably to keep the Frenchman from exposing himself.

"Yes, Mr. Coletrane, let us hope so. Young men can be careless of their futures, don't you think?"

And she let her gaze simmer on him for just a moment before returning to her plate.

By Jove, a threat? thought Darrell.

The Monsieur murmured something to her before excusing himself from the table.

Then Darrell settled into eating a hearty breakfast, and noticed Monroe on his right; who was nearly finished with his meal. His wife addressed her tea as she chatted with Cecelia Betterton about one of her children.

"Understand you are from London, Mr. Coletrane. Do you often come to Bath?"

"No, I can't say I do, since London was my chief location for some years, and my father is there."

Sizing up this stranger, Darrell came to the conclusion he was forthright.

"And you are from Bristol, I believe?"

"Yes, we have been friends of Lady Betterton all our lives, having grown up in the same area."

"So, you knew your charming wife all your life also?"

A warm smile softened his face as he glanced at her.

"Yes, Mr. Coletrane, I am a lucky man."

So, Darrell bowed his head in acknowledgement.

"Did I hear that you are in shipping, sir?"

"Yes, and my father before me."

"Has this long war caused you trouble?"

"The one in America is a challenge, Mr. Coletrane, since our chief markets have been there and the West Indies. Now we must get creative and seek alternatives."

Having continued their interesting discussion, he was amazed at how people in all kinds of occupations were affected by the war, but America was a region he did not think much about.

After his late breakfast, Darrell took a walk outside. Not many people walked about since a party had departed for Wally's excursion. As he strolled into the garden, he saw several others deep in conversation; Pelletier and Fornier among them. One man he did not recognize; certainly not one of the guests.

Turning another way, he showed interest in the row of boxwood that were sculpted into attractive shapes. A breeze brought an occasional word from the group; more so when a voice was raised. "By next week," "dangerous man," "committed," "worth it," carried on the wind. He turned on another path to remove himself from the area and wished he could see them clearly enough to see whether any of them were in the Cathedral.

So, the plot thickens, he thought. The fact they met where anyone could come upon them showed their brazenness. What were they planning? That was what Darrell must find out.

At luncheon, he went in on time; curious if the French group would show any embarrassment, but they didn't.

The excursion had not returned, so he chose to sit by William Renwick, since he wanted to see if his observances were correct.

"How are you enjoying the party, Mr. Renwick?"

The young man said, "Fine, sir."

"Understand from your aunt that your estate is in the north. By-the-way, I was sorry to learn of your father's passing."

"Thank you."

Knowing of his reticence, he debated whether to press for more or let him be, so he turned instead to his left to speak with Mr. Weatherbee, to whom he had been introduced.

"You are not one of the excursion party?"

"No, I did not relish such a long ride today."

"My thoughts as well. Captain Finchly thought me a poor sport, but one must follow one's instincts."

Then he smiled when Weatherbee looked up.

"Are you acquainted with Finchly?"

"Yes, since Harrow. Of course, he was at sea over the years, so I did not meet him as often as I would like. Have you known him before?"

"Yes, by his outstanding naval career."

When he didn't enlarge on his statement, Darrell raised both eyebrows as he said, "Are you connected with the Navy, sir?"

He thought before replying. "Yes, you could say that, I suppose, since I have some connection with the Admiralty."

This intrigued him even more, but he sensed that to pursue it now would be a mistake. Better to ask Wally.

"Glad to hear it," he said, reverting to his "foppish" persona. "So, you reside in London, do you?"

"Yes, some of the time."

As he hesitated, he thought, *there is something important here.* Then he switched the conversation to Weatherbee's son.

"I am pleased to see so many young people present, sir, and I had the pleasure of meeting Tyler. Thought he expressed himself well last evening of his high opinion of the Navy."

"Thank you, Mr. Coletrane, he is not afraid to speak his mind and I had to agree with him. Did you?"

Astonished, Darrell said, "Yes, wholeheartedly."

The excursion group did not return until late afternoon. The party of tired riders included several women; whose bright riding costumes added colorful splashes as they rode into the stables.

Wally was boisterous in his greeting, "You missed a fine time, my friend."

"Even so, I'm not sorry, since I needed today as I told you. Are we still going out in the morning?"

"Of course, unless you need more beauty sleep."

Smiling, he assured him he would be ready as early as need be, since he was anxious to see something of the country.

Before dinner, the Ainsworths arrived and explained that their coach broke an axle yesterday, delaying their trip. As Darrell tried to see the reactions of the various guests to the new arrivals, he noted Ainsworth settled into the French group.

Meeting with Clint later that night, he told him about Weatherbee. "The man is still a mystery, even though I got the feeling we were on the same side; but his admiration of Wally brought questions to my mind."

Since he had no new revelations, except that Jake arrived late and was not talkative, they said good night.

The riders departed when the sun came up. Heading north-west into the hills, they chatted and joked as they rode. After an energetic gallop over an open field, they settled back into a comfortable canter.

Again, Darrell wondered how to broach the subject of Weatherbee, since he had not told Wally of his mission and debated what to do.

Riding in silence for a while, Finchly mulled over his friend's bizarre behavior and knew he must have a plan.

Darrell said, "There is something I must tell you."

With a questioning look on his face, he said, "Go ahead, tell me."

"I have not been straight with you and I know I shouldn't tell you, but I also know I can trust you with anything."

"Well, it is obvious to me that you are acting weirdly," he said, holding back a chuckle. "But go on, tell me."

"Well, I am here on a mission for the Foreign Office. There is a suspected nest of French spies at this party and I must expose them."

After studying Darrell's face for a moment, he erupted in laughter.

Devastated, he became angry.

"Sorry. This is not funny, it's just that I didn't know what you were up to, but now I can tell you."

"Go ahead, let me know the worst."

Keeping himself under control, he said, "I'm on a mission here too!"

The horses had stopped from inattention and chomped on the grass.

"Do you work for the Admiralty with Weatherbee?"

Then Wally nodded. "The Admiralty's intelligence division heard a rumor of a plot being hatched, so they got us invited here."

"And you were so kind to find me and invite me too!"

"Yes, we learned you had joined the Foreign Office and, from snippets of information, considered you do the same work."

As he blinked at the coincidence, he said, "There is so much we need to share, Wally. I have made observations and heard bits of things that could be combined with yours. There is something dangerous in the works and the last of the French group arrived late yesterday, but I don't know what they're planning. Do you?"

"Yes, we anticipate an attack on the Navy. They are mad as hatters at our success, but the proof is evasive."

As they pondered how to proceed, they heard a twig snap. Both men reached for their pistols, but then Darrell's horse snapped another, so they relaxed.

"We must be careful," said Wally. "Even trees have ears sometimes."

"Can we arrange a meeting in a safe place and include Weatherbee and Clint? He's acting as my valet, looking for clues in the servants' hall."

"Surely, we can come up with something that won't look suspicious, but we better head back! I'm hungry for breakfast."

Returning from their ride, they had to change into morning clothes before appearing, so Darrell rang for Clint. While he changed, he told his partner of the revelations of the morning.

"Never expected that. Were you surprised too?"

"Yes, I was. The clue was when Weatherbee seemed to know about Wally, but I had not connected them. But when he admitted his attachment to the Admiralty, I couldn't help but conjecture."

They talked about the proposed meeting until Darrell left for breakfast.

Being such old friends, it was easy to put on a show for everyone at the table; light banter and some teasing, along with Darrell's absurd behavior should cast out any doubts. When he told Weatherbee about the need for a meeting, they started to outline a plan. Wally told them of an old friend who had a residence near Warminster. Darrell, Wally and Clint could leave the house party to go for a visit.

An express rider was sent to ask if George would accommodate him and his friends, and waited for an immediate reply; so, they completed their plans. While on this trip, he would drop his act as a foolish fop since he had to trust them completely, and they had to do the same. If what Darrell overheard was true, the French plot would be enacted "next week."

The story put about was that Wally was taking them to visit an old navy buddy.

As they prepared to leave, Darrell made an issue of what to pack—will he need his best evening dress or not? Will he need his riding costume? So, he acted like a fussy fop, worried how he will look.

CHAPTER 6

The Four Agents

The three men left for Warminster after an early breakfast. The Weatherbees would leave to visit their friends in a different town later in the morning.

Their party arrived at Birches by noon, where George Freeman greeted them.

"This is my wife, Mary, and my children, George, Jr. and Grace."

"Welcome to our home," Mrs. Freeman said "Pleased to see you, Wally, it's been a long while."

At luncheon, the men refrained from any in-depth discussion until after the family removed, then Wally explained the Admiralty's concern about a plot, and that they had been sent to expose this threat before it's too late.

"Darrell overheard a few comments from a meeting in the garden. The French group—as we call them, said it would happen 'next week.' That doesn't give us much time."

"Do you have any idea what that is?"

"Well, Weatherbee thinks the Admiralty is the target, but we don't know what they plan to do; may be individuals or certain ships."

George took the men outside, where they observed the house. It was in the elegant Palladian style, surrounded by regimented gardens, and the stables beckoned them to view his prime hunters.

"Do you belong to a Hunt?" asked Wally.

"Yes, I ride with the Cotsmores, and had a great run this Fall."

A short walk took them down to the lake, which was picturesque in the sunshine.

By mid-afternoon, the Weatherbees arrived. After greetings, they received light refreshments, and the ladies departed; the men removed to the library. Weatherbee filled in with further details.

"That is audacious! Count on me to help in any way I can."

"Thank you, George, just providing us a private meeting place helps the cause, and having your input is welcome."

At dinner, all was comradery and good old boys after the ladies left the room. Then Darrell told them about his disaster at the Émigré party in London when he was *uncovered,* livening it up to make it funny, but they still felt how dangerous the situation had been. Now they must get to the hard work, so removed to the library.

"What are some names of these plotters?"

"So far, we've identified Pelletier, Gantre, Ainsworth, Fornier, and maybe Fleur, and Tanner," said Weatherbee.

"In addition, Samuelson and Timberleigh are suspicious characters. We don't know why they are at the House Party," said Darrell; so, he recounted his experiences at Bath Cathedral and Clint told his experience with the valets and Ainsworth.

Next Wally and Weatherbee told them the contents of their portfolio from the Admiralty. Captain Morgan reported a turn-coat on his ship Manfold some months ago, and under questioning, he revealed a plot, claiming he did not know names, but had been selling navy information for money—a clandestine operation with codes. Finding solid facts was a problem. To tie this in with the émigré community would help.

The name Ainsworth kept coming up. How to find out his connections and history?

"All right, I will send a letter to the Admiralty by express, with any other questions we can add," said Weatherbee.

Next, Darrell told of his suspicions of Lord Smithson, who was attached to the Foreign Office; which meant they couldn't make inquiries there in case he may learn of it. Chad Peterman's imprisonment and torture was disclosed. There might be a connecting clue in any of these things.

At midnight, they broke up, agreeing they would meet again after breakfast, which would give them time to review the information.

Comparing notes, ideas, and suspicions, the plot began to materialize, and the two teams became one, seemingly trusting and sharing.

Several important things needed to be discovered:

Who are all the plotters and their leaders?

What is their target, and when would it be carried out?

Lady Priscilla Gantre orchestrated the gathering at the house party, and Darrell's observations at the émigré event in London and in Bath Cathedral were shared.

The Admiralty contributed facts also, as well as suspicions.

Clint identified whose valets and maids had made suspicious remarks.

Pelletier was as strong a suspect as Gantre as the probable leader. Ainsworth had been said to have many Frenchie friends by his valet, and since he arrived late at the House Party, he was obvious in his friendships. Plus, he looked worried. Had he gotten in too deep? Did he regret being part of a treasonous plot?

Mrs. Fornier was a supporter of Pelletier and Gantre, and Fleur was also inclined to stay around with the French.

Whether Betterton was in the group, or just playing host was not sure. Did he have any reason to harm the navy? And there was Tanner, who was still ambiguous in his intentions.

What is the target? Could it be the assassination of a key person in Britain's government or someone of value to the Navy, like the First Lord, Melville? But who would cause the most destabilization if they were killed?

Perhaps a well-placed bomb to damage the navy? Or the shipyard? Could it be a new ship being built which would increase the British Naval Power?

Might it be at the Admiral's Mess in Whitehall—to take out the cream of the officers? Was there an event planned where a gathering would take place?

So, he asked, "When is the opening ceremony for Parliament, where the Prince Regent would be present?"

"Well, where would the most damage be done?"

They thought it over and decided Wally should deliver the letter instead of using an express rider—to give the warning sooner.

Proof—every effort must be made to obtain it and the particulars, so Darrell offered to search Gantre's room for notes or letters. Since Ainsworth was a nervous Nelly, perhaps Weatherbee could evaluate his situation.

Could Gantre have involved her nephew?

When Darrell and Clint returned to Allen Court, there appeared to be trouble; tempers were edgy, and Renwick lurked about the hall when they entered.

"Hello, William," said Darrell.

"Sir," and gave a slight bow. "I would like some words with you in private if you are available. Will you come to my bed chamber?"

He controlled his reaction—the boy appeared to be very troubled.

"Yes, I will. Do you mean now?"

"Yes, if you don't mind."

He went upstairs to William's bed chamber in the far reaches of the house, where he locked the door behind them. The room was small; with a bed, chest, and one chair. The one window overlooked the kitchen garden.

"You appear to be troubled, William. How can I help?"

"This is hard for me, sir. It is about my aunt, who is involved in something dangerous. She will be angry that I told you, but you knew her before and perhaps you can stop her."

"I promise to do what I can. Tell me all you know."

Taking a deep breath, William said, "No doubt you are aware of my aunt's close friendship with the Frenchman, and I believe he is using her for his own ends, and I suspect he is hatching a plot which could be treason. There, I've said it, as ugly as it is."

"No wonder you are worried. That is dangerous."

William put his hands over his face. He looked like someone had stepped on his grave. Darrell's heart went out to this young man who had just taken on all his late father's duties and now faced betraying his aunt.

"Let's meet this head on and discuss it. What led you to this conclusion?"

"Well, I overheard snatches of conversation between them about an upcoming event of great consequence and I saw a lot of them meeting in the garden and in secluded areas of the house. There have even been other Frenchmen on the estate for meetings as well.

When I confronted her, she laughed at me, 'Not just men seek revenge against their enemies. This may go down in history; one of the best!' When I tried to question her about it, she pushed me aside like a useless piece of trash."

"Have any proof of this, William? Did you notice notes or letters being exchanged?"

"I don't know who keeps their papers."

"Better keep some distance from it. Leave this to me, and thank you for your bravery in coming forth. We will try to save her."

As Darrell mulled over this information, he realized it wasn't much more than they knew, but from a different observer; one with a lot at risk. He admired William's courage.

At dinner that night, the tension was evident, but polite conversation carried them through, as Darrell kept a close eye on everyone. Soon it became obvious that the Timberleighs watched Diana, who showed an angry flush on her cheeks, and they noticed Tanner had been placed near Lady Betterton again; but was not his usual *gay blade*. Had something occurred between them?

Most of the French contingent seemed tense, but endeavored to carry on politely. They did not display the smugness of success, so things must not be working out as they wanted.

The scene at the table during Port and cigars was subdued. A few subjects of no importance went around, but no one cared to bring up anything of interest. Tanner sulked and wouldn't make eye contact. Was he smarting from a set-down? When the gentlemen joined the ladies, cards and games entertained until the tea tray was delivered.

Darrell left early; when he arrived at his chamber, Clint was waiting.

"That was uncomfortable."

"Something happened in our absence, shall we share our findings?"

First Clint told of the tension below stairs and how several valets had words. Those of Pelletier and Ainsworth appeared defensive; Timberleigh and Tanner aggressive.

"Yes, I saw that at dinner as well, but I think it is about Diana."

"The French group was trying to be polite, but their tenseness told volumes. They did not show signs of success."

"No, I detected worry more than anything. And that brings me to my news."

So, he related his conversation with William and his reading of the boy's feelings.

"He felt distressed to speak against his aunt, but worried about the plot she is involved in."

Since this was confirming their own suspicions, they discussed possible action.

"Shall we search some rooms?" said Darrell, "to find real proof?"

So, they talked it over and assigned them; which was a touchy undertaking and could blow up in their faces if one of them was caught.

Late the next morning, the Weatherbees arrived, and at luncheon told about their trip to their friends' home.

"It is some time since we met, so in catching up, we overstayed our visit. They even held a dinner party last night, so we could meet some of their neighbors and a dance afterward. No wonder we were late starting back this morning."

The speculative look in Pelletier's eyes made Darrell consider that he was suspicious.

"That's what I like," he said at his most frivolous, "good food and conversation, topped off with a little dancing! Remember, Mrs. Monroe, I promised you a waltz while we are here!"

Lady Betterton became effusive over her plans for a "grand ball" on the last night of the House Party.

"I am looking forward to it, Mr. Coletrane. Sorry Archibald, but you understand."

"Of course, my dear. My skills at dancing are limited."

During the afternoon Darrell mingled with other guests and displayed his foppish side. Some, like the Effingtons, showed their disgust at his behavior; with her repeated "Really" comments.

He had an opportunity to join a few people on a walk about the extensive gardens; Harold Tanner being one of them, he arranged a tête-á-tête with him.

"How are you enjoying the party?"

"Could be better." Then kicked at a pebble on the path. "Some people here don't give a man any credit, accuse him of things he didn't do."

"I say, who is giving you trouble?"

Then he struck another a little more ferociously.

"You wouldn't believe."

After another pause, the need to unburden his feelings overcame his judgement, and he said, "My intentions toward Diana were serious, but her father misconstrued my objective and accused me of being a fortune hunter, and didn't give me any credit for my sincere desire to make her my wife!"

"But how does the lady feel; is she happy at your attentions? Such a beautiful young woman."

The strained face softened at the compliment, but he still struggled with his emotions.

"I thought she was receptive since we went out riding a few times—she's a superb horsewoman. Also, she was friendly to me and I may have read more into it than she intended. Perhaps she isn't ready for marriage yet, but a man doesn't like to be rebuffed."

"Any hope of reconciliation? Maybe she will reconsider after thinking it over."

"But her father stands in the way. I think his hopes are for a higher match. She's already twenty and had a couple of Seasons, so she'd better be careful of spurning a willing man."

Darrell was surprised at his attitude, and guessed he had been correct in his first opinion of him.

"My advice, if you care to hear it from someone with more experience, is to let things cool off. Apologize to her father for not approaching him first. Show your best side. If it's meant to be, and you still want the attachment, it will work out."

He slapped Tanner on the shoulder before turning away.

When they were at a distance, Monroe asked, "What is he so upset about?"

"His offer for Diana has been rejected, and he is angry; but I still gave him advice; his behavior was atrocious, so I told him to apologize to her father. Didn't even ask for her hand properly."

Smiling at his indignation, Archibald said, "That poor lad has not had a proper education, if he thinks he can make his own rules. I'm glad she said no–he doesn't deserve her."

As they rounded a corner of shrubs, they came upon several of the French group; who were deep in conversation, but they fell silent.

"Good afternoon," said Darrell. "I see you are enjoying a walk in this splendid garden as well."

After a pregnant pause, Lady Gantre said, "Hello, gentlemen, it's enjoyable to seek some fresh air."

The glare she aimed at Darrell was not missed. *What was she mad at him about? Surely, she had not learned of William's confession.*

So, he let a smirk play over his face for a moment, then he raised his expressive eyebrow at her.

"My dear lady, who can blame any of us for coming out? It is such an opportunity to share private thoughts with one's chums."

Surprised, she recovered enough to say, "You shock me, monsieur. One would hesitate to consider that you have many friends."

Putting his hand over his heart he said in a sugary tone, "But Madame, how can you think me so low; one who has known you all these years?"

The implication was not missed; her face flamed, but she let the subject drop, since she knew she was no match for Darrell's tongue. Then everyone bowed and went in different directions.

Archibald put his hand on his shoulder.

"My friend, now you're done it."

"Serves her right; gave her back some of her own. Now she'll be worried about what I know." And they laughed.

CHAPTER 7

Worried Nephew.

As Darrell entered the house, William Renwick invited him to go to his room again.

"Oh, I overheard my aunt and Marie Fornier talking about the "big bang" at the Admiralty soon, and I am even more concerned about her. She is pleased about something, but when I tried to caution her, she flew into me.

'You are nothing; don't realize the perfidy of enemies and you were sheltered all your life; never been forced to be a man!'

So, I told her that she was mistaken, that I learned about the world through study, not action. "You are putting your family at risk! The games you play with these friends of yours may get you hanged! Stop before it is too late!"

After a pause for a deep breath, he continued, "She glared at me venomously; as though weighing the danger I posed and a heinous look crossed her face. 'I do not want to hurt you William, but if you say anything to anybody about this, I will turn my friends on you.' And I said, tell me what they are planning because I am worried about you. Perhaps I can assist."

And she threw back her head and gave one of her guffaws.

'So, you want to help? But you are nothing but a boy and I play with men; men who know how to deal with enemies. Don't become an enemy, William.'"

Now Darrell was sure that he was putting himself in danger.

"May be best if you keep this to yourself since I believe she is in earnest about her threats. Let's go back to what you heard. Where did this take place? Any of her friends around?"

"Yes, in the hall and there were no others near, I was reading at the East window seat and the draperies blocked me. This is serious, isn't it? If it is treason, all is lost. She will ruin my family. How can we stop her?"

"Perhaps you should take your sister back to Bath; I know you want to help, but the risk is too high."

"How can I leave, Mr. Coletrane, knowing what I do? How can I turn my back on her? What reason would I give for leaving since Sarah is enjoying her time here with her new acquaintances?"

"This is not a nice question, but who is more important to you—Sarah or your aunt?"

As he stared at him, Darrell thought, *he had not come down to such a simple choice in his mind. If she is involved in treason, he should shelter Sarah.*

He straightened to his full height. "Put in those terms, I must always choose my sister since she is my responsibility and I must protect her from the ugliness of the world."

"Yes, you must come up with a believable reason to leave; for your sister and for everyone. Might you receive an express message with an excuse? Even to go back home?"

That took William back again—go north?

"Going back to Karlsford would be best, wouldn't it? But I must give some thought to this. How can a missive be sent to me?"

"I have a few acquaintances in Bath; I will ask one of them to send one. Now, what reason should it be that would require your immediate return?"

William paced his room. Karlsford was his now; what might call him home?

"If I can come up with something, I will tell you."

"Time is urgent. Could your steward be injured or ill? Would the other staff be able to run your estate without him? Think along those lines. Any possible alibi will do for the letter; and you can explain it all to your sister after you're on your way. Did you bring a carriage or will you hire a hack chaise?"

Now he wanted to get William thinking about specifics of a journey. The trip was one thing but planning would move his mind into logical thoughts.

Pacing some more, he realized that these were totally new considerations, and he must become pragmatic and put the protection of his sister first.

Rising to leave, Darrell was stopped when he said, "You are right, Mr. Coletrane, I think a fall from a horse and broken bones could be grave enough to call me home."

"I will arrange for a letter to arrive in the morning. Don't make any preparations until after it comes. Don't deviate from your normal schedule and don't let your sister know any of this, I pray."

Then he gave him an encouraging smile.

When Clint came to dress him for dinner, Darrell told him and asked him to go to Bath and find Clarence Young on Gay Street, and wrote a note of explanation and gave it to him.

"Use my horse, Sultan, and you may stay over if you wish, but do not bring the letter; let it be delivered by a regular express rider to avoid suspicion. I hope the young people will be out of here by noon tomorrow."

"How will Gantre react?"

"Well, I imagine she will be pleased to see her troublesome nephew on his way, since he has been making her nervous lately. The difficulty will be the niece—she will not want to leave. If Gantre tries to keep her here, it will be worse."

A twinkle came into his eyes. "Perhaps if I indicate an interest in Sarah at dinner, Gantre will be glad to send her north. Now, I think you need to procure something for me as a reason for your sudden trip. Is there anything I need to replenish in my wardrobe? Some new cravats? Some special cigars?"

"Do you mean something frivolous? As outrageous as your behavior here?"

"Exactly! What do you think?"

Clint chuckled, and thought about what might be atrocious enough. His eyes brightened.

"How about the London papers or a play bill for the Bath theatre next week?"

"That wouldn't do because I might be looking for something about their plans. The theatre's not bad, but not enough. If you got my mail from the hotel, it might be misconstrued too."

Silence reigned as Darrell completed his raiment.

"Since I will set up a flirt with Miss Renwick tonight, it should be something—like a nosegay! Is it outrageous enough to send one's valet to Bath for it? That should raise some eyebrows and put Gantre on her guard! Get something out-of-season; hard to find. What color are her eyes? Let me check at dinner, then you can leave right after."

"I'm sorry for the girl! Since she is young and inexperienced, you may be too much for her."

"Oh, I will be gentle, my friend, I don't intend to hurt her in any way."

When the guests gathered in the drawing room before entering the dining room, Darrell walked to Sarah's side, where she was standing with Rose and Connie, talking about bonnets.

"Ladies," he said as he bowed to them, surprising them into giggles as they curtsied.

"Did I hear you mention hats? I can't refrain from joining in, if you permit."

Then he hesitated, raising his expressive eyebrow.

Since no one objected, he continued,

"It is a study for me. The ones from Paris used to reign supreme, but London now boasts of some fashionable milliners." He turned to Sarah, taking in her blue eyes and said, "Do you have a favorite style, Miss Renwick?"

Flustered by the directness, she glanced quickly to Rose for guidance, and he waited as she struggled with a reply.

"S-sir, being newly from the north, I have not had enough experience to make a choice."

The butler announced dinner and Darrell expertly took Sarah's hand and placed it on top of his sleeve.

"Now we will continue our interrupted conversation, shall we?"

And he gave her a brilliant smile and proceeded.

Gantre was by her friends as usual, so he took seats as far from her as possible, since he did not want her to hear.

Then he gently bantered with Sarah, who was soon at her ease with this charming, handsome man. After the subject of hats ran its course, he talked with her about the House Party.

She asked him a question, "Mr. Coletrane, is it true that you have known my aunt for some time?"

"Yes, Miss Renwick, I have, and I was also acquainted with Lord Gantre. Did you ever meet him?"

"No, I was never in London. Tell me about London, Mr. Coletrane."

As her blue eyes shone in anticipation, he told her of the grand buildings and parks; the theatre and entertainments, but tried not to make it too enticing—heaven knew when she could go there.

"Since I have never been to Yorkshire, Miss Renwick," said Darrell as desert was served; "do tell me what it is like."

Starting with a general overview of the country, she gave a description of Karlsford, her home, and sadness overcame her as she remembered her father.

Bending low he said, "I must express my condolences, Miss Renwick. I have talked with William about your loss. Do you realize how fortunate you are to have a brother who will take care of you?"

Looking into his eyes for a moment, she said, "Yes, I am, he and I are very close. Do you have siblings?"

Darrell let a look of regret cross his countenance before replying, "No, I am sad to say."

When Lady Betterton rose, the ladies adjourned to the drawing room.

As William's eyes met Darrell's across the table, he was about to burst with curiosity and anger, not pleased by his actions toward his sister.

"Sorry Captain Finchly has left the party," said Samuelson. "Probably you will miss his company, Coletrane."

So, he raised his gaze.

"Yes, sir," said Darrell with a smirk. "And I trust he will return in a few days since he owes me a rematch at whist."

A knowing chuckle ran around the table.

"You know, his children reside with his mother since his wife's passing. Perhaps he needed to go see them."

Several of the men nodded in agreement.

"What is this about a gathering at the Admiralty?" said Effington. "Don't believe they did it last year. Do you think it is related to the war?"

Everyone sat silently; it was like a cat had been thrown among the pigeons. *This should be interesting,* thought Darrell, and gave a look to William that said, *don't say anything.*

The first response was from Fornier.

"Well, I believe the Admiralty likes to keep us guessing."

Several eyebrows rose, but Tanner spoke first.

"Those old guys probably needed some entertainment. Maybe they want to give themselves congratulations or pass out some more medals."

Betterton bristled.

"Be careful what you say in this company. Not many here could agree with you, sir. Even our émigré guests must admire the British Royal Navy."

Darrell held his breath. The French appeared stunned. How would they answer?

After a few moments, Pelletier spoke to break the silence.

"Yes, Monsieurs, the achievements of your navy are unequaled, and they have much to be proud of, your Admirals."

Both Fornier and Tanner seemed surprised at these conciliatory words from Pelletier.

Struggling, Fornier said, "Yes, it is true that they are great, but one must agree that the secrecy causes questions."

Effington shouted, "What? Do you expect the military hierarchy to broadcast their plans to the enemy?"

Betterton attempted to temper the discussion, and said, "All nations of the world must keep their methods close to the chest. How could they operate otherwise?"

Mumbled agreement could be heard and Darrell wished that the subject would be developed. Instead of passing the Port again, Betterton rose, ending the gathering.

When the gentlemen joined the ladies, he searched for Sarah, and saw that she was in a group of her friends; so, he did no more than meet her eyes across the room, and she flushed prettily. Making it a point to keep a distance from William also, he stole away long enough to speak to Clint.

"Blue", he said; reviewed his note to Clarence, then bade him goodnight.

As Gantre sipped her tea, she saw Darrell coming her way and obviously had something to say to him.

"Well, you can't even keep your word, Mr. Coletrane."

"But Madame, I did not know how enticing the lady would be."

"Still, you will keep away, for I will not permit it."

"Is that a delicious challenge?" And, raising both eyebrows, said, "I love a dare, my dear."

"You will not like it when I take vengeance."

Darrell let his eyes slowly rake over her person. It unsettled her.

"Revenge can be sweet, but can just as easily be bitter. Be careful what you wish for."

And he turned away from her and strolled casually to the tea table for a piece of cake. Out of the corner of his eye he could see her fuming.

When he saw that William was leaving, he caught up to him on the stairs.

"An update on events, stop at my chamber."

"The express letter will be here in the morning, so you may remove your sister tomorrow."

"Sarah! What are you thinking, to flirt with her!"

"There was a perfectly good reason. Now your aunt will be inclined to let her go to get her safely away from me."

He stared at him. "Well, I hadn't thought of that, but I hope you won't break her heart; she's an innocent, you know."

"Yes, I am aware of it. But I will be making one more contact, since Clint will bring back a nosegay tomorrow and I will make a scene of presenting it to her, to solidify your aunt's desire to protect her from me. You can assure your sister that I was just finding a way of entertaining myself at her expense. Perhaps her wrath will turn her against rakes. And you can call me a rake, I used to be one." William was confused, could not understand this man, so he said goodnight and left.

When Clint arrived early in the morning, bringing a nosegay of little white flowers tied in a narrow ribbon of blue satin, he was soaked from the rain and rushed to the fire in Darrell's chamber to warm himself.

"Well, you got here in good time; sorry about the miserable weather." He opened the box to see if they were crushed, but they were not.

"Your friend Clarence obliged us with the messenger, and he should arrive this morning," he said through clattering teeth.

"Here, get out of those clothes. Wear these." Then he put more wood on the fire and pulled the bell cord for tea.

After he changed, he gave him some brandy.

"When you go below stairs, take your wet things, and let them know about the flowers. That will look outrageous and will spread. My objective with Miss Renwick is to make her aunt glad she will be heading north after the express arrives; and William already knows what will happen; they must be distanced from her before the arrests."

The breakfast room was not crowded when Darrell arrived, carrying the nosegay like a treasure. Both Sarah and William were there with Gantre. Then he sauntered over to her and presented the flowers.

"For my newest friend, Miss Renwick!"

His eyes held hers as his brilliant smile made her catch her breath; her hesitation was endearing.

Lady Gantre interrupted.

"What is the meaning of this, Coletrane?"

"But, my dear, you interrupt an important moment; I sent all the way to Bath for this little token of my affection. Do not spoil it."

Having looked imploringly at her, he shifted his gaze to Miss Renwick, who sat still, unsure how to act. Her eyes turned to her aunt for direction; whose face showed signs of wanting to snatch it from her. Gantre glanced at Pelletier, who was watching the tableau, his head gave an almost imperceptible shake; Gantre must not make a scene. She glared at her niece, giving a resentful nod.

Sarah held the nosegay, still unsure of herself, but glad of the gift.

"Thank you, Mr. Coletrane. That is kind of you."

The Bettertons arrived in time for this acceptance.

"How charming!" said Lady Betterton. "But where did you find such pretty flowers at this time of the year?"

"In Bath, of course," a smug grin on his face.

"But how did you procure them? Surely you have not been there and back."

Darrell almost preened himself like a peacock.

"Why, I sent my valet for them!" Looking as though there could be no other possibility.

"Must have been a wet ride for the lad," muttered Jasper.

"As you say."

Now he had the attention of everyone in the room, so he had to say something audacious.

"Miss Renwick," said Darrell with a bow, "would you permit me to take you for a walk in the garden later? For I declare the sun is just waiting to shine."

Silence held the room for moments, all eyes turned to Miss Renwick, who was in confused blushes. Gantre was struck dumb, and William kept himself back with great effort.

Then Lady Betterton broke the breathless pause.

"Oh, go ahead, my dear, it is an honor to you to have the attention of such a gentleman as Mr. Coletrane." Her face glowed with smiles.

Darrell looked hopefully at Miss Renwick, stretching the tension to a breaking point. She looked up at him again, still holding the precious flowers.

In a small voice, she said, "Thank you, I would be pleased to walk with you."

A bright smile sparkled as he stood even taller before bowing to her again.

"You make my day, Mademoiselle!"

Wanting to kiss her hand—he held back. *Too much,* he thought.

He smiled at Lady Betterton, who was a most interested observer.

"Now I must eat some breakfast, for I am prodigiously hungry!"

Laughter rang through the room but did not include everyone: Gantre seemed like an ice statue; William was concerned, and Pelletier pretended to not notice anything; since Mr. Coletrane's bizarre behavior always confused him.

The rain diminished into a drizzle, but no sun shone, and Darrell was grateful, since he did not want to further entice this poor young lady.

So, he sat in the library with Monroe and Effington, chatting about the navy again and recounted several stories of the support sometimes received when needed at sea. The Atlantic storms could damage any ship not in top shape and cargoes would be lost, but the men might be saved if a British ship were on hand.

When the doorbell sounded, Darrell hoped it was the letter arriving and sauntered out to the hall in time to see William following a footman down the stairs, receive the dispatch from the rider with a scowl on his face, bestow some coins on the man, then proceeded to open the missive.

After perusing its contents, he cursed and looked up, his eyes catching Darrell's, but then swung his gaze to Monroe.

"This is terrible news! I must go home right away!"

Monroe laid a hand on William's arm.

"Sorry, what happened?"

So, he gave him the letter to read, acting as though he was speechless. After reading it, Monroe passed the missive to Darrell.

He said, "Trouble at Karlsford, poor lad! Can I be of any assistance? You will want to start as soon as possible."

Passing it back to William, Darrell said, "By Jove, yes, you cannot delay and I will offer my help as well."

"But now, I must tell my sister," and he turned and ran up the stairs.

The rest of the morning was spent getting them ready for a speedy departure. Several of the young ladies helped Sarah, who was overcome with tears of regret because she didn't want to go!

Gantre fell into Darrell's trap and encouraged her to accompany her brother.

"It might be months before he can come south again, and you do not want him to bear this all alone, do you?"

That worked, since her love and devotion for him helped her do as she should.

Next, Lady Betterton asked cook to prepare an early luncheon for them and a hamper of food to take in the coach.

Darrell bade farewell to Miss Renwick with a balance of regret and wishes for their safe journey; and commended William on his swift actions.

"Yes, you are doing the right thing. Your sister must get away before the fireworks start. Thank you for your levelheadedness and courage. After it is over, I will write to you."

Almost everyone was on hand to wave goodbye and Gantre put on a good show, including tears.

Luncheon was a somber affair that day, with most of the guests making comments on the ill-fortune of the Renwicks.

"Such lovely young people, and I hope they have a safe journey since Yorkshire is a long way."

The men speculated on how many days it would take and trusted the steward was getting proper care.

Fortunately, by the time luncheon was over, the sun came out. A couple of the young ladies made attempts to befriend Darrell, but he deflected them gently.

CHAPTER 8

Fear Grips the Soul

Soon Francis Weatherbee asked Darrell to go riding with him.

"Splendid idea, mustn't waste the sunshine."

They chatted until they moved well away from the stables. Knowing Darrell's horse had been ridden hard this morning, they kept a sedate pace.

Then he explained his behavior toward Miss Renwick and how it achieved his goal.

"Yes, I wanted them safe from their aunt's machinations, and I hope it will lessen the effect of her treason."

" Yes, I do as well. What a thing to do when she must be aware of how it would ruin the family."

"Wrapped up in the scheme; she lost her sense of reality. All she cares about is getting her revenge—foolish woman."

"Yes; well, I have been chatting with Lord Ainsworth and it was not easy, but I got an inkling of his involvement. Apparently, he is accepted by the émigrés better than the *ton*. Wife is the problem; a merchant's daughter. So, his objectives must be to do damage to England with the French group, which amazes me. He is a peer of the realm and is allowing his personal anger to lead him into treason."

"Astonishing! And I suspect that at least Gantre is the same; and perhaps Fornier and Fleur as well. Did you know Mr. Fornier left for London this morning? How foolish to let resentment of trivialities lead one into such dangerous actions."

"And we trust we can stop it before the damage is done; Wally will have informed the Admiralty."

"Let us hope they will act quickly. Will he bring back the law to make the arrests?"

"Yes, he plans to, but it is unfortunate we found no proof."

"Perhaps they may slip up yet or one of them become too worried. The risk is great, hanging at least."

Then they talked about the old days when treason was punished by being drawn and quartered.

After a silence, Darrell said, "What surprises me is that it is being pursued even though Napoleon is heading for defeat by the Allies. What good would this do to help him or are they trying to cause chaos as a delaying tactic?"

They examined the question as they ascended a hill. The view from the top was breathtaking.

"It all looks so peaceful; while vipers are coiled to spring a deadly trap."

"Getting poetic, are we Darrell? But seriously, how might this help Napoleon?"

Riding in silence for a while, feeling there must be something missing; they then talked over all the possibilities, and still thought these plotters were intent on hurting the English.

"One of the reasons people do drastic things is often for money. Let's consider how destroying the Admiralty building might bring them monetary rewards. Are they being paid to do this?"

Darrell said, "Who would pay for it? And what benefit would they receive for it?"

"If successful, it could put them in disarray and weaken their forces; who would profit from that? Let's think world-wide while we're at it."

"My mind goes to the colonies; the Navy has a controlling hand in all those areas. Plus, there is the war with America, but I can't think of any value for them."

So, he looked off into the distance for a moment before continuing.

"It just doesn't make sense," said Darrell.

Then he stopped Sultan again, and looked out over the valley as though to gain perspective, and Weatherbee pulled up beside him.

"Let's review the plotters again. Why did they gather here to make their plans? Is it because the location would not be suspected; a safe, bucolic setting? The fact some émigré community members in London are involved should be significant. Who will benefit?"

"This may go back to the intrigue on the Manfold; which is the first clue, when someone got to that man and recruited him into spying for them. Those plotters must have chosen that particular ship for a reason, and they must be sophisticated enough to involve codes. Not everyone knows how to write codes, usually intelligence groups. In England, it would be the Admiralty or the Foreign Office," said Darrell. "Might someone in either of those departments be the kingpin, or working for the leader?"

Suddenly he thought about the possibility of someone like Smithson, who might set up a trap for him. "The first clue is Chad's arrest in Paris; perhaps Smithson is now setting me up!"

Weatherbee looked shocked at the idea, but since they brainstormed, they must check every angle.

"Maybe that is why this is so elusive; it is not what it seems. Remember, I knew Lady Gantre for some years. My cover was blown at the émigré party, and my partner trapped in Paris."

"So, what do you think they are after? To arrest you for treason?"

"Perhaps, but it is convoluted and may be drawing tighter around me. Would you consider Wally or yourself might be a target? I don't think Clint is."

"No, I don't see any signs against us, as I haven't had any unusual things happen to me, or Wally."

Then they sat, lost in their thoughts for a while.

"How do we get to the bottom of this? Any possibility of false documents being planted on you, here in your chamber or even at the Inn in Bath? Should we make a search?"

Darrell's nerves were drawn as tight as steel bands and his head hurt. *That devil has been out to get me for years. Maybe this time he'll succeed.*

"Yes, we must do a thorough search, I don't like this at all. Makes me feel like a plucked chicken contemplating a hot fire. Why didn't I have some suspicion before this? They played a devious game and I've fallen for it."

Then a new thought even more distressing. Had his father received any mail or packages for him? Might they be planting incriminating evidence at Broom Street? Should he write home? No, it would do no good and might implicate his father. He must do this on his own, find out their plans.

"The implications keep expanding in my mind; they may use my father in their diabolical scheme, like send documents to our home on Broom Street."

"Hold on a moment, Darrell! Let's not run off on a tangent, because this could be totally wrong, and it might not be a plot against you at all. What would be the payoff for these people to trap you? Even if Smithson or his backers are paying for this, the potential for gain is too little. Just to get revenge on a school antagonist would not be enough to warrant this extensive scheme."

Now Darrell was taken back again, he had allowed himself to think it was true. What if he wanted to discredit him, to ruin his reputation? What would be his reward?

"Yes, you are right, Francis, I jumped to conclusions. But the circumstances are too coincidental to ignore and I'm sorry."

They both became silent to reflect on this. Darrell's mind went back to school days and Simpson.

"Francis, I have known him since Harrow and we were always at odds. He used to terrorize the new boys and I used to fight him for doing it. Those poor little boys were scared and missed home. We were often at fisticuffs over it, and as we both grew, our fighting increased. He was vicious, lashed out at everyone. He was as strong as I, but couldn't prevail over me. Actually, we learned a lot about boxing during those days.

Then, at Oxford, it continued and we both grew stronger. I used to get at him because I could always steal the girls from him, and usually beat him at athletics. So, you can see, there could be a reason for him to try to hurt me now."

Francis was amazed at this story—not having dreamed how deep the rift was between these men.

"I acknowledge this goes much deeper than I realized, Darrell, and you have good reason for your feelings. Let's walk for a while. Physical activity can stimulate the mind and bring us back to earth."

Getting his feet on the ground did make a difference. So many thoughts crowded his head that he had to let go of these outlandish ideas and concentrate on reality.

"All right, let's review the facts:

First is the Manfold affair, the selling of navy secrets by the turn-coat, but who are the buyers?

Second, Chad's arrest via a cleverly-laid trap in Paris, and Smithson is a suspect.

Third is the warning at the émigré party which led to my cover being blown.

Fourth are the orders from Foreign Office to go to Bath to follow French plotters.

Fifth is the Admiralty's command that you and Wally come here and invite me to the same event.

Sixth is we did find a number of them here.

Seventh, word leaks out of action "next week", and Gantre tells her nephew of a "revenge" and overhears Gantre and Fornier talk of a "big bang."

Eighth—Wally goes to London to warn of a possible blowing up of the Admiralty Mess during a gathering of the admirals.

Ninth—no firm proof."

Weatherbee followed the listing of facts. "I agree with your conclusions so far. Now we dig deeper."

"Yet we must still consider that at least part of this plot is a trap; it came to me all in a flash, like a revelation."

"Yes, intuition can be strong, but sentimentality can be involved. People seek revenge in lots of ways without setting up such an elaborate plan. Let's just keep that at the back of our minds while we consider the whole picture."

"Oh, you are right. Let's review the cost and benefits angle again."

Soon they realized they had been out for a long time.

As they rode back to Allen Court, Darrell said, "We should agree where we went, and how long we were out before we are asked."

"One of the horses needed a rest, maybe yours, since I think people are aware that Clint went to Bath last night."

"Yes, that will be the truth, too. So, we will turn my room inside out. Perhaps he can search Pelletier's room again during dinner."

Emotionally exhausted, he rested until his valet came. Somehow, he must rid himself of this whisper of fear.

"Let me tell you of my discussions with Weatherbee today. Went riding up in the hills this afternoon and did some brainstorming, a terrible thought struck me."

He revealed his suspicion of a trap, and also divulged the list of facts they worked out.

Clint was shocked. "So, you suspect Smithson of being behind this? Why? How?"

Then Darrell went on to tell him of the possibility of someone paying these people to set up the plot. The question—whose money and what would be the benefit?

"It's possible he may have a rich backer, but how would he profit? Doesn't make sense,"

"If we come upon one proof, such as a letter from the head man, we would go forward with an arrest."

"If we don't find anything, can the Runner do so?"

"No, but in the meantime, can you gain access to Pelletier's chamber during the meal and search it again? Tonight, you and I will look into this one thoroughly for any planted material, and you should do yours as well."

The dinner became a blur for Darrell that night, so he didn't do any flirting with the ladies, or be as aware of other conversations; and he hoped Weatherbee paid attention.

Tanner asked him, "Missing the young lady, are you?"

"Yes, I suppose I am. Hopes dashed and all that." *Let them think that,* he thought.

Soon, he left the drawing room and went to his chamber, because he just couldn't put on a show tonight.

Later, he and Clint turned out everything and made exhaustive incursions into the fireplace flue, under rugs, behind furniture—anywhere that might hide a document; including each piece of clothing.

Nothing was found, so Darrell felt relieved.

"I did a thorough search in Pelletier's chamber, then my own. Although he had a letter from a mademoiselle in London, I couldn't detect any code or anything."

Then he smiled. "Rather risqué in places."

"Can you recall any of the contents?"

Doing his best, he recited the lines and Darrell made note of them, but there was nothing sinister.

The night seemed endless.

Again, he went over all they knew but no new insights arose, and he wished he was able to talk with Chad, who had such a long experience that he might make sense of all this. Only a week passed since Darrell came to Bath, but it might make a difference. Another one here, and he would go home, but something lurked just out of his consciousness, some clue that might break the case wide open, but he couldn't grasp it.

If Smithson played a double-agent, he would do much damage, but it all required evidence!

By noon the next day, Wally returned. When Weatherbee saw his coach approach the house, he made sure he greeted him first.

"The story is you went to see your children," he said in low tones while shaking Wally's hand, and he gave the slightest nod of comprehension.

The boisterous greeting surprised Wally, but he reacted pleasantly to seeing lost friends, so Darrell waited inside for the commotion to lessen before he came out.

"Welcome back, I hope you found your children and your mother well."

"Yes, quite well thank you, did you behave yourself? Any broken hearts?"

For a moment he was surprised, how did he know?

"Nothing of consequence, old man; a little flirtation to pass the hours."

Details must wait, for there were too many people within hearing; then Betterton took him to the library.

"Glad to see you're back safe. How did you find your family?"

So, he spent some minutes in extolling the joy of seeing the children again. "At least I can visit them regularly now that I'm ashore."

It was much later before Darrell and Wally talked in Wally's room, where he told of the ploy to remove the Renwicks to safety, including the flirtation.

"Yes, they left yesterday for the north, after Gantre became aware of William's knowledge of the plot and threatened him with harm. It was necessary they go before arrests can be made."

Then he relayed what William saw and heard. All the agents would meet tonight in Darrell's chamber to review everything and decide how to proceed, and Wally could give his report on London.

Waiting was hard, even making a great effort to be in his foppish persona didn't work because he'd lost his edge.

Engulfed by everyone, each trying to get his attention, Wally endured.

"Wow, I have been anxious to get to business all evening."

"Yes, it is a test of fortitude for us all," said Weatherbee, "and we are all bursting with curiosity about your mission."

"Well, I had some success with the Lord of the Admiralty, who gave me the opportunity to explain the danger they were in. Of course, they knew something was going on, but not the details, so they changed the date of the meeting."

Looking around the group, Wally continued, "When I talked with the head of Navy Intelligence, he told me the turn-coat had been killed in prison; the lead person had not been exposed and the whole affair closed up like a clam. Didn't seem like there would be any more information forthcoming there, so I gave him the names of the suspected plotters, but that did not help.

I asked if they had anything relating to inter-department communication with the Foreign Office, and he said they learned of an arrest of a clerk there who stole some strategic documents."

A sigh of disappointment ran through the room, for their hopes were high.

"How about the Bow Street Runner?" asked Darrell.

"That, at least, is taken care of. A friend recommended a Mr. West. After meeting him, I hired him to come to Wiltshire to work on the case. So, he will put up at The Huntsman at Westbury and will nose around the area until we request him to come here."

Silence filled the room as all four men reflected on their disappointment.

"Well, I don't know what we expected, but more success than this. At least the Admiralty danger has been spared. Let's consider how to go forward."

"It will be interesting to see if the plotters will learn of the disruption of their plot," said Darrell, "and if they hear of the change"

"If they do, it will show they have an informer,"

"That's right!" exclaimed Wally. "Another turn-coat or a plant? And we just learned of the stolen documents at the Foreign Office, the same might happen at the Admiralty."

"Let's get back to the benefit," said Darrell. "What is the pay-off that could out-weigh the risk? Let's take M. Pelletier, for instance. How would he profit by this?"

Blank faces showed their bafflement, as they did not imagine anything except money, and who was the backer?

"Would it bring this to a head if the Runner came to ask questions of the plotters?" said Clint.

After a moment, Weatherbee said, "I think it would drive them underground, and if they go, who is behind them to continue the intrigue? Wish we had a hint to follow. Is there someone in this country who made a noise about the Navy? Perhaps someone in Parliament or rich enough to pay for what he wants?"

"Yes," said Darrell, "because we have considered this was a French plot so far. Maybe we should think bigger, like a powerful Englishman with revenge in mind, and is using the émigrés to make trouble."

Everyone stared at him for a moment, before turning their thoughts to this new possibility.

"Wish we got the newspapers," said Clint, " so we could see who is making news."

"But if he's behind it, he would be sure to keep quiet, don't you think? From the Navy standpoint, we need to think of someone who was demoted or brought up on charges. Even a Captain. There was the sailor accused of treason, but he did not go to trial yet, and that would go back to revenge."

"Could someone with means be using this plot to fulfill his schemes?" said Darrell.

"The issue of payoff is still on my mind," said Weatherbee.

The hour was getting late, so the meeting ended—this would give them all lots to think about.

As he lay in his bed, sleep was far away, so he reviewed the situation once again: the house party was half over and four hand-picked agents had not found evidence of the plot by the French group. The Admiralty changed the date of their gathering. The Runner was situated at an Inn near Westbury, waiting for the order to arrest the plotters, but lack of proof was holding him back. *And I fear that I am the target of a trap--a set-up for a charge of treason.*

The thought of going home to see his father was strong, and he also needed to talk with Chad, whose experience in Paris may shed some clues on this situation. But he had already left for the meeting a few days ago—it would look odd for him to go away again. I *must continue to do my work with the other agents, but we have hit a wall.* Is there a weak-link? Breaking just one of the plotters would help find out the plan.

The Royal Navy was the center of it. If the Admiralty brass is the target, might there be another reason to go after them? To stop the blockades? What about timing?

What if it was crippled by losing many of its leaders? Would it cause an immediate repercussion? Ships were on missions all over the world; how long would the news take to change their orders? To interfere with them in European harbors? To end patrolling the Channel, the Mediterranean, the Atlantic, the West Indies—it would take as long as it takes to travel those distances. So, there would be no immediate benefit.

The communications were slow and happenings in Europe were reported by Castlereagh's staff by diplomatic bag to the government in London. The Foreign Office would have the information as soon as it was received, but getting it to agents in the field would be delayed.

Now Darrell was out of the loop while on his mission in Wiltshire and Wally's trip to London was to the Admiralty, not privy to all the news, only what affected the navy. The four agents must proceed as best they could. One would assume the plotters were similarly handicapped, and probably acting on instructions given to them before they came to Bath; unless the outsiders were bringing them messages.

How to break the deadlock? How to get proof of who was guilty of planning the treasonous plot?

Could they bring more of the guests in on the dilemma? No, they thought they had identified them all, but what if one or two were so well undercover they were fooled? How had he done with his acting? Did they think him foolish? If Darrell was a target, didn't it mean that his real identity as an agent was known to the plotters?

What if Smithson was behind all this? What if he duped the émigrés to do his bidding? The plot seemed so ambiguous.

Should he withdraw back to London? To the Foreign Office? It was as though his hands were tied. Could he do better in London? There, he could talk with his friend, who may help. How might he fight Smithson? And who to trust there? What a dilemma.

When he went to London, would he have to take Clint? And who was he? He had been pushed on Darrell after Chad was hurt. *Was he a plant? A mole?*

All this intrigue and supposition was driving him crazy, and he faltered. If he didn't know who to trust, why trust anybody?

This was a whole new thought which kept him awake through the night; he felt like he was working blind. What if all this was true and the net was closing in around him? Now he felt suffocated. He had to break away.

What if he sent an express message to Clarence in Bath and requested another letter? Perhaps his father was ill. Maybe he was called home from the House Party? Why not go to Westbury and hire a rider?

So, he wrote: *"I have another favor to ask of you, old friend, and I'll find a way to thank you when this is all over. Send this note to me by express as soon as possible to Allen Court. The previous one arrived exactly as I expected and served the purpose. This one is a family matter. Yours, etc."*

The missive he included was supposedly from his father's valet and explained that his father was under his doctor's care and requested his son be summoned; Sir Giles was having another occurrence of his gout and his heart was not strong. *'Please come soonest, Your servant, Anthony Strange.'*

The horse was saddled while most people were at breakfast. A note was left for Clint, and he advised the butler he would be absent today.

After he located an express rider, he went to the Inn where the Bow Street Runner was staying and took breakfast there, keeping an eye open for Mr. West. He had the appearance of a boxer with large shoulders and well-muscled arms, so he introduced himself and was invited to sit at West's table.

Darrell bought him ale, and they talked of the area and the people until he finished his meal.

"Wish to speak privately with you, sir. Could we go to your room?"

After they were seated by the fire, he said, "I don't know how much Captain Finchly told you about this job, but I have a few questions for you."

"Certainly. Are you one of the gents who are trying to break up this plot?"

"Yes, I am working for the government."

"What is it you want to know?" he asked, as he rubbed his huge hands together.

Then Darrell talked about the plot, and said, "Have you learned anything new?"

West sat back, studying him, then said, "What might a poor bloke learn in this little village about the plots set up by the posh gentry? Can't very well go around naming names or describing them, can I?"

"Thinking more on the lines of gossip in the pub about unusual happenings here or up at the manor, like some strangers talking too much over their whiskey."

"Oh, well now, that is another matter. People do be free with their speech when in their cups. There was one feller who was that mad over being taken advantage of. Said he was promised a fine reward for following a bloke and reporting on who he met. He was from up at the manor, he was—don't know his name, though soon a big dark man came up to speak to him and they talked a while, then had a bit of an argument."

"Do you have any descriptions or names?"

"Now, is it likely I was close enough for that? Except the second was a nasty one. Was all dressed in black with a black hat and his hair was long enough to fall over his collar, but no mustache or beard. When he shouted, he said something like, 'That's all you know? What good are you? I need to know where he went.' The other bloke was cringing, 'I told you, he went riding up in the hills with another feller,'" he said.

Oh, he thought, *that could have been himself and Weatherbee.*

"When was this watchdog on the job?"

"Last night they met, so yesterday or the day before," he said.

So, they had been followed! But maybe the fellow hadn't heard anything. Sounds like Pelletier was the dark one. If he was able to describe him and Weatherbee, Pelletier would now know they were working together. More reason to go away for a few days. Should he warn Weatherbee? That was the question.

Late afternoon, Darrell returned to Allen Court, and went to his chamber without seeing any guests. Then Clint came to dress him for dinner.

"Did you have a good ride? Go anywhere special?"

Hiding his suspicion, he said, "Just getting some air to clear my head. Had lunch in Westbury and scouted around the hills. Sultan is holding up well with all this riding. Always has good endurance."

Since Clint had turned to brush his dinner coat, Darrell couldn't see his reaction. It was an uncomfortable feeling to be suspicious of one's partner.

A footman interrupted—an express was being delivered; so, he followed the fellow, and received the letter from the rider. Opening it, he reacted as expected upon receiving bad news, and uttered a curse before heading back to his room. But he didn't show it to Clint because it was in his own handwriting; then made a scene of distress at his father's illness.

"Well, I must leave at first light and I will ride Sultan, so you can stay here and keep an eye on things."

"Ride all the way to London? Hope you have good weather."

"Yes, it will be faster. I am anxious to get home because of my father's illness."

Well, he can make what he wants of that, thought Darrell.

"Do you want me to pack for you?"

"No, I can do it, and if my father is improving, I will be back before the end of the week. If not, you will need to gather everything, go back to the inn at Bath and wait for me there."

"Very well," said Clint with downcast eyes.

During Port, Darrell gave the news to the others, explaining the express letter and his father's worrisome illness.

"Stands to reason you must go," said Effington pompously. "A son's duty and all that."

Muttered agreement went around the table, and Pelletier's raised eyebrows showed his surprise.

Then Tanner said, "Too bad, you'll miss the Ball, and someone else will have the pleasure of dancing with Mrs. Monroe."

After he stared for a moment, Archibald said, "I'll care for my wife, thank you. The waltz is not that important." Then he turned to Darrell. "Sorry, old man, about your father, I hope you'll find him improving."

So, he bowed to him, but kept a serious expression. "If I am delayed, I will miss my farewells and I have enjoyed meeting you."

A damper fell over the group and Betterton soon rose.

CHAPTER 9

Escape in the Rain

Rising early, Darrell ordered his horse, and traveled a number of miles before stopping for a late breakfast; taking a break from the frigid rain.

He stayed his course and reached Newbury by evening. The wet penetrated his clothing, and he was stiff from the cold when he entered the inn. He stepped over to the fire and took off his soaked great-coat, then ordered a room and his dinner. Having tipped the ostler to give Sultan a thorough rubdown before throwing a blanket over him; he hoped that would suffice. Maybe tomorrow the rain would cease.

But it continued to plague him all the way to Richmond, where his concern for his horse made him stop at an inn for the night; but he would reach Broom Street in the morning.

The grooms were surprised and took Sultan into the snug stable.

"Yes, he's had a hard time, so give him good care, as you always do." He flipped them some coins, and went to the house.

Whenever he thought of those days—of the turmoil of his mind—it was hell. By the end, he had succumbed to a cold.

His father looked shocked. "Well son, I thought you still in Bath!"

He took his father's proffered hand in his.

"So glad to see you, Father. Sorry to drop in unannounced, but I had to come to London."

Sir Giles lead him to the fire." Is something wrong? You look worried,"

"Found unforeseen developments, and I will tell you all about it after I get out of these wet clothes. Is Trent here?"

What a relief to be comforted by the tender ministrations of his long-time valet.

"If I may say, you got yourself into it now," Trent said, "have you taken anything for your illness?"

"No, I have been traveling for days in cold rain. Sultan suffered for sure."

"Do you mean you rode from Bath, sir? Where is your carriage?"

"I needed a swift journey, so I came on Sultan."

When he inquired about Chad, he was informed of his slow improvement.

"The internal injuries are still a worry, as well as his mind, and he has some terrible nightmares."

"Not surprising, he will relive the terror for some time."

Then he soaked his aching body in the tub until the water cooled and dressed in clean clothes.

Next, he found Chad reclining against pillows in his bed and his face lit up when he saw Darrell enter the room.

"I say, you are a sight!"

"Hello, Chad, I hope I find you better than when I left."

"Slowly improving, thank you." Now his facial swelling had declined somewhat, but many scars remained to be healed.

"Did you successfully complete your mission in Bath?"

As he surveyed his old friend, his heart ached for him, he may never be like his old self again.

"No, no success, I think I hit a wall, Chad. Hope you can re-direct me."

"Why, what happened?"

"Well, first, the Admiralty sent two agents there also, so the four of us did our best identifying the plotters. But we could find no proof against them, only hints and overheard phrases. I had the crazy idea that the plot was to trap me into a charge of treason! Can you imagine? Fear and suspicion made me even suspect the other agents! So, I made the excuse of my father being gravely ill to leave."

"Oh, Darrell! So sorry. Once trust is lost, it is hard to recover. What do you plan to do here?"

"First, I want to talk to you, then go to the Foreign Office, and I even have concerns about who I can depend on there. I keep thinking Smithson is out to get me. Did you remember anything from the time of your torture?"

Chad sat staring at Darrell in disbelief, then gathered his mental resources and steeled his feelings, because he owed it to him to help if he could.

"There is something," he stuttered," but it is not very clear, I got the impression of someone in the wings, stirring up the guards during the worst of the beatings. And I also got a fleeting image of a sneering Smithson. May have been mistaken, but it stayed with me."

"Well, that is something, even if the perception is blurred with pain. If it's true, I hope we get the bastard, for they did a thorough job on you, Chad, and I'm so sorry." Then they sat in silence for a while.

"There is another matter also, Suspicions have surfaced about Clint Warden, who was with me when we brought you back from France. He was thrust upon me when the exchange was set up, then he did work in the émigré community and went to Bath with me. He's been my valet at the house party, so he's privy to everything we've uncovered. I can't trust him to be what he claims anymore, so I left him there. I'm going to inquire about him at the Foreign Office."

"Yes, I need to talk with you b…f-fore you go," said Chad. "Be careful who you speak with there—not P-p-e-e-body. I recommend Mr. Bart since I would trust him with my l - l - ife."

"Tell me more about him." So, Chad stuttered through:

"Has been there for many years and will know who is trustworthy. When you go in, go in disguise, and ask to meet with Mr. Bart; he will know what to do."

The next day, Darrell arrived about 10 o'clock and asked for Mr. Bart. He added a wig, eyeglasses and a mustache, and doubted anyone would know him; plus, he had a short note written at Chad's dictation.

Mr. Bart listened to Darrell's story and concerns, then asked many questions before agreeing it looked bad and Darrell could be in danger.

"If Lord Castlereagh was here, I would take you to him straight away, but not Peabody—he's an ass."

"Yes, I agree with you, sir. Couldn't even get a rise out of him when I suggested there may be a double-agent involved in Chad's arrest and torture."

"Not surprised, but now leave this to me and I'll see what I can do. Just lie-low and come back tomorrow."

As Darrell returned to the street, he thought Mr. Bart looked like a dog with a juicy bone to chew on, and he felt better.

Father and son had lots to talk about over dinner, but he must screen the secret parts for his father's protection.

"That is a tough spot to be in, trust is important in your line of work. Is this fellow at the Foreign Office going to help you?"

"Yes, he will do some background checking. We'll hope he will find something to give me direction."

Sir Giles reported the Beckworthys had not resolved their dilemma. "Seems Bernice still has some time before she talks with her suitors, but I wonder which she will choose."

Darrell said, "What a terrible position to be in. Perhaps I will stop to visit her when I return from Bath after the House Party."

The next morning, he came to Mr. Bart's office again.

"Well I issued a false report to try to trap our suspect, and we will see what the results will be. I also checked on Clint Warden. Nothing distinctly troublesome showed up, but I'm worried. The boy was too new to have an extensive record, but too weak to entrust him in such an important mission. Maybe someone is using him for his own purpose—like Smithson?"

"Oh, I'm afraid I told him all about that. Raises new questions, doesn't it?"

"If, in fact, he is working for him, it puts him on guard. The other two are highly esteemed by Admiralty Intelligence, so don't worry about them. Now, young man, here is what I want you to do; go back until the end of the house party, and you can tell the agents what you found out about Clint Warden, but you must all stay alert and check your rooms for planted documents."

In the Hansom Cab on the way home, he thought over the situation and knew he must continue with Clint until they leave the house party, but be careful what he says to him.

He left Sultan at Broom Street, and hired a Hack Chaise for the return trip, and though it was slower, he didn't suffer from the elements.

When he arrived late in the evening, Wally was all curiosity, so they set up a meeting of the three in Wally's chamber after the guests retired.

"Yes, I went to the Foreign Office but did not meet with the regular people since my friend put me on to a man he trusted implicitly. He was receptive of my story and didn't think me an idiot, and he put out a little trap for Smithson; to flush him out with some false information."

"What else did you check on, Darrell?" asked Wally. "There must have been other things on your mind."

Grinning at him, he knew he was taunting him.

"Yes, I also inquired about Clint, since I had begun to suspect him; he did find that he was too inexperienced to have been assigned these missions, and he told me to be careful what was said in front of him."

The grin came back to his face and his eyes twinkled. "He said the Admiralty had high praises for both of you."

Darrell smiled as Wally said, "Why you . . ." then they all laughed.

"Well, I must admit that when those demons danced in my head, trust went out the window, but I couldn't believe you were deceiving me. By the way, Francis, when I talked with Mr. West, he told me about a "dark" fellow who put a tail on us when we rode up into the hills. So, it's possible Pelletier knows we are working together."

"That must be why he's been acting rather strangely around me."

"While you were gone nothing of great significance happened," said Wally. "The rainy weather kept everyone too close, so tension is showing. But we didn't stumble on any proof or any news about the group, so we weren't able to call in the Runner."

The next morning, Darrell went late to breakfast. Only four guests were present.

"How is your father doing?" asked Monroe. "Assume he is improved since you are back."

"Yes, sir, thank you, and I was vastly relieved to find him better, but am glad I went—it seemed to ease his mind. We had a chance to review estate matters and make some decisions; although I hope he will have more years if he obeys doctor's orders."

Effington made some pithy comments about doctors and Lady Effington shushed him.

"Now I must leave to assist her ladyship," said Mrs. Monroe; "as she may need help with details for the ball."

Monroe showed great interest in Darrell's travels, which soon drove the Effingtons from the room.

"That horse of yours must be a real trooper," he said. "Sounds like a rough trip."

Darrell replaced his coffee cup in its saucer, and said, "I can't remember a more uncomfortable one—freezing cold rain all the way, so I left Sultan behind for a rest. What a grand stallion. Bought him in Ireland last year."

"You can find excellent breeds there, which breeder did you go to?"

Darrell told him all about the stud farm near Dungarvan and was surprised Monroe was so interested, being a seafaring man; but he had to admit that he knew horses. So, they took a walk to the stables after breakfast to check on their teams.

The head groom took them around, and Darrell's Troy joined them as well. "The blacks are out to pasture today, sir, since they need some exercise after several days of rain, but we'll be leaving here soon, won't we?"

"Yes, within the next few days. Sultan will be well-rested before I get back."

Frowning, he said, "I hope he took no hurt from the rough trip, sir."

"Your concern is not misplaced, Troy, but he is strong and did well, and I had the ostlers take extra care of him at the inns; not as good as you do, of course," and he gave him a bright smile.

"Thank you, sir, he's a grand horse." He pulled his forelock and walked down the aisle.

When Monroe finished checking on his team, they returned to the house.

"Thought I would check your evening clothes," said Clint. "Will you wear all black or the mulberry?"

Darrell studied him as he spoke, but found nothing untoward.

"Don't you think I should be audacious on the last night?"

And he noticed the devilish look in his eye. "Of course! End as you began."

"Why don't you pick out things for me to consider? Your valet days are nearly over, you know; we may leave tomorrow."

As he looked through the wardrobe, he picked out not only the Mulberry with grey, but a turquoise coat with yellow trousers; so bright as to make one blink.

"That's it! I remember I had it made for a special occasion," touching it as he spoke. "A shirt with lots of lace should add to the splendor." And he threw back his head and laughed. *This should be fun, Lady Effington might faint.*

Clint was not surprised at his choice since he did his best to be outrageous.

In the afternoon, Wally and Darrell took a walk around the park. Plans had already been made with Weatherbee to search the rooms during the ball and Clint would not be included, so secrecy was total. Surely no one would suspect such a thing. The three agents would break away separately to not raise suspicions.

Darrell made a scene when he tore the lace at his wrist. "Oh no! Look what I've done." Glancing around the ballroom in a panic, he said, "I'll go get it repaired."

Four chambers had been assigned to him to search, so he proceeded. A letter was well hidden in Gantre's unmentionables drawer—a Promise-to-Pay for services rendered, signed by Comte de Maitree! After reading it, he replaced it for the Runner to find. Next was Effington, nothing there, nor Tanner, but Ainsworth was productive with another promise note.

Keeping his excitement under control, he stole back to his room. Finally! Some proof! The first to find something should send a servant for Mr. West, so he repaired his lace haphazardly and approached the butler.

"Can you spare a footman, Wilson? Need a message delivered to The Huntsman Inn at Westbury." said Darrell.

He sputtered before agreeing—he wasn't surprised by Mr. Coletrane's request since he considered him most frivolous.

He gave a sign to Wally as they sought a beverage, telling him of success, and he slipped away.

In Marie Fornier's chamber, he found a letter about the plans. In Timberleigh's, he discovered a Promise-to-Pay note shoved under the mattress. Monroe was clear, as he expected, and he returned to his room before going back to the ball, where he asked Connie Betterton to dance.

Soon Weatherbee told his wife he needed to go to their room for an aspirin for his headache, but she wanted to go with him. So, he turned to Darrell, indicating he should dance with her.

The first room on Francis' list was Pelletier's. Nerve endings tingled as he began searching. Soon he was disappointed and about to leave when he spotted a framed picture of a hunt scene that looked crooked, so he turned it over and discovered a folded note stuck into a corner of the frame—an encrypted message! He thought of the Manfold troubles. This could tie this plot to the previous event, and he returned it all as it was.

In Fleur's room there was no success, nor in Samuelson's. But he was elated. As soon as Mr. West arrives, his search can turn it up, enough for an arrest. Perhaps the others found things as well.

He went to his room then back to the ball. A waltz was playing, and he watched Darrell and Mrs. Monroe twirling around the floor. Her face told it all, she was experiencing a little heaven. Of course, he was at his best; gallant and handsome; each step perfectly in harmony with the music. Even his outlandish turquoise coat added to the ambiance.

So Weatherbee smiled to himself. It was a good night.

When Mr. West arrived well before the end of the ball, Wally was waiting around the hall for him, then whisked him up to his chamber to give him directions. Darrell and Francis had provided him with information of what they found, but the runner had to search every room. Footmen accompanied him as he went from room to room, and one kept a list of whose produced the prized documents.

So, he talked with Wally before descending to the ballroom; and must make the arrests before the guilty parties could escape. He went to Betterton and brought him over to West, who said, "When the orchestra finishes this number, my lord, you need to make an announcement." And he told him what to say.

"Ladies and Gentlemen, let me have your attention please," Jasper called out.

The room quieted and everyone looked at him expectantly as they wondered if an engagement would be announced.

"This is Mr. West of the Metropolitan Police, and he requested that the following persons step forward: Lord Ainsworth, Monsieur Pelletier, Mr. Timberleigh, Mrs. Fornier, and Lady Gantre." Pelletier made a rush for the side door, but a footman guarded it. Confusion reigned, but they came. When Lady Betterton protested on behalf of her friends, it made no difference. Tanner's face was ashen, as was Samuelson's.

The group was ushered out and taken to the library where they were informed of the searches and the results, and that they would be detained and removed to Bath in the morning for arraignment.

Pelletier was outraged and protested, the others all made a protest for show and Gantre trembled with rage. Both Ainsworth and Timberleigh looked frightened.

Once the prisoners had been told of the charges under which they were arrested, they were taken upstairs and locked in their chambers. Consequently, it was very late before the rest of the guests retired. *Little sleep would happen tonight,* thought Darrell. But it was a good feeling, success. He thought of the Renwicks and was glad they were not here to see the arrest of their aunt.

Francis Weatherbee sought out Lord Betterton, and they went to Jasper's study, for he deserved an explanation of the fracas which ended his wife's ball.

"Well Jasper, I can now inform you I am with the Admiralty and was sent here to uncover a French plot. We now have enough proof to bring the plotters to justice. So sorry you and your wife were incommoded."

"I guess I'm still confused, Francis. What has this to do with them?"

"Well, it all started months ago with espionage on a Navy ship; secrets being sold. Then I was sent here because there appeared to be a French plot in the works with the involvement of the émigré community in London. This is all hush-hush, you understand. Now that some arrests have been made, the Admiralty should be able to find more complete information from these traitors. It's like a jellyfish with tentacles going in all directions."

But Jasper still seemed confused. "What will we tell our other guests, Francis?"

"As little as possible, I'm afraid. You can say, truthfully, that you knew nothing about it, that you are as surprised as everyone. In the morning, they will leave and the house party will be over."

"I hope the policeman can move them out of here swiftly in the morning; because I don't want any of them in our breakfast room; let them eat in Bath," said Jasper with passion. "Oh, it makes me so mad to think we were entertaining the dirty traitors; and I trust they will get what's coming to them!"

The exodus in the morning was orderly. The ones with coaches were advised to use them—under guard. Extra men had to be recruited to watch the prisoners as well as their valets, ladies' maids and coachmen. Gantre's maid refused to go with her, but would still be interviewed in Bath like the others, and Weatherbee wanted all this mess to be removed from Allen Court right after dawn broke.

Lord Betterton was told Finchly and Coletrane volunteered to work as guards. Clint had packed everything during the night, and Weatherbee would stay until after breakfast to help the Bettertons deal with the remaining guests. He had decided the best way to move this lot to London was by ship. The Navy frigate *Freedom* was in Bristol now and would be commandeered by Captain Lord Wallace Finchly.

Darrell was relieved when the five prisoners boarded and became the Navy's responsibility. So, he told Clint that his mission was over when they reached Bath, and he could leave for London by stagecoach.

CHAPTER 10

A Cousin's Visit

As expected, Darrell received a warm welcome at his uncle's home. Lord Hector took him to the drawing room and offered him a brandy.

"Chilly winds out there today. Where are you coming from, London?"

"No sir, from Bath, where I attended a house party for a few weeks. How is the family?"

"Could be better; still upset about the wedding."

"That's not surprising; rather earth-shattering in fact."

Sitting in silence for a few minutes, they were not quite sure how to proceed as Lord Hector gazed into the fire.

"Perhaps you may be able to help Bernice sort it out; she has always been fond of you; just cries whenever I mention it."

Darrell imagined the stiff formality his uncle would use. No wonder the girl dissolved into tears.

"Yes, sir, that is my main purpose for coming since I have worried about her."

At dinner, his cousin looked pale and thin.

"Glad to see you, Bernice."

She lowered her head, searching for words. "Hello, Darrell. Nice of you to come."

"I'm on my way back to London after a sojourn in Bath, so I couldn't pass by Basingstoke without coming to visit, and I hope we can spend some time together."

Nodding her head, she turned as her mother spoke to her, so he turned to Lord Hector, and they talked about horses, and in particular, Darrell's Sultan.

The dinner table conversation was on general subjects, but it was obvious they all thought about the situation; like a huge dilemma filling the room.

The next morning Darrell asked Bernice to go for a walk with him, and they were pleased to find that the sun was shining. They walked in silence for a while, then he spoke.

"I wondered how to start the conversation I want to have with you, for I wish to tell a story of my own which might help with your problem, Bernice. A little over a year ago I lost the woman I wanted to marry to another man. Though I came to recognize I was not the best match for her, I still feel regrets, but now she is happily married to a wonderful man, and I am happy for them."

Then he paused, scraping his boot in the gravel of the walkway, bowing his head

"The decision was taken out of my hands because I did not behave the way I should and I did not deserve her love. My angry actions proved it so."

Watching his face as he spoke, she looked amazed by his story.

"But both of my suitors acted in anger. What's the difference?"

"Well, it is complicated, Bernice, but let's look at each of them. Do you have a preference now?"

"No, I cannot decide, they each have good and bad points."

"Yes, but how did they act it out? Humphrey showed a terrible temper and did not esteem anyone, thinking only of himself and even called me out for a ridiculous reason. But Captain Mark was a gentleman. Once your father recognized him, he showed respect to everyone involved, and I believe he wants what is best for you, Bernice, because he loves you."

"Are you saying I should choose him?"

"No, I'm not trying to steer you, but pointing out some important character traits which appeared during that terrible scene. Why did you not wait for him? Had you decided he was not the one for you?"

Lowering her head again, she wished he did not ask such hard questions, then she relented. "My friends were marrying all around me, leaving me behind, and I wanted to marry also, but he was not here; not knowing when he would be, if ever. The war takes many lives. So, when Humphrey proposed, I accepted and put Mark out of my mind, as I had not heard of him for a long time, and I wanted a big wedding at St. George's like my friends, and I was impatient to move on with my life. I didn't even think past it, that was my only goal."

A little surprised, he saw the shallowness of her decisions.

"What are you thinking now? Do you want to marry either of these men now?"

"Well, I don't think I want Humphrey after his behavior. But I don't even know if the Captain still wants me, after what I did."

After Darrell studied her for a moment, he said, "Your father put restrictions on everyone for a month, but would you want to discuss it with Mark?"

"Oh, but I am so embarrassed I don't think I can. Would you talk with him first?"

Then he sighed—he hoped she would not do this; did not want to be the go-between.

"Where is the Captain staying?"

"Well, I believe he is at his mother's in London, on Adams Street. Are you on your way to London?"

"Yes, but first you must tell your father what you intend, because it won't get any easier if you put it off."

So, she agreed to talk with her father as soon as possible, as she could not stand all this tension.

After Bernice and Lord Beckworthy had their meeting, she came looking for Darrell in the library. He loved his uncle's room with its plethora of fine volumes, all bound in leather. The room was redolent with the smell of tobacco as well, a man's retreat.

"There you are. I talked with Father, and he relented, and said he didn't mind if you meet Mark. Will you?"

Smiling at her breathlessness, he said, "What do you want me to say to him?"

This stopped her, she hadn't thought it out that far.

"What do you want to ask?"

"Well, I want to know if he still wants me!"

"If he still does, will you agree to see him and talk with him?"

"Oh, it is so hard, Darrell, I don't know if I could do it."

"Well, if you can't even speak with your betrothed now, how do you plan to make a marriage work? I'm aware you're embarrassed, but you must overcome that and proceed as an adult. The embarrassment will cease once you enter into conversation with him. Think how he must feel; he's the one who was hurt," said Darrell ruthlessly.

Now he had to move her past this girlish behavior and have her act like a woman; a woman who knows what she wants.

Bernice looked aghast at his words; thought he would do it for her, like her father always did. But here she was being forced to take action and it irritated her. Why couldn't he just do it?

"It is all about what you want for your future; not just frivolous dreams. How do you see yourself in five or ten years, Bernice? Do you imagine being in a loving marriage, probably with children? Or do you just want to float along, letting others plan for you?"

Blinking at the harshness of what he said, she finally realized she had to take control of her own future. What was it she really wanted? Mark, or Humphrey? Was it to wed, or spinsterhood? Did she want either of them? Yes, she wanted her brave officer, if he would accept her.

"Yes, you are right, Darrell, I abdicated my life to others. Now I must stand up for what I want. I do feel bad about the pain I caused him in my thoughtless actions, but I want to know if he can forgive me and move forward together."

"That's more like it! So glad you made decisions for yourself; I will meet him in town or would you like to come with me and see him?"

She started at this option. Could she handle it? Could her mother come with her? Yes, she could take action for herself.

The next day, he set out for London, and was followed by the Beckworthys in their coach. They would open their house on Albemarle Street for their visit.

A note was sent to Captain Mark Littleton at Adams Street, asking for a meeting. A swift response showed eagerness, so he assumed he was still interested in his cousin. He had liked this young man, the little he had seen of him.

This is no shabby-genteel establishment like I expected, he thought as he glanced around the apartment.

Thrusting out his hand, he smiled as he greeted him. There was anxiety and some fear in Littleton's eyes, but his handshake was firm.

"This is my mother, Mrs. Littleton, Mr. Coletrane."

"Pleased to meet you, ma'am." The lady was friendly, gave him a welcoming smile and chatting briefly.

Mark led Darrell into the drawing room. Both men wanted to get to the purpose of this meeting, for he half expected to hear that he was out of the picture.

"Captain Littleton, I have been to visit the Beckworthys in Basingstoke, and had the opportunity to discuss this awkward situation with Miss Beckworthy. There is a question I must ask you: do you still want to marry her?"

Mark's eyes grew wide and his brow rose at this frontal attack. A flush crept up his face.

"Of course, I want to," he cried with passion, "more than anything in the world—I love her, sir."

Darrell smiled and said, "Just as I thought."

There was a pause as each man watched the other. "How is it you are here; not Miss Beckworthy or his Lordship?"

"Miss Beckworthy is very embarrassed by this horrible situation, and she would like the opportunity to meet with you, but first had to ascertain if you still wanted her."

Mark rose; walked to the window and his tense shoulders relaxed as he turned toward Darrell.

"What of this other *gentleman?*"

"Well, I have had no contact with Mr. Beales, nor any news of him, so he is another matter altogether."

"But he still may fight for the marriage."

"Between us, Mark, I think he showed himself in an unflattering light. Don't think he is the man for my cousin at all; but that is my opinion."

"No, he didn't show any concern for Miss Beckworthy, did he? Since we're speaking frankly, I suspect her dowry was of greater importance to him."

"You may be right, but I must state the second part of my mission, sir. Will you set a time when you can meet Miss Beckworthy at Albemarle Street?"

Mark started. "Do you mean she is in town?"

"Yes, she just arrived last night with her parents. Would two o'clock this afternoon work for you?"

The time was agreed on and as Darrell took his leave, he murmured, "Wear your regimentals," with a mischievous smile.

She felt a mixture of joy and apprehension, since she had always avoided confrontations, but this was too important to put off.

Stiff civility ruled the greetings when Captain Littleton arrived; resplendent in his best dress uniform. Lord Beckworthy was limited to the briefest conversation by his lady wife, who soon excused them and left the room.

Bernice sat uneasily on the sofa, and Mark was seated on a chair across from her. He wanted to gather her into his arms and tell her his feelings but had to refrain.

"Miss Beckworthy, I am appreciative of this opportunity to talk with you and was pleased by your cousin's visit this morning. I trust he told you the answer to your question."

She found the courage to look up at him, and what she saw emboldened her.

"Captain Littleton, can you ever forgive me for my stupidity? I told you I would wait for you and I did not, I became impatient for marriage—all my friends were marrying; but I should have written to you."

"My place in Portugal was tenuous and mail could not be counted on. A letter from my mother took six months to reach me; so, I understand how hard it must have been for you when you knew nothing of my position. I can't say that I enjoyed the situation at St. George's, but I could not let you go and I pray we can work out the details."

"So, you still want me?" she asked in a small voice, wringing her hands in her lap.

Mark was surprised at her question, so he rose from his seat and came to sit beside her, took both of her hands in his, looked into her blue eyes and said, "Miss Beckworthy, will you marry me?"

She sighed. A smile changed her face into the Bernice he remembered, so full of life it dazzled him.

"Yes, Mark, I will!"

The lengthy embrace that followed was interrupted by a tap on the door and the entrance of her mother.

"Excuse me," she said, "but I wondered if your conversation was complete and it is." Then her face broke into a smile.

"Oh Mama, it is all right," said Bernice, and she rushed to her mother and threw her arms around her neck.

Captain Littleton rose to his feet upon her entrance, with a rather sheepish grin on his face; but joy shone from his eyes.

"So glad," said Lady Beckworthy as she shook his hand.

When Lord Beckworthy heard the news, he was pleased, but knew it was not so easy to settle the dilemma.

Captain Littleton requested his daughter's hand in marriage, and he said, "Not so fast; we have another bridge to cross first."

A pall fell over the group for a moment.

"I shall meet with Mr. Beales and inform him of her choice," said his lordship, "Where may I call upon you, sir?"

Mark gave him his address.

Lord Beckworthy sent a note to Mr. Beales, requesting a meeting at Albemarle Street.

Humphrey Beales walked into the house as though he owned it. The butler had trouble keeping his countenance blank.

Beckworthy said, "Thank you for coming."

"Good day, sir, I assume you reached the decision I have wished for."

"On the contrary, Mr. Beales, I don't believe you will like it."

So, he studied the arrogant man before him—must handle this with care.

"Miss Beckworthy has given her full consideration and decided she still wants to marry Captain Littleton, and she is sorry for the unfortunate situation in which you were embroiled."

Then Humphrey's temper went out of control again.

"Sorry! For shattering all my hopes?"

Lord Beckworthy took a step back as though he expected blows; a startled look on his face.

"Yes, she is. Now she realizes she made a rash decision when you offered for her."

He hesitated and said as an after-thought, "And why did you offer for her, sir? Since you don't appear to like her."

Humphrey snorted. "Why should I like the woman I would marry; since she'd soon learn to behave the way I wanted. There are other more important considerations, as you well know!"

Lord Beckworthy raised his brows at this statement, *alarmed that he had agreed to give his beloved daughter to this man!*

"By that I would expect you refer to her dowry! Are you a fortune hunter? Had I known that I would not have let you near her. Perhaps you should leave now, Mr. Beales."

Then Humphrey sneered. "Not so fast, your lordship. There are things to be settled, marriage or not."

Beckworthy's eyes narrowed. "Now you wish to threaten me, Mr. Beales?"

"There's such a thing as breach of promise. It does not matter how I get the money, but I will get it. My solicitor will be in touch."

With that, Humphrey smirked and went out the door.

Lord Beckworthy sat down with a 'plunk' at his desk, thunderstruck at the audacity of this creature. Then he took out writing paper and a pen to write a note to his man-of-business. This was outrageous! He wanted Beales investigated.

CHAPTER 11

Darrell was glad his father looked well and Chad was improving. Now he might sit with him often, talking about the Bath mission, although it was out of his hands now, and he would turn his mind to the future. So, he went to Mr. Bart and discussed the situation about Smithson.

He was greeted with a smile by Mr. Bart, who asked, "How does our friend progress, Mr. Coletrane?"

"It is slow—the wounds heal but the thoughts are troubled," said Darrell, a frown creasing his brow. "And I fear for the outcome, so I am taking him north, out of the city for a while, where he will find quiet at my father's estate, as well as the best of care. But I came to learn of your progress also, what of our scheming friend?"

"Not surprised at your question; we set several things in motion but no results yet."

Of course, Darrell looked concerned. "Is he so smart to avoid the traps?"

"There is no proof of his possible treason. How cunning he is, we do not know, for we found no evidence of harm to any of our other agents, so we will continue our watch and put out more misinformation."

Darrell hired a Hansom cab to White's. News often spread around the club, so he ordered a drink and sat in a corner to read the paper. He skimmed through the Times, and came upon a small article that aroused his interest. Another body was pulled out of the Thames, but this one was a gentleman, with no identification.

As he put it aside, his eyes narrowed, and he realized this unusual occurrence smacked of intrigue; so, he finished his drink and left.

At Bow Street, he spoke with the detective in charge of the case. What he learned only caught his interest more, so he asked to look at the body. Officer Clarke watched for his reaction.

"Well, do you recognize the gent?"

Now Darrell struggled to maintain a bland countenance.

"No, I do not know him, but I believe I have seen him at some social event."

"What kind of party, sir?"

"A ball, I would say. I will let you know if I find out more."

On his way home, he searched his memory. The man was about Darrell's age, and well-dressed; but he had the look of trouble, like he had suffered a great deal of stress, and he didn't equate it with gambling debts; perhaps blackmail or threats on his life?

Going up to Chad's room, he found him sitting by the window, reading.

"Hello Darrell," he said, a part-smile on his face, but when he saw the way he grimaced, he added, "What's amiss?"

Taking a chair by the desk, he said, "I've just viewed a body, Chad, the one they pulled out of the Thames. The man was a gentleman, and a little familiar to me."

"Any idea where you've seen him?"

"Maybe at a dance—seems to fit into that kind of surroundings."

"Recent or some t-time ago? What one did you last attend?"

"Except for the House Party in Bath; the Castlereagh Ball."

"Did he dance or talk with someone? A man or a group of men?"

He let his mind drift back, and remembered he did not go to many social events in the past months. So, perhaps last year? But then, he stayed in Ireland until late in the Fall.

"Can't connect him with a lady, more likely in conversation with a man."

Now Chad's eye brightened, and he sat straighter, intrigued by the puzzle.

"Where you close enough to hear his voice? Did he have an accent or any peculiar expressions?"

"No, I don't recall a voice. About my age and height, Chad; maybe someone mistook him for me?"

Now Darrell was feeling that pinch of fear again. Was someone out to get him? Thought he had gotten over that episode at Allen Court, but he had been thinking of Smithson again today and it refreshed his persistent fears of being set up. Then he sat with his head in his hands and pushed down those troublesome thoughts.

Watching him, Chad showed concern for his friend.

"The best thing to do is find out this man's identity, to find out if there's any connection with your work."

Then Darrell straightened in the chair and shrugged; trying to pull himself out of his dread.

"Now I have to take some time to think it through. Thanks for all the questions, it helps me focus on it. Are you up to taking the air today? Feels warmer than usual for the season."

Chad turned to look out the window—his friend was right, but he didn't want the world to see him yet.

"No, I'm not able to go out"

"How long before we can go north? Perhaps a little walking within the house would help get your muscles working."

When Darrell smiled, it transformed his face, and Chad was glad to see it, and said, "Maybe another week or two."

While father and son had dinner that night, their conversation ranged over many subjects before coming at last to the body.

After relating the details, he said, "I have to remember where, then I'll recall his name or who he was with."

"You are rather keen on this, Darrell; is there a reason to be concerned? Do you think this might be related to your work?"

"Yes, it has renewed my fear of being caught in a trap. At the Foreign Office today, I checked up on Smithson to learn if there was any progress. This dead fellow seemed about my age and height and dress. Could someone think it was me?"

Looking into Sir Giles's eyes, he was hoping for understanding. His father remembered his difficulty when he thought he was being trapped at the house party; had hoped he had gotten past that.

"Oh, anything is possible, but the likelihood is remote. I think you should advise Mr. Bart about it, so he can look for clues."

The next morning found Darrell back at Mr. Bart's office, where he relayed the case of the dead body and his suspicions.

"Had a report on that; doesn't seem to be related to our work, but we'll keep an eye on it. Got you rattled?"

"Yes, it crossed my mind the gentleman resembled me, Mr. Bart."

"When do you go to Banford Grange?"

"In a week or two, if Chad is able to make the trip."

"Some quiet time in the country is what you need."

He turned this all over as he rode in the Hansom Cab. That trace of fear still lingered, and thoughts of Smithson bothered his peace of mind. Why couldn't he resolve it?

CHAPTER 12

Two weeks later they headed north in Sir Giles's best travelling coach to help smooth the inevitable bumps. For the middle of March, it was an exceptional spring-like day.

"How are you doing? Is the roughness causing you pain?"

Chad looked at his concerned friend, and knew Darrell would take it on for him if possible.

"Nothing I can't tolerate. Most generous of you and your father to send me to the country on a repairing lease."

"No thanks needed and I hope you like the estate. Have you been in Northamptonshire before?"

"Yes, I did travel the North Road when I went to Yorkshire as a youth, but don't remember much."

"The area around the Grange is pastoral, but with sufficient woods and rivers for interest; you may enjoy some fishing when you are able."

Nodding in acknowledgement, he did not mention his ignorance on the subject, just wanted to go to a bed; so, he rested his head back against the swabs and soon the motion of the coach rocked him to sleep.

Glad he could rest; Darrell knew the pain was worse than Chad admitted, for he could see it on his face. During his nap, Darrell reviewed the situation of the corpse, including his movements since the beginning of the year. The wedding, so abruptly interrupted, brought him no results.

In Bath, he had attended the Pump Room, but could not remember seeing him there.

At the house party, he got to know the guests through his investigations and wondered if any of the émigrés might seek revenge on him. Gantre had been enraged. Would she hire men to kill him? If that is the case, he felt sorry for the poor man who died in his place. Soon he would contact Wally Finchly to find out if he learned anything new. That brought him back to the Castlereagh Ball and his odd meeting with Smithson. *Always back to him,* he thought, and he scanned his memory of the people at the ball without success. Perhaps he should be more observant, but something caused him to recognize the poor man in the morgue.

Darrell brought back the images of the bloke's face, and remembered it swollen from the immersion in the river. The hair was a dirty brown, and he had no facial hair, so had been clean-shaven when he died. The clothes were rather expensive, and his hands well-manicured, so he must have had a valet. His eyebrows slanted, his nose was average, and his chin appeared to be receding. Perhaps he spoke with a lisp? Oh! Had he heard a man speaking that way?

When Chad stirred after a sharp bump and opened his eyes, he seemed to be confused, not remembering his location.

"Just coming to Barnett, and we will change horses there."

Looking out the window to get his bearings, he sat up and smiled. "I would prefer to remain in the coach if you don't mind—I'm still not comfortable in public."

"We will order refreshments, what do you want?"

He ate sparingly, but enjoyed the fine ale.

When Darrell returned from the Inn, he asked "Do you recall a gentleman speaking with a lisp? Yes, I know some young bloods effect one for interest, but this fellow had a receding chin which could result in distorted speech."

Chad thought for a moment. "Do you remember more about him?"

"Yes, I went over his appearance and discovered the facial defect, dirty brown hair, slanting eyebrows and well cared-for hands and dress. I systematically reviewed my various social events so far this year and only came up with a couple suspicions. There were at least two people who might seek revenge: Lady Gantre and Humphrey Beales, the spurned groom, and I will be inquiring about them."

"So, you are making some progress."

As they proceeded on their way, talk turned to reminiscence of their youth at school. In no time, they arrived at Banford Grange; the miles shortened by their memories.

One day the butler announced visitors, "Sir Arnold and Miss Forsyth are here to visit, Mr. Coletrane."

Looking up, he saw the young gentleman and lady. The expressive eyebrow rose and a slight smile changed his demeanor. As he walked forward; his hand was extended toward the gentleman, since he knew the Forsyth's lived at a neighboring estate.

"How do you do?"

"Pleased to meet you, Mr. Coletrane. Let me introduce my sister, Miss Charlotte Forsyth."

Miss Forsyth dipped into a curtsy as Darrell made a bow; still breathless from her first glimpse of the tall, handsome gentleman before her.

Then he ushered them into the drawing room and indicated a sofa.

"Rather a brisk wind blowing today, isn't there? Come to the fire and I will order tea."

Sir Arnold seated his sister. "We wanted to come to meet you since we learned you were here, Mr. Coletrane."

"Well, I have rarely come here. My father has lived in London for some years now and I often travel."

"How is your father?"

"His health gives him some trouble, but mainly it is his gout which is often painful."

He took the opportunity to observe these young people. The young lady was flustered and the gentleman kept the conversation away from her—she reminded him of Sarah Renwick in her shyness.

"Yes, you are fortunate to still have your father with you. Our father died a few years ago, while I was away at the wars."

"Sorry for your loss," said Darrell as he bowed to them. "Is your mother with you?"

"Yes, but her health is poorly."

Soon the arrival of the tray interrupted them. The maid distributed the tea and biscuits before leaving.

A silence prevailed as they all sat by the fire and enjoyed the refreshments. The color had returned to Miss Forsyth's face, and she was trying to restore her composure. As she placed her empty cup and saucer on the tray, she picked up the plate of cakes and rose to offer it to the gentlemen.

"Or would anyone want more tea?"

They did not, but accepted another cake, and the tension was broken by the homey activity.

"You appear to be experienced at this, Miss Forsyth. Do you stand in for your mother?"

"Yes sir, Mother is often unwell."

As Darrell nodded his head in acknowledgement, he said, "I compliment your gracious comportment."

Her blush was charming as she lowered her head again.

"Mr. Coletrane, is it true that your friend is staying with you?"

He tensed, and took a moment to determine what he could reveal about Chad. A seed of annoyance passed through his mind. *So, that got out, did it?*

Then he smiled and said, "Yes, he was injured in the wars and is here on a repairing lease."

Sir Arnold, unsure of how to continue, decided on a straight-forward approach.

"I also suffered injury in the Peninsula a couple years ago. The recovery can be lengthy. How is he doing?"

Darrell continued to evaluate this young man. *What is the purpose in these questions?*

"My friend is still recovering from the journey here, so is not receiving visitors yet."

A protracted silence fell on the room until a servant came to remove the tray. This pause gave everyone an opportunity to sort this information.

"I am sorry he is not well enough to see us. After he is better, we would enjoy meeting him. During my recovery, my sister used to read to me and it helped pass the time. She also is talented at the pianoforte and sings. It helped me take my mind off my pain for a while."

Smiling toward Miss Forsyth, Darrell said, "Yes, I appreciate that, and I am sure your brother benefited from your reading as well as the music, since your voice is charming."

She glowed under the compliment. "Thank you," she said, a smile playing on her lips.

Then her brother rose from the sofa, and said, "We will be going, but we hope to meet you again soon; you are welcome to visit us sometime."

Nodding, he walked with them to the hall. After they left, he went up to Chad, who was sitting in a chair by the window, looking out over the gardens, and turned upon Darrell's arrival.

"You had some visitors; who are they?"

Grinning, he said, "Well, I believe they were more interested in you than in me. A young couple—brother and sister from the neighboring estate.

Miss Forsyth has a desire to come and read to you, as well as sing. Shall I encourage her?"

He broke into a mischievous smile, eyes gleaming in jest.

Chad grinned. "Sounds interesting. Is she pretty?"

"Yes, she's an attractive young lady, but a little shy."

"Perhaps she was overcome by your magnificence, she may not have met anyone so handsome before."

They laughed again, and it felt good. There had not been much to laugh at recently.

"I will accept their invitation to visit them, for I need to clear them of any doubt before I let them visit again."

Now Chad was surprised. "Suspicion? Why would you feel that way? Aren't they just a couple of neighbors?"

"Yes, but he was injured at the wars also and I think I should learn more about him first."

Studying him, he realized his objective was to protect *him*! Was he in danger here in the country?

"Was something said to cause this suspicion, Darrell?"

"Not in particular, but it crossed my mind; we can't let down our guard, even here, since you already suffered and I still have not determined whether the body was meant to be me. So, we can't be complacent."

Then Chad turned back to the window and considered this; had he relaxed too much here at the Grange, thinking he was secure? Was any place really safe? Or was he falling into Darrell's paranoia? Perhaps not until Smithson was either found innocent or was arrested will they be able to totally relax.

"So sorry, Darrell, if I brought trouble to your quiet country home."

"And I regret I let my uneasiness spill over; you are here to heal, not worry, so I will refuse visitors for now, OK?"

Chad sadly nodded his head; he would have liked to meet this young lady who desired to help him through his healing time.

A letter arrived the next week from Lord Beckworthy.

"My solicitor reported the results of the investigation into Beales' background, but I wish to God I had done it before I consented to his marrying my daughter! For he is a scoundrel, Darrell. Not only has he charged several fathers with Breach of Promise, he also married an heiress some years ago. In less than a year, she was dead, probably by his hand. I turned this information over to a Magistrate, and I hope they put him in jail as least; society is not safe while he's on the loose.

My solicitor filed a counter-suit against him, but his man does not possess a satisfactory reputation and may be a crook. Thank you again, nephew, for talking with Bernice, she and Captain Littleton married by special license last week, and they seem happy.

Fond Regards,
Uncle Hector"

Darrell was amazed at the audacity of Humphrey; seems he was more dangerous than they thought, then he shared it with Chad.

"Well, I almost wish we had fought a duel, maybe I could have accidentally killed him!"

"But he just isn't worth it, not to risk arrest. Let's hope the law will deal with him."

"When I think how close my cousin came to marrying him, I shudder; because she was in grave danger—saved by her warrior hero!"

They continued to review and analyze the situation; they always did well at that.

But still, Darrell looked forward to hearing from Wally. He had concerns about the circumstances around the body in the river, and he wanted to hear what was happening with the plotters. When was their trial?

"Would you like to play chess this afternoon?"

"Yes," said Chad with a crooked grin.

The next day, Wally's letter came while Darrell was out visiting the Forsyth's, so he took it to his chamber for complete privacy.

Settled at his desk, he spread it out before him and it began;

"*Greetings,*

I cannot say I solved your riddle, but there may be something important here. The traitors were tried separately, as is the custom. Pelletier was not co-operative but did let a few things slip; when asked about Comte de Maitree, he became flustered, admitted to the coded letter being from him and then tried to back out and say he didn't know how it got into his chamber. Imagine! I think he is deathly afraid of him and his group. Nor did he point a finger at any of the other plotters, just a close relationship with the ladies Gantre and Fornier.

Ainsworth caved under questioning as we expected. However, he was guilty of treason as were the others, and Fornier tried little miss innocent, but it didn't work. The facts did her in. As you would expect, Gantre attempted to bluster her way through, denying the charges and acting 'Holier than thou'. But the evidence was her downfall, then she spewed out her diatribe of hatefulness. Timberleigh brazened it out also, but the evidence was too strong. His wife was released because of lack of proof, since she claimed she was not aware of the plot. There will be at least three of the five at the gallows. Don't understand how any of them can avoid justice, but it is not always served.

My own feeling is that de Maitree is involved, but there's someone higher than he. Considered it might be Fouché because his hands are in everything in France and have been since the Revolution; he is not above any nasty work that needs to be done. And he also plays both sides—Napoleon and the Bourbons; the Austrians and the French. I heard that he hasn't any morals.

As far as revenge, Darrell, I can't say I've found out anything solid. I don't know why you would be targeted and not myself or Weatherbee. I continue to hope the corpse will be identified and will have no connection with you.

The most important thing to remember is that we all did an excellent job and had a great success. We saved a disaster from happening.

In closing, I will say how much I enjoyed seeing you again, and wish you peace and happiness in the future.

Best Regards, Wally"

Darrell sat back in his chair, took a deep breath, and let it out slowly. He had anticipated answers, but this was rather vague. Perhaps his fear had led him to his conclusions. Perhaps it had nothing to do with him after all.

After a time of meditation, he went up to see Chad, passed him the letter and went to the window while he read it. Then he sat in the chair by the bed, and they had a long, rambling discussion about the information Wally had sent. They had to agree that the revenge scenario now seemed dimmer.

"I wish the body would be identified; then I could let it go."

Chad was exhausted, so he took a nap. Darrell needed to get outside, so he went to the stables for a horse – he needed a good run, both he and the horse.

Yes, Chad was right; spring was here. He inhaled a deep lung-full of the sweet air. His thoughts wandered, reviewing his dealings with the Forsyths and then naturally back to the body. Why couldn't he remember? He wondered if the Runner had found any more information—a mother missing her son? Surely someone was missing him, so he relaxed and let his mind sift through images of people.

All around him the grass was thickening in that wonderful fresh spring green and the birds flitting about, gathering nesting materials and taking them into the trees, on which the leaves were filling out more each day. As he stopped to let the horse chomp on some grass, his mind idly moved over those images some more. Then he imagined how the lost man would have looked, all fitted out for a ball or a house party and his receding chin stuck out in his memory, and he tried to see him in his former looks, and the Castlereagh Ball came to mind. A minuet came to his vision – it was the chin that did it.

He stayed still so as not to disturb the image. Who was his dance partner? Like a flash, the sultry face of Lady Strangford appeared, taking the man's hand to swirl around before changing to the next dancer. The man was not a smooth dancer – a little awkward in his movements, and he tucked his chin back against his neck. Was he shy? Embarrassed?

Now, Darrell thought, I can get in touch with Lady Sophia and get his name!

He came back to Chad's room after his rest.

"Chad, I have good news; I have remembered his dance partner and it is someone I know."

"That's great, who is it?"

"Lady Sophia Strangford, and I have to find her to get his name."

"When are you going back to London?"

" I must go soon, but I wanted to take you out to see the park first, so you can ramble around after I'm gone."

Chad smiled through his scars. Perhaps it was time for him to venture out.

"How about a walk in the gardens?"

"That sounds perfect for a start. Would you send a footman to tell me when you are ready?"

Darrell noticed how tenuously Chad took that first step over the threshold, like he was heading into danger. Just a few months ago he had been full of confidence and bravado; but that had been beaten out of him by those monsters. Now he had to learn who he was again.

Chad had a cane to steady him—his injured leg was a problem, and he carefully maneuvered down the front steps and stood for a moment at the bottom. Darrell refrained from talking so Chad could take his time and experience all the sensations of being outside. He was eyeing the gravel drive, but finally put a foot forward and used the cane to steady himself; so, Darrell stood by but waited to see if he needed a strong arm. After he reached the garden path, he stopped to look around, to feel the breezy fresh air on his face, to hear the birds calling. It was Spring! He looked at Darrell and smiled at the joy of it.

"This path is smooth and level," said Darrell. "We should see some early flowers and there's a bench under the Linden tree."

Chad took his time, stopping to look around frequently. When they reached the bench, they both sat down.

"Is it causing you pain, Chad?"

Putting his hand to his chest, he said, "The ribs are much better, but still tender. My leg feels stiff and the exercise is probably good; to get the muscles working again."

He looked around, "I think the springtime which is bursting with new life is a good tonic, don't you agree?"

"Yes, Chad, I relieve you have recognized the truth. It's marvelous!"

The sun was beaming down on them and Chad lifted his face to it, and sent up a prayer of gratitude to his maker. He might have died in Paris, never to enjoy another spring, so he resolved to make the most of what he had and let go of what he'd lost.

They walked along several paths before turning toward the house. Chad stood and looked.

"How old is the house, Darrell?"

"It's just over a hundred. My great-grandfather built it after the previous one burned down, and also bought up land to enlarge the park."

"It's a grand house. I like the soft gray of the stones—such a good foil for the greenery. Your father must have an excellent gardener."

Darrell smiled, realizing how fortunate he was to have a family home in the country, and he should come here more often.

As much as Chad had enjoyed the outing, he was relieved to get back to his chamber to rest his battered body.

CHAPTER 13

Whose Body?

A week later, Darrell left the Grange since Chad was doing better; going outside every day and the Forsyth's often visiting—so his thoughts turned away from his memories; perhaps the nightmares would lessen as well.

When he talked with Wilkes, who smiled for a change, he said, "Well, you will take excellent care of him. Send a message to me if needed, but I think you'll be fine."

"Yes sir, I believe the worst is over. Thank you for the young visitors—that is helping him as well, for we know what a pretty face can do."

Sir Giles was glad his son was back, looking more relaxed.

"Hello, Father, how are you feeling?"

"Very well, and you look like a weight has lifted. Is Chad better?"

"The country is the place for him now. Also, neighbors are visiting him. Do you remember the Forsyths, Sir Arnold and Charlotte?"

Then he told him of their circumstances, since he had known the parents.

"They are fine young people, and I think it helps Chad to adjust to his changed looks. But the reason I came to town is about the body—I remembered more about him. Do you know the Strangford family, Father?"

Surprised, he said, "Strangford? Haven't heard of them in years. They had a house on Berkley Square, but sold it some time ago."

"Wonder who Sophia stays with when she's here, because she attended the Ball in January."

"Her mother was a Crewe; perhaps Lady Crewe would know of her," he said.

At White's, Darrell asked around and received bits of information. Later, he stopped in at Brook's Club with no luck. There was a Soiree at Metcalf's house, so he attended, and there were a few acquaintances but not Sophia. Then he thought of Lady Jersey and her cronies at Almack's, and knew her well enough to call the next afternoon. She was surprised to see him, as were her other callers, who overwhelmed him with questions; one questioned him about Bernice's wedding.

"Where have you been? We gave you up"

"Been traveling."

Then she looked at him and said, "Where did you go?"

There was disbelief in his eyes. *Rather bold, but might have some information to share since she's so inquisitive,* he thought. So, he gave her vague answers, and inquired offhandedly about several people, including the one he sought, and learned she was staying with her aunt, Lady Hayward, on Porter Street. Then he made a point of asking further questions about Lords Smithson and Yarrow, and got some news on both to cover his interest in Sophia.

The next morning, he asked his father, who told him enough to permit a visit. Although not a fashionable location in Mayfair, it was respectable. The butler ushered him into the drawing room, where he found her with several ladies; so, gave a graceful bow and a bright smile. Then she stood, curtsied, and said, "Mr. Coletrane, how nice to see you." He took her hands and looked into those dark eyes.

"Yes, I am pleased also, it's been months. Would you ride in the Park with me today?"

The older lady rose, so she turned, keeping one of Darrell's hands in hers, and politely introduced him to her aunt, and the other ladies.

The obligatory tea and biscuits were offered, so he had to take a seat. After a half-hour of conversation, he stood to leave and Sophia did as well.

"Let me get my hat, I'll just be a moment."

After setting out in his curricle, they headed for Hyde Park, steadily chatting. He drove down Rotten Row, then took a smaller path toward the Serpentine, and pulled over in a clearing; where he helped her down, so they could take a walk by the trees, arm in arm.

"Something unusual has happened, Sophia, which I must discuss with you. Sorry, it is not a pleasant story and I'm sorry to ask you, but it is important."

Those dark eyes did not leave his as he spoke and had darkened even more.

"Several weeks ago, a drowned gentleman was found in the Thames River, and when I read it in the newspaper, I realized that it was not a normal happening; so I went to Bow Street and learned that they couldn't identify him—all identification had been removed, so I studied his face, and remembered I had seen him before. I searched my memory to try to recall where I saw him; and the other day, I recalled you dancing with him at the Castlereagh Ball."

Her hand flew up to her mouth, and she cried, "Oh!"

"I'm hoping you can remember his name, so his family can be informed."

She stood there, her eyes huge, her hands to her mouth, staring at him, and she gasped, "Tell me about him," so he gave a concise list—height, hair color, clothing, and of course, his chin.

"Does that remind you of anyone?"

"Yes, Mr. Drummond," she said, " Chester Drummond. The description fits him. Oh, the poor man!"

"Can you tell me about him; where he's from, or his family or anything?"

While they talked, he led her to a bench, and she took his hand and began squeezing it as if to hold her back from the abyss of terror.

"Well, he came from Devon; parents are deceased. Also, I believe he has a sister but I don't know who she married."

They sat in silence for a while, giving her time to take it all in and to get accustomed to the shocking facts.

"Sorry to be the bearer of this bad news, Lady Sophia," then he placed his arm around her shoulders, and she leaned her head against him for comfort. Tears rolled down her cheeks.

After some time sitting, watching the river through the trees, she remembered that he had been drowned and, pulling herself away, she looked at Darrell.

"Please take me home, Mr. Coletrane."

After he reached her door, he said, "You can write to me if you think of anything more—perhaps some friend he was close to, since I think they would want to be told." She nodded her head and entered the house.

Again, Darrell probed his memory, and it meant nothing to him, so hoped that after she got over the shock, she would have more information for him, but he would wait a few days before providing the name to Officer Clarke. It would be better if some family member or close friend claimed the body.

"Father, I learned a name; Chester Drummond from Devon. Does it mean anything to you?"

"No, but I'll think on it."

That afternoon, Darrell put on his disguise and went to the Foreign Office.

"Well, how are you? Back from Northamptonshire I see."

"Thank you, I am fine sir, and I came because I have the name at last." Then he told Bart what he learned.

After turning it over in his mind, he said, "I knew a Horace Drummond, but he's dead now—could be his son."

After looking at some papers, Bart said, "Just as I thought, Drummond Senior was with the Home Office several years ago. Didn't hear of him getting into any trouble, but if he was, someone could have gone after the son to find something, so I'll look into it further."

As Darrell sat looking at Mr. Bart, he wondered what that trouble might be.

"Asked the young lady who I remembered had danced with him if she knows any of his friends, and I am waiting for her reply. Would still like to find out if his death had anything to do with me."

"Be careful, since you might uncover something dangerous. By the way, how is our friend Chad doing?"

"Well, he's much better, thank you, and he's in a safe harbor out there with some new friends to take his mind off the terror; which means fewer nightmares."

"Glad of it. The countryside in springtime must be good for the soul."

Then he chuckled as he said, "Yes, and a beautiful girl who sings like an angel doesn't hurt. Neighbors of my fathers' have been visiting to entertain him while he's recuperating. The brother, Sir Arnold Forsyth, was injured in the war too."

"Keep me informed as you learn things, Darrell."

And Darrell noticed the look on his face, which made him curious— what did he know?

Some days passed before he received a letter.

"Mr. Coletrane,

After recovering from the shock, I did recall a few things: that his father had been with the Home Office and died, with his wife, in a carriage crash—Mr. Drummond mentioned it in sadness, and we joked about us both being orphans over lemonade!

Then his friend, Adam, joined us; they seemed to be good friends, but I don't recall his surname, and I am sorry that is all I remember. I feel sad for him, assuming he was killed and dumped in the water, and hope his killer will be punished.

Lady Sophia Strangford"

He wondered who Adam might be as he folded the letter.

The message from Mr. Bart was short: "*Please come in soonest.*"

CHAPTER 14

Serious Business

After he donned his disguise, he took a Hansom cab, and found Bart with a sharp look instead of his usual smile.

"Called for you because there is a mission. Lord Peabody will give you details, but as you know, since Napoleon abdicated, Paris is in chaos. Looks like Talleyrand and Tsar Alexander have taken control, but King Louis XVIII is on his way back to Paris—he was in exile here in London. Go home and await Peabody's summons."

Stunned by all this news, Darrell said, "At least the long war is over."

"Yes, but now the work of resolving conflicts between the Allies will begin in earnest."

After a few moments of silence, he said, "I checked into the Drummond case. There's no proof, but the accident which killed his parents may have been staged. Had left his position at Head Office without notice, so something was not right. Have you learned anything else?"

"Only that he had a sister —married name unknown; about the carriage and the first name of one of his friends, Adam."

"Well, I think that Mr. Drummond's death had no bearing on you, but I will follow up on details and let the Officer know his name. That's all you can do, so you must turn your thoughts to this new mission."

Darrell reluctantly took his leave, pleased at the proposed job, but he wasn't ready to give up the mystery of the body. After he arrived home, he talked with his father, who always had some wise words, but he agreed with Mr. Bart in his evaluation. Let it go.

Later that day, a messenger came with a note from Peabody, requesting his immediate presence.

"Oh, there you are, Coletrane," he said in his regular disinterested voice.

"Good afternoon," said Darrell as he bowed.

Searching through some papers on his desk, he came up with an envelope.

After spreading out the contents, he said, "Yes, we have a big job for you and Clint Warden, Coletrane."

Surprised that Clint was with him again, he hid his disappointment, realizing that a new partner would be hard to work with on such an important case and memorized the details as Peabody rambled.

"Here are the documents you will need. Meet Mr. Warden and the two delegates in the morning, ready to travel. The situation may be dangerous."

Then he stuffed them into the capacious inner pocket of his Benjamin and took a cab to Broom Street. The hair on his nape had reacted, and he realized that he would be in for added tension on the mission, and thought, *I wish I could prove Clint's trustworthiness.*

When he found Sir Giles in his library, he told him that he would be away again, and they talked about Chad.

"Perhaps you will write him a note; since he will be expecting you back soon."

"Yes, I will do so now, and I must prepare for my journey."

In his chamber, he chose unmarked paper and began his letter.

"*Hello Wilkes, you may share this with your master,*" and he carefully wrote in code so that only Chad would understand. He smiled to himself as he recalled Chad's early instructions: *Stay in character.*

After he reviewed the orders again, he turned his attention to his appearance, deciding to bleach his hair, lighten his short beard, and chose eyeglasses that helped disguise his eyes.

Since his persona, "Percy Enfield," would be a debonair diplomat-type, he picked a stylish black coat and a silver vest, with just a little lace and a pearl pin in his cravat because ostentation would not suit. Next, he practiced his mannerisms at the tall cheval mirror. Now he must act the part, and recalling the 'fribble' persona from the House Party, he incorporated some of it. Since it was a trade mission, it would be more serious.

As arranged, they met at the stated place, their hats pulled down to help hide their faces.

"Hello, I see you have prepared well. How do you feel about it?"

"To tell the truth, I'm rather excited to be going abroad again," Clint said, with a grin.

Then they discussed their cover names; Clint would be Stanley Marsh, and Darrell — Percy Enfield.

At the appointed time, they went to the hotel to meet the delegates. Sir Keith Louder was the first to arrive and his demeanor showed an attitude of superiority. The introductions were performed as Anderson Semple came in. Next, he inquired into the interpreters' qualifications in his abrupt way, and confronted the other delegate with his questions, like where did Mr. Semple come from and what his business was. So, he learned that he came from the Midlands, and was in agriculture; friendly but a little reserved.

Refreshments were served, and Percy took the lead by commenting on the purpose of the Trade Mission.

"Now that France lost the war, the Continental System is ended, permitting the re-opening of business with Europe. My partner and I will act as interpreters for you gentlemen while in Paris and during the convention."

So, he looked around the table again and said, "Sir Louder, do you reside in London? A grand city with the theaters and entertainments, is it not?"

A frown on his face, he said, "That may be, but such frivolity is of no interest to me. My shipping business keeps me busy."

Then Stanley turned to the other gentleman.

"Did you say you are from the Midlands, Mr. Semple?"

"Yes, I am involved in agriculture and I think there will be a high demand for food and animals now in Europe, because farms have been decimated by twenty years of war when huge marching armies ravaged the land. So, they will need to replenish their stock."

"How will these goods get there? On our ships!" said Louder, pounding his fist in emphasis.

All three men sat back, took a breath, and sipped their wine. Now, who would follow that?

Then Percy spoke up in a calm voice, "That is just what we are setting out to do; cooperate in the production and the delivery to fill the needs. Expect great things from this Trade Convention, gentlemen; we can help set up the future after this prolonged war."

After they rose from the table, they proceeded outside where the coaches waited to take them to the docks. At the Isle of Wight, they transferred to another ship to take them across the Channel.

The two agents had to be cautious whenever they talked, so they stood on deck by the rail if they needed to discuss details. By the time they got to France, they both had a clear picture of their mission, and had been practicing their new names, to get used to them.

"Oh, Stanley, please pass the salt?"

"Yes, Percy, the soup tastes rather bland, does it not?"

As they conversed, they became more secure in their disguises. By the time they reached Paris, they felt comfortable. The delegates did not mix much with them, but kept to their cabins, and Darrell hoped they would learn to work together at the convention.

After meeting their contact at the hotel, they got settled into their rooms. The two gentlemen indicated they would stay here for dinner, since they liked their privacy.

While they dined at the restaurant next door that evening, Stanley created a commotion when he swung around and knocked a wine bottle out of the waiter's hand. Profuse apologizing brought even more attention, and Percy stood to wipe the splatters from his breeches, fuming.

"What are you doing? Pray, be more careful!"

"Terribly sorry to ruin your clothes."

The waiter was standing by, appalled at the commotion, right in the dining room!

" Please, sirs, do not be distressed for Pierre will help."

So, he cleared away the offending bottle and dishes, coming back with clean linens.

Stanley whispered something to Percy, who raised both eyebrows in reaction.

A gentleman at the next table had been amused by the fuss over a few drops of wine, so he said, "An unfortunate accident, Monsieurs. Let me introduce myself, Armand Duplessy at your service. How may I help you? Would you care to join me at my table?" He hesitated, glancing at Stanley.

"That is kind, Monsieur, Merci. This table is no longer comfortable."

Soon they all settled, and his companion was introduced—Madame Frome; a formidable-looking matron of about fifty years, dripping with jewels. So, Percy turned on his charm, and she talked about herself and even shared that monsieur was with the Council of Commerce, and knew everyone of importance in Paris. Soon food and fine wine appeared, and the servers' cow-towed to them, particularly to M. Duplessy. The urbane manner of the diners had overcome the embarrassment and conversation flowed. Not missing the expertise of Monsieur in asking just the right questions, Percy noted he soon had all the details of his new companions. Whether Armand realized or not, Percy was doing the same thing, enjoying himself, and Stanley did well in keeping Madame entertained with quips about British life and praise of French charms.

After a lengthy meal of extraordinary cuisine, they said their farewells, and kept their conversation strictly blasé until they were safely in Percy's room.

"Well Clint—I mean Stanley, you did well this evening."

"Yes, I was nervous at first, but your reaction helped. What do you think of Duplessy's behavior? Had he prepared for our meeting?"

Darrell thought he had seemed more than willing to divulge information.

"On purpose or not is hard to tell, but he's an experienced gentleman whose country suffered a terrible reversal, so, we must investigate what the counsel does, and we can evaluate his discourse."

Poor Stanley did not sleep well that night. The volume of wine and rich food effected his delicate digestion, which was accustomed to simpler English food, and he had a nightmare in which he was drowning in a thick, gooey whipped cream. His partner felt amused, but had compassion for a sick friend.

Most of the next day was spent exploring the city with their delegates. The shining glory was missing from Paris, and everywhere one saw evidence of the recent unrest, even battle damage. The presence of the military was evident, but the uniforms were mostly Russia, Austrian and Prussian.

"Have you seen the ladies, Stanley? All are dressed in their best gowns to draw attention. I've seen their smiles and gestures working on the foreign soldiers."

Stanley nodded, and said, "I hope they stay away from the Cossacks, who look very fierce."

As they strolled by a busy sidewalk cafe, Percy suggested they take a table to observe people, since it would be to their benefit to learn about the attitudes and behaviors of the residents.

Louder was impatient and Semple awestruck as they sat there. Many of the people showed grudging acceptance on their faces, but there was also fear and anger lurking; so, Percy tried to imagine London under foreign rule and could not.

"Remember that France's problems started with the extreme excesses of the Aristocracy, which caused a revolution, which lead to the Reign of Terror. The upstart, young Napoleon Bonaparte, seized the moment and grew into a tyrant. History stories are amazing, are they not?"

"For more than twenty years, he and his Grande Armee rampaged over Europe, bringing a large portion under his control, then Russia stopped him, but he never totally recovered from his disastrous defeat in Moscow. Now, the Bourbon King is back, but not everyone is glad." said Stanley.

Percy added, "A new government was set up, and new men of power run it—like Talleyrand, who took the opportunity and became Chief Minister and Tsar Alexander has his ear. The Tsar thinks himself a savior, a liberator."

Suddenly, Percy saw a familiar face, and remembered that he wore a disguise and would not be recognized. Turning to Stanley, he informed him that Smithson was passing the cafe.

He quietly said, "We must stay in character; for he shouldn't recognize us."

They proceeded to converse with their guests on 'touristy' subjects, such as the beauty of the Seine and the magnificent Cathedrals until he passed down the boulevard, and Percy surreptitiously looked at the man he was walking with. For a moment, he thought it might be de Maitree, but changed his mind, the man was too short.

After they all left the café, they walked in the opposite direction, casually entering several shops, where Darrell bought a gift for his father.

Back at the hotel, he said to Stanley, "I realized the potential of seeing familiar faces, but was not prepared to see Smithson here. So, we will adjust our disguises to guard against exposure, since I can't help but recall my trouble at the émigré party."

"Yes, I can understand your concern, since you have distinctive features and bearing, I could recognize you without seeing your face. Can you change your motion?"

"Well, action is not easy to change. As a diplomat, I try to be 'smooth'. Perhaps I need to be less arrogant and use a cane. Do you think a limp is too hard to maintain?"

"Yes, it would confuse everyone when we see them again."

"What might I alter at this point? Maybe I could have an accident which injures my foot? No, I must practice my walking, to be more unsteady, because I remember when I saw Jacques in Bristol, his movements gave him away. I think I will adjust my hair more. What do you think?"

Then he studied Percy's appearance from all angles before replying.

"Your usual style was dark, curly hair, longer than normal. The light brown worn shorter should be enough. Also, your short beard draws the eye and the glasses disguise your distinctive eyes. Perhaps some pomade would control your curls, or always wear hats. If we could find a different style of hat than your regular tall English one, it might help."

"Very astute, Stanley. Thank you for your suggestions. Let us go to the haberdashery shop on the next street."

They looked at hats until they chose one with a wider brim and lower crown.

"That is the latest style, Monsieur," said the young man. "And I think it suits you well, if I may comment."

"My friend requires a new one also," said Darrell. After much debate, one was chosen for Clint which made him look more distinguished.

That afternoon, they received an invitation to a banquet at the Grand Hotel, organized by the counsel, and Duplessy would be pleased if they would all attend.

So, they accepted, and studied the documents Peabody provided to refresh their memories on facts, figures, and British manufacturers who would welcome renewed trade with France.

Some bleach was applied to some dark hair showing through Percy's disguise. The ends were trimmed before dressing in his exquisite evening clothes. So, Percy disembarked clumsily from the coach, and made an issue of using his cane. Stanley grinned to himself; pleased with the alteration.

Inside, they were greeted by M. Duplessy and introduced to many of the guests. The gathering was International, and they were glad they had studied their facts to help Louder and Semple. Trade representatives from several countries made a point of meeting the gentlemen from Britain, and it was plain that everyone was eager to open trading now that the war was over. They made notes, including names and addresses of interested parties to assist their delegates and wondered about Duplessy's agenda as he moved among the crowd with an ear trained on the conversations.

The banquet was an elaborate feast, so Stanley ate sparingly. The delegates required help with conversation as the dinner proceeded, and Percy outdid himself in a party mood. One of the French gentlemen was in his cups and shared his views on France's past and future. No one disputed him.

Before retiring, they went over notes and wrote down their memories of the evening.

"Yes, I believe this period will offer many opportunities. The political wrangling will go on for some time before things are settled, but trade can resume now."

"The representatives appear eager to get things started," said Stanley, "Duplessy enjoyed the limelight, didn't he?"

"Yes, he thinks of himself as a leader and is looking out for France's interests, as he should."

"Now that we've finished, we should retire, it's gone 3 o'clock!"

First, they put the papers in a safe place and would encode them and send them to London tomorrow.

A shock greeted them in the morning—someone had entered Percy's chamber and stolen their notes!

"Must have been professionals," said Percy, "since they were quiet as mice; I am not usually a deep sleeper, but I did drink a lot of wine at the party. I wonder who did it and why?"

"Yes, who might benefit from them? There was nothing of great importance."

"Well, it might mean someone is suspicious of us. What harm would we be doing at a trade convention?"

Stanley held his head in his hands, and searched his memory. Since he had not imbibed at all, he should be able to recall the events. After some thought, he suggested, "I think we should try to write them again, Percy. That might nudge our memories."

So, they ordered breakfast and wrote as much as they could, not as complete as the original, but couldn't find anything important or threatening in them.

"The impression they hung around the periphery of our group came to me. Did they hear something they didn't want us to share? What might it be about? Did Louder or Semple say something that would create a problem? Want to ask them, but it would tip our hand," said Percy.

Stanley was thoughtful, then said, "Shipping. The subject of shipping drew the most attention from the guests, or was it Louder's arrogance that turned some heads? Well, he was not shy in drumming up business for his company—did he step on someone's toes?"

"Might have to talk with him about how his conversation was received. Wish I could recall more faces. Let's write down as many as we can."

They each took a sheet of paper, then compared the lists. The names brought back some snatches of talk as well.

"Yes, I think we need to ask our delegates who was most interested in their conversations. Perhaps they noticed if anyone was in strong competition. Since it starts tonight with the grand opening, we must work hard on our preparations."

"Shipping is big business. If there are many people here with shipping connections, we must pay attention. Wish Sir Louder were more friendly with others, too stiff-necked by half."

They invited their delegates to luncheon and Percy had to keep the conversation going in the direction he desired. Also, he and Stanley kept watch for eavesdroppers.

"Well, gentlemen, tonight is the opening of the convention, as you know, so we thought we should discuss your objectives so that we may assist you in any way you need."

Louder did not hesitate to speak, "Well, I told you, I am here to further shipping opportunities for England and I hope to get agreements from many merchants for business. Do you have any suggestions how to proceed?"

With that, his haughty gaze bore down on Percy—like a challenge.

"We are in an unusual position and need to remember that we are representatives of our government, and I think that a friendly approach will benefit you with these Europeans, who are still struggling to overcome the lengthy war; so you can consider yourselves as ambassadors."

Reticent Semple followed the conversation, and he glanced at Sir Louder before saying, "Yes, goodwill is my motto, and my objective is to build bridges and thereby increase trade and help heal the past."

"Bravo, Mr. Semple. That attitude will be well-received, and we can be comfortable representing our country and opening up the trade routes again," said Stanley. "How did you find conversations last night, Sir Louder, for you had many opportunities to further your interests."

"Certainly, that is why I am here! This is not a picnic we are attending; this is serious business!"

"Did you stir up any worthwhile responses? Who showed the most interest?"

Then he leaned closer and said, "There was a fellow who was interested in what I offered, and I believe he is in shipping here in France. Had a lot of questions about our operation and services, so I think we can do some business. Name is Charles Ouest, and he will be there tonight."

"Glad to hear it, but until you know more about him and who he represents, perhaps you should protect your information. We could do some checking on him if you wish."

Louder glared at him. "Well, I guess I might be at a disadvantage here, so I would appreciate anything you can find out."

Then they went to see Duplessy in his office in a government building, who said, "Bonjour, Monsieurs, glad to see you."

"How do you do," said Percy, and Stanley nodded.

"Are you prepared for the convention this evening? Do you have any questions for me?"

"That is why we are here. One of our delegates asked about a gentleman he met, and got a name, but nothing more. Do you know Charles Ouest, Monsieur? What can you tell me about him?"

A shadow passed over Duplessy's face, and he hesitated before answering.

"Yes, I know who you mean; always eager to investigate anyone interested in shipping and I believe he represents a French magnate."

"Thank you. My man would be happy for any information I could gather for him since he hopes to do some business. What is the name of the Frenchman?"

Again, he hesitated, pondering how to reply. "Well, I can put you in touch with Monsieur Ouest, and he can give you what you want."

Then Percy and Stanley looked at each other—they could recognize a prevarication when they heard one. *Why was he stalling?*

"That will have to do if you cannot divulge information about one of your delegates. How do we find Ouest?"

Shaken, Duplessy worried because he did not like to admit his inability to be open with them, and he liked these two Englishmen and wished he could oblige. So, he gave them the address of Ouest, and they took their leave.

Back at their hotel, they acquired directions to Ouest's, and hired a ride.

"Good day, M. Ouest," said Percy in flawless French. "Our Sir Louder talked with you last night at the Banquet, so we offered to meet with you to learn about your business before the Convention tonight, since he is at a disadvantage with the language, you must understand."

The man hesitated before inviting them in, then he took them to his library, and after some small talk, Percy brought up the subject again.

"Well, he is most interested in shipping connections, and he understood that you represent a magnate and wants more information about the owner. What is his name and where are his headquarters?"

He hesitated, looking distressed. As they waited for his reply, they became guarded, but Ouest was debating with himself, moving objects about on the desk.

"Well, you can understand him being select in giving his information. When one has such a big stake in a business, he must always be on guard."

So, Percy gave him a "Louder" glare, causing more unease, and rose from his chair.

"Well, it is evident that our delegate cannot work with a shadow, sir, so we will inform him to look elsewhere for trade. Good day." As they started for the door, Ouest said, "Wait!" They both stood their ground before Ouest, who had become quite flushed.

"Well, you won't even tell us this person's name, so we have nothing more to discuss."

Then he struggled to find his words, and said, "Francois Eynard, from Bordeaux."

"Why, thank you monsieur," said Percy, "we still don't understand the secrecy, but appreciate the information."

After they left Ouest, they went to the board of Trade. The secretary also had a secretive attitude and was not generous with information. *What is this man, an ogre or something? Why is everyone frightened of him?*

Back in Percy's chamber, they reviewed what they had learned. There seemed to be a mystery worth investigating.

"Well, I think we should caution Sir Louder to search for other shipping interests, since this does not feel conducive to honest trading to me," said Percy.

Stanley was puzzled, and said, "It has such a sinister feel to it, Percy, I would stay away from him and try for other leads."

"Yes, we will investigate through the Foreign Office when we get back. That will be safer. Now, let us concentrate on tonight and how we can assist our delegates."

The convention was a whirlwind of men trying to further their business dealings, so they stayed with theirs; assisting them in their communications, but Stanley had to remind Semple several times to keep to business since he tended to be too sociable, and he was finding that most areas of France and some other countries were in need of the agricultural supplies he represented. Contacts were solidified and plans made to start sending the animals and produce as soon as possible.

Yet Percy had a challenge with Louder, who kept forgetting the goodwill part. After he informed him of the clandestine operations of Eynard's company, he steered clear of it. In no time, he met other promising contacts and initiated future business.

The next day, when M. Ouest tried to approach, Percy stepped in to block him while his client was talking with another delegate. At least Louder was following Percy's suggestion and refrained from telling too much. The fact that Ouest still sought him out caused concern and he would be interested in what the Foreign Office could find.

They all agreed that the convention had been worthwhile as they reviewed the event. Then Semple talked with Sir Louder about some orders he had received, making plans for transportation. By the time they all disembarked in London, a positive feeling prevailed.

CHAPTER 15

A Little Vacation

When Darrell and Clint reported to the Foreign Office, Peabody behaved as his usual careless self; not asking for any details.

Later, when he told Sir Giles about the mysterious shipping magnate, his father was surprised he could do business like that. What would it gain him? Since Bordeaux was wine country in France, perhaps he was only interested in that trade. So, he decided to go to Mr. Bart about it, since he could do some investigating through channels.

A letter arrived from Chad.

> *"Have to admit I worried about you and Clint being in Paris, and will be glad when you are home. Will I ever be comfortable there again? I can report I made progress, now that my ribs are not so painful, and I am getting out every day to exercise as my leg is less stiff. Let me know soonest how you are.*
>
> *Always, Chad P."*

Happy he was healing, Darrell picked up a pen and began to write to him.

Pleased when he came, Mr. Bart sensed that he had finally put the fear of entrapment behind him. Then he gave his report on the mission, and told him about Eynard. How bizarre!

"Did you ever hear about this man or his business? The agent, Ouest, was too reticent to share his name, so it makes me think this person is involved in illicit activity."

"Yes, I will make inquiries, Darrell, since it has potential of unlawful practices, things like sabotage, so I hope Sir Lauder did not give away too much."

"Also, I must report that Clint did well, and I am relaxed with him now. I received a letter from Chad, who is doing so much better, and I wouldn't be surprised if he is nearly ready to get back to work."

"Well, I'm glad and will let you know when I have more information on the Frenchman. Are you going to Banford Grange soon?"

"First, I must find out if he is prepared to relocate. He will need new rooms in the city, but there is no rush?"

"No, unless a new mission is needed. Maybe you can enjoy yourself for a while."

A week later, Darrell got tired of the London scene—maybe because he must be on guard constantly. Plus, having renounced his old lifestyle, he avoided many of his old friends who still lived that way, so he went to Brighton for a change. He enjoyed the peaceful British countryside in late Spring and the small villages he stopped in. When he heard of a horse race planned for the next day, he stayed over in a tolerable Inn, where he saw an old friend, Samuel, and they attended the event together.

After getting to Brighton, he toured the Preston Barracks, although the soldiers were mostly away at the wars in Europe and America. Recruits were being trained to fill the need. Next, he visited the Royal Pavilion again, remembering how he used to go to many social events there in earlier years—being an acquaintance of the Prince. After a few days, he headed back home.

Several letters had come for him, so he opened the one from the Foreign Office first, finding out Mr. Bart had not learned anything of interest on the

Frenchman, but still worked on it. But Chad's held a surprise; he was ready to return to London, so Darrell wrote back he would be happy to see him and invited him to use the coach and four in the Grange stables, asking him to come to Broom Street first.

The one from Clint was not a surprise, voicing his interest in the Frenchman—was there any news? Then he smiled at Clint's curiosity.

CHAPTER 16

Sovereigns in London

The dinner with the Coletranes felt like a welcome home for Chad, and they marveled at him since he had adjusted to his new looks and was comfortable with himself.

The next day they went together to visit Mr. Bart at the Foreign Office, where they talked of potential jobs which they might handle. Now that the war was over, the leaders would gather to celebrate in London.

"It will be an opportunity to sort things out between the allies," said Bart. "And I expect there will be a mission in that for you two; we will await Lord Castlereagh. The Grand Duchess Catherine already arrived with the Duke of Clarence, which was a surprise, and I also hear that she is a pushy, demanding individual, so it will be interesting how she will fit in with British society."

His eyes shone in jest at the vision, and they all laughed.

"So, we will anticipate hearing from you, Mr. Bart," said Chad.

The search for rooms was successful, and Wilkes arranged it all; even procured everything they needed.

Soon they each received a note from Mr. Bart, saying that Lord Castlereagh, the Foreign Secretary, wanted to see them. The meeting was private, with only Mr. Bart included. Then Lord Castlereagh outlined the proposed plans, and had hopes that this could be the beginning of the Congress of Vienna; perhaps even to set timetables for meetings.

"Mr. Coletrane, you will act as my assistant since you know people of the *Ton* here. Go to parties and balls to mingle with the foreign dignitaries and their staffs. Your previous reputation will allow you to associate with the ladies, sometimes they are attracted to rogues."

A mischievous grin softened his serious countenance.

"Now, Mr. Peterman, do you still have the opportunity to wear a military uniform? Yes, I know you have just recovered from your grievous injuries in Paris, but it would let you associate with officers of the Allies. Entertain them and see what information they may share. Keep in touch with me as you progress. But be cautious around the Tsar and his people. Do you know any Russian?"

"Yes sir, I have a little and I will endeavor to improve," said Darrell.

"No, I am afraid that mine is almost nil, but I will work to learn as much as I can." said Chad.

Lord Castlereagh acknowledged them, and said, "The Tsar sees himself as the liberator and it has gone to his head, but he loves to dance, so will go to all the parties and balls. That might offer opportunities, Mr. Coletrane, to find him relaxed and jovial, but don't give him too much attention; there will be a plethora of others doing the same." Then he turned to Chad, "Mr. Peterman, the officers will no doubt be posturing and maybe bragging of their grand victories. Be careful with them, as their bravado could go beyond bounds at times, but in the excitement of telling, they might drop something of importance."

"Give these gentlemen everything they might need on this mission, John. Include the latest weapons and any information that might help them. This may prove to be valuable, but will be dangerous as well. Now I will bid you all a good day."

With that, he was gone, and they all stirred.

"That was not what I expected," said Darrell, " What do you think, Mr. Bart?"

"What I think is that he has honored you both by showing his trust with this mission; will have expectations, and I will assist any way I can."

When they received their assignments from Bart, it put it into perspective; they would use their own names here in London and Bart would procure necessary invitations for them to attend events, and also get permission for Chad to use particular uniforms. Since he had not sold out, he just needed approval; would his old Hussars uniform still fit?

Mr. Bart would set up a meeting with his Russian acquaintance to help with language.

They went to Broom Street to talk over all the details.

"Yes, I think this is an honor, "said Chad.

Darrell added, "He put his faith in us, and we must do the best job possible to produce results."

"The fact that we can almost be ourselves interests me. No wigs or glasses, no hair dye to cause discomfort."

Now he smiled at his friend who had been through hell for his country and was grateful! How humbling.

"Perhaps you need to practice salutes and marching to prepare. It could be tricky though—doing this mission as ourselves and having to think about our actions as well as those languages. Do you know any German?"

"A fair amount, since I have done some missions among the Prussians and Austrians. The most important thing will be to understand what they are saying to each other." Chad did not take the hackney all the way to his rooms, but got out elsewhere and took another to get home, wanting to be careful.

The next day they met the Russian scholar at Young's Hotel, and found that Mr. Orloff was a sharp fellow. Since he had been informed by Bart about the job, he got down to work. By the third meeting, Darrell was able to converse somewhat, but Chad found it more difficult, and tried harder.

By June 5th they felt confident with their mission. The old uniform was well-worn, so a new one was procured, and he looked striking in it; the eye patch and stiff leg enhanced his image as a seasoned veteran.

The arrival of Tsar Alexander I and General Blücher were enthusiastically awaited. People of all classes traveled out of London on the Dover Road; the carriages overflowing, and some took up strategic positions on hills or steep banks for a better view.

On June 6th, Alexander I, Frederick William, Nesselrode and a host of German Princes and lesser ministers embarked at Boulogne on HMS *Impregnable*, commanded by the Duke of Clarence in his role as Lord High Admiral, and Blücher, who along with Hardenberg had been made a prince the previous day, sailed on the yacht *Royal Charlotte*. Others took passage on the escorting frigates.

That afternoon they reached Dover, where a lavish reception was held. A strong wind made it difficult to disembark the carriages, and there were delays. So, Alexander accompanied Countess Lieven and her husband, the Russian Ambassador to London, in their private coach; unknown to the anxious crowds. At his request, they took him to the Pulteney Hotel to join his sister.

The Prince Regent had made arrangements for The Tsar to stay at St. James Palace, but he stubbornly went his own way. People came to the Pulteney, trying to get a look, and they cheered wildly when he showed himself at a window. Then the Prince of Wales was stopped by the mob, unable to greet him so Alexander later visited him at Carlton House; still followed by the anxious crowd.

The bustle in the streets increased as people tried to trail the foreigners, cheering as they ran along. Trades shut down as the workers moved about; the city had gone wild with excitement. As days passed, numerous banquets and balls were held; each group trying to outdo the other, so Darrell did his best to attend wherever he was invited. Getting there was the problem. Lavish coaches, some of them Imperial, brought travel to a crawl.

The Lieven Ball offered the opportunity to see and meet many of the important people. The Tsar made sure he was the center of attention, and always sought the most beautiful and youngest partners for the dance, and he turned on his charms relentlessly, dazzling the poor ladies. His audacity amused Darrell.

While Alexander waltzed, he approached a member of the Tsar's staff.

"Does your Emperor always enjoy dancing?"

"Yes." The gentleman said as he bowed.

"What does The Tsar expect at this gathering? Do you think the leaders will use the time to plan for the Congress?"

Petro replied, rather tensely, "It is a shame to waste time here for business. What is your attitude?"

Surprised, Darrell watched the gay abandon with which The Tsar swung his partner around the floor, and said, "But it would seem that one cannot dance constantly. Perhaps some time could be set aside for planning."

"What is your position, sir?" asked Petro.

"An assistant to Lord Castlereagh."

So Petro stood taller and said, "I beg your pardon, but I do not associate with secretaries." Then turned on his heel and moved away.

Darrell's grin was hidden with a poorly-arranged frown, and he followed with his eyes to see who Petro talked to, helping him determine the Russian hierarchy. He picked up a glass of wine from a waiter and sipped it slowly, searching for his next subject, and sauntered over to a small group of ladies to ask for a dance. The lady he chose was definitely from Europe by her dress, and they spoke in French. Soon he learned that she was Francene from Austria, and they exchanged a few sentences before the set ended. He took her arm and walked to the opposite side of the floor, separating her from her group.

"Must compliment you for your attire—a Paris design?"

"Oui, Monsieur."

"Has Paris settled into the peace?"

Surprise on her face, she said, "Do you know Paris well?" As his appraising look passed over her, he said, "Yes, Madame, I had some connections there and used to delight in the society. But alas, that all changed. Do you have family there?"

Reaching the double doors which stood open to the terrace, he led her out for some fresh air, keeping close, and she did not pull away, so he continued to a shaded corner.

"My father was an attaché in Paris before the war, where I lived as a child and keep fond memories of it. Now I only go there for the shops. What takes you to Paris, Monsieur?"

"Well, I used to go often for the enjoyment and had many friends there."

"Do you find London too staid?"

"Never, Madame, if you know where to look for pleasure."

Almost flinching at his inference, her interest increased.

"Now Mr. Coletrane, I believe you must be a naughty boy!"

He glanced into her eyes and saw mischief there; and had to control himself not to continue the risqué conversation; must keep to his purpose.

"Dear lady, will not your husband be looking for you?" She stepped back, as though struck.

"No, he is in the card room with his cronies, enjoying himself. Probably going on about his politics and making plans."

"For what, Madame?" His hand rested on her shoulder, and she moved a little closer.

"For this opportunity to prepare for the congress; setting their agenda."

Then he leaned in also and said, "That sounds intriguing. What group is he in?"

Oh, his lips were tantalizing, so close to hers, and she struggled to keep control.

"Yes, he is attached to our Foreign Minister, and must plan how to get what they want in Vienna. Will you be there?"

"Possibly, if my services are needed."

The look in his eyes made her think of some she might enjoy. Another couple stepped out on the terrace, so he led her back to the Ball.

Next, he made an appearance in the card room to see who was there, paying close attention to faces and behaviors. A seat was vacant, and he settled in to play a hand. The others kept to light conversation with a stranger in their midst, so Darrell played carelessly; like having too much wine, then they relaxed and soon got back to their interest—the congress.

"There will be competition from all sides," said Simon.

Looking around the table at his friends, he said, "We must make a plan before it is too late."

The gray-haired man with the great mustachio nodded his head.

"Yes, Talleyrand will be negotiating with everyone to keep what he can for France and himself, and he's a shifty devil."

"Well, Austria needs to get back what we lost in the war," said a man dressed all in black, with a cigar in his hand, striking the table for emphasis.

"Now, Max, keep calm, we all have the same objective, and Metternich will do his best for us," said Simon.

"No, he will be too conciliating, with his mind taken up with the Duchess Wilhelmina."

The group laughed heartily, and that was all they would say about the congress, so Darrell took the opportunity to leave the game.

Since Chad could not dance because of his stiff leg, he joined a group of soldiers by the refreshment tables. The wine flowed and the talk got rowdier. A large fellow in Austrian uniform was boisterous, edging into some bragging.

"Now Dom, watch your tongue, we're in genteel society here," said his friend as he patted his shoulder, but he shrugged him off.

"Look, we got invited like everyone else. Have some more wine, Nick, and let's talk about a battle. How about Laon; we gave them a show, didn't we?"

Nick rolled his eyes and looked at another of their group.

"What will we do with him? Now he's reliving our victory." But his companion looked nervous.

"Well, he did earn his glory. Captain Huber put in his name for a medal."

Then Chad said, "I say, that's good news. Too often it goes to the leaders. Good show, Dom."

He reached out to shake his hand, and Dom was stunned, but took the hand.

"Thanks, what battles did you fight in?"

After hesitating for a moment, he said, "Well, I was in several in Portugal. Brought home some lasting mementos." And he indicated his eye patch.

"Bravo," said Nick and the others raised a glass in salute.

The talk turned to the upcoming congress in Vienna, and they hoped their sacrifices would pay off for their country.

The next day they reviewed the results of their evening, laughing over Darrell's repulsion by the Russian, and he told him about the card game conversation. Was anything of consequence said?

Now Chad told of his time with the officers, noting their attitudes.

"Had to stretch the truth about where I got my injuries, Darrell, and felt bad about it."

"You received injuries while in the service of your country. A battlefield is not required; just seems more glorious in hindsight—you are an unsung hero, my friend."

When they reported at the Foreign Office, Castlereagh was not in, so they gave their information to Mr. Bart, and he filled them in on what was happening.

They kept a list of who was who, and noticed if someone showed interest in horses, so they would be invited to visit Tattersall's, or if they liked trick riding, Astley's was the place. A ride in Hyde Park was enjoyable for some, like the Officers, and conversations could spill over into gossip.

The enchantment of the visitors soon wore thin; weary of the mobs that followed them everywhere. Blücher, attended by Stewart acting as guide and interpreter, was pleased at the drink being abundantly offered. He and the Cossack Commander, Platov, played to the gallery and the crowds adored them. But even they began to falter as time passed.

The Prince Regent requested Lawrence to paint a portrait of Blücher and the crowd pushed their way into his studio and caused disruption. A few days later, General Platov came for a sitting; and brought his Cossacks to stand guard.

Soon everyone was agitated by being followed, as well as all the long dinners. The King of Prussia became surly, hardly returning the civilities of the people.

Since Hardenberg didn't arrive until 9 June, he had to greet the crowds of people who practically carried him to his lodgings in Berkeley Square. The Prince Regent invited him to Carlton House for dinner, where he invested Frederick William, Lord Liverpool, and Lord Castlereagh as Knights of the Garter.

Then he was taken to the Opera with Stewart, and on to Lady Graham's. The next day he drove down to Ascot with Blücher where they were mobbed getting from their carriage to the Royal Box, so his tolerance was wearing thin, and he was exhausted. So, Darrell met with Hardenberg's chief-of-staff and listened to the complaints patiently, but was surprised with their irritation. *What did they expect?*

"Yes, it must be fatiguing, but you realize it shows the gratitude of the British people for the services of the Europeans, and they are beside themselves with joy, sir."

Their conversation turned to the up-coming Congress. Nothing of interest was dropped, but Darrell invited him for a ride in Hyde Park the next day.

The team met at the Foreign Office often to report, and Mr. Bart took notes and gave them more instructions.

"Well, I hope you are using these opportunities to befriend some of them."

"Yes, I have been able to get close to several aides and assistants, so I expect they will reciprocate if we go to Vienna," said Darrell.

"If?" he said with a frown. "Did Castlereagh not settle that yet?"

"No sir, just a couple of hints. Do you think we will go?"

"Yes, I do. Your qualifications and experience should assure it. Keep up the good work and it will pay off." Then he actually grinned.

When they left, Darrell said, "What do you think, Chad? Will you go if Castlereagh asks?"

"Well, it may last for months, and it also could be dangerous, but I will be pleased with the assignment."

"Yes, I would like to serve him because he is a great man, and will be in charge of the British delegation at the Congress—it would be an honor."

One afternoon, Chad took Dom riding in Hyde Park. Luckily, he had ridden some at Banford Grange.

As Dom looked at the verdant vegetation, he said, "Your city must be proud of this." A carriage needed to pass, and the ladies saw the uniforms and cheered and waved with broad smiles, Chad was embarrassed by the show, but Dom was used to such display.

"Shall we call them hero-worshipers?"

"Yes, I guess you are right. Should we leave this avenue for quieter lanes?"

So, they trotted past stately oaks, and he looked at his new friend with concern.

"Do you have something on your mind?" asked Chad.

"Yes, I would like to hear about your capture and injuries, as I am wondering why they treated you so harshly, and who captured you."

Chad struggled to control his countenance, thinking frantically of something to say when his horse reacted and shied away from a hedge; so, he calmed enough to speak; and came up with a likely story.

"Well, it was in Portugal, and I was taken by the French. Those were tough days for they were not doing well, and I was separated from my reconnaissance group and captured.

"Since I would not talk, they decided to beat it out of me, and they kept beating what seemed like forever. They had this big brute of a fellow, arms like a boxer, and he concentrated on my face first, hence the damaged eye. Broke some ribs too, and I was lucky he didn't kill me. Sometimes, through the pain, I wished he had. By the time they realized I could not speak because of the swelling and bruising around my face, they left me as though I was dead." As Dom listened, he winced at the harshness.

"Sorry that happened to you."

"Thank you, but that was not the end. At my next battle, I took a ball in my leg, breaking the bone and resulting in this limp. War is hell, isn't it?" Then he turned his gaze from him and stared at the river.

"Yes, it is at times, but is also glorious when we achieve our goals." When he turned back, he had a melancholy look.

"Glad we have achieved peace at last, now that Bonaparte abdicated, we all must sieve through the ashes and divvy up the spoils."

"Well, now we all have an opportunity to create a kinder, gentler future at the congress. Expect some posturing and bullying, but there are many good men who will negotiate for an improved Europe."

"Oh, a philosopher, are you?" laughed Dom.

"Let's just say I've had a lot of quiet time to visualize a better world. What do you and your countrymen hope for?"

They pulled up by the river, which seemed perfect: the water pouring down it like troubles flowing away, and Dom glanced back at him, a frown on his face.

"Yes, I have my concerns. There are those who almost want to replace Napoleon as ruler, but this time it could be much worse. The new leader might not be as big a man, might be puffed up in his own importance. So, we will all have to handle him carefully."

Surprised by this slur against Alexander, Chad thought, *what did he know?*

The Tsar went his own way in London. Although he never missed a ball, he also did things in his interest; attended a meeting of the Bible Society, met some Quakers and told them of his plans for the regeneration of the world, met with Wilberforce to discuss the slave trade, avoiding mention of the serfdom in Russia; and took every opportunity to further his ideas.

Then he sought out the chief Whigs, hoping to win them over on Poland; to no avail. When his friend, Czartoryski, called on Castlereagh to explain options for it, he listened politely, and also talked to Sir Samuel Romilly, Grey, and Holland; none of which would accept Poland under Russian rule.

Since Emperor Francis declined the invitation to come to London, Metternich could move more freely than his colleagues. Lord Aberdeen offered his house on Oxford Street for his use. The bad behavior of the others made him appear both civilized and sensible, and made himself popular with the Prince Regent. He went out of his way to associate with Hardenberg, and they discussed the rearrangement of Germany.

Insolent as usual, Alexander refused to join in discussions unless it suited him, and he was determined to pursue his Polish plans.

The ministers held several hurried meetings. By the 15th, Castlereagh and Hardenberg reached agreement on the fortress of Mainz and that Luxembourg should be garrisoned by troops of the future German federation, and two more meetings took place to deal with incorporation of Belgium and Holland.

The next day they reviewed how the work of the congress would be organized. The plenipotentiaries of Britain, Russia, Prussia and Austria, along with France, Spain, and Sweden would form a committee to handle the project for the arrangement of Europe; by the plans previously chosen by the four courts, so they should meet two weeks before the start of the congress.

The starting date was to be 1 July, but on 15 June the ministers agreed it would be August, having decided to be in Vienna early in the month to set up a steering committee of the seven powers. This was upset by Alexander since he must be present, but needed to go back to Russia, and he was not prepared to come back before the end of September; insisting that the congress open 1 October.

This caused anxiety and raised doubts about his intentions, so he pledged he would make no decisions or take any action on territorial settlements in areas occupied by his troops. Still, Metternich was worried and sent word home to not have their army stand down yet.

The festivities continued at full force. The repetitions of parties and the people who attended started to wear on everyone. By mingling, Darrell and

Chad established that the attendees were more interested in the entertainments than talking about the future. Reports to the Foreign Office became slim. Even though Lord Castlereagh would be glad to see the visitor's backs, he was deeply disappointed by the lack of progress with negotiations.

That night going home, Darrell saw an altercation in the street. An elegant curricle had tangled with a farmer's wagon loaded with cabbages. The wheels locked together and the horses reared and screamed. The two drivers argued and all traffic was blocked, and the gentleman was shouting in Russian. Luckily, the farmer knew enough not to strike him, just tried to argue with him, so Darrell felt the need to translate. He got their attention, and begged one to be quiet while he conversed with the hopping-mad foreigner. A difficult task, but he was able to calm the gentleman, pointing out the need to untangle the wagons so each could leave.

Then he called to several men who were enjoying the commotion, asking them to come help him clear the wheels. This was accomplished, the horses calmed, but the fight was not over. The Russian pulled out a pistol and shot the farmer where he stood. Darrell was able to get his name before he died, and someone brought a constable to take charge, then asked him to translate. Since he knew this could be an international problem, he would contact Castlereagh in the morning.

Soon it became clear that a Russian gentleman felt he could take the life of any farmer that dared to confront him. English law was alien to him and it would require diplomacy to settle the affair without further disaster.

Mr. Bart made sure his men got invitations to the banquet on 18 June at the Guildhall, presented by the City of London.

The event was for males only, but the Grand Duchess demanded she should attend, so two more ladies had to be invited as well. As they paraded in to make an important entrance, The Tsar insisted on stopping to talk with the chief Whigs he encountered. This holdup forced the Prince Regent to wait behind him, and tempers rose.

When a large band began to play for the diners, the Duchess demanded that they be removed. No, she did not like the music. Then Metternich rolled his eyes at Castlereagh, not in amusement, but in chagrin. Would there be no end to their selfishness?

The Mayor of London presented a speech, thanking the visitors for choosing his city for their gathering, as they made a lasting impression on the English people high and low.

The mood was frantic as arrangements to go home were made.

The Tsar and his sister were the first to leave and their entire entourage were transported to Dover.

By now the Londoners had had enough and went back to their normal lives and carriages could now traverse the city without the long waits.

Soon they were summoned to the Foreign Office to give final reports and Bart greeted them with smiles.

"That fiasco is over," he said.

"Yes, finally," said Darrell. "Here is my report on the Russian issue and on the dinner last night at the Guildhall."

"And I have written up my outing with the Austrian soldier," said Chad, "he had some interesting comments."

Bart went through each one thoroughly, asking questions as he went.

"Tell me about him." So, Chad related his ride in the Park and expanded on their conversations.

"I was particularly struck by his reference to a proposed replacement for Bonaparte, for it appeared to refer to The Tsar, but he did not have good things to say about his character because he thinks he is dangerous."

"Yes, I have surmised Alexander's objectives are higher than we can let him be and his harangue over Poland has upset many, but to want to replace Napoleon to be head of all Europe is much too aggressive."

Then Bart turned to Darrell, "What are your feelings on it?"

"Well, I certainly agree on the Polish question, and I observed his play for our Cabinet members—especially the Whigs, but I don't think he would want something that big; Emperor of Europe, let us say. Yes, he would like the power, but not the work, because he likes to dance too much for that."

And they all laughed.

After further discussion on general matters, Bart said, "I have talked with Castlereagh about Vienna, and he would like you two to go, and gave me instructions for you, including cover names."

So, Darrell would be Bradford Allen and Chad—Norman Rowe, and they would lodge at a house close to the Palace where the meetings would be held. There he would appear as a secretary and his partner as his assistant.

For a week they worked out their wardrobes and disguises and got their personalities down, but they would not see Castlereagh again until they arrived at Vienna in early September.

CHAPTER 17

Congress of Vienna

The early meetings were being held to organize the Congress; and Darrell took notes as a secretary to Lord Castlereagh.

The various plenipotentiaries had already struggled to gain the best positions. Even though it was about peace, past hurts and humiliations ran through their thoughts, and sometimes were spoken. Since Darrell had a knack for analyzing behavior to find the root of a conflict; it helped Castlereagh keep his eye on the goals, instead of reacting to emotional outbursts. Their positions in London during the gathering of heads had prepared them for aggressiveness at Vienna.

Meanwhile, Chad patrolled the streets and taverns, keeping on alert for conversations which may contain a nugget of information.

With so many sovereigns and their entourages present, something was always going on; lavish dinners, balls, and entertainments, hosted by Metternich or other aristocrats.

Soon Castlereagh became determined to confront the Tsar on his Polish plans, because they were an obstacle and prevented progress. This was difficult, because Alexander did not appreciate arguing with this mere Foreign Secretary, claiming his own benevolence and personal integrity to try to silence him.

Lord Castlereagh wrote a memorandum on 4 October, stating his case to the Emperor—a long document in which he reminded Alexander of all the agreements he had entered into at Kalisch, Reichenbach, and subsequent treaties; of the plan for the tripartite of Poland. Then he suggested he should combine with Prussia and Austria to establish an independent state.

The Tsar's response was disappointing.

A second memo reminded him of the ideas he invoked as his armies advanced into Europe in the spring of 1813.

"If moral duty requires the situation of the Poles be improved in a manner as decisive as the re-establishment of their kingdom, let the task be undertaken according to a wider and more liberal principle, and by making of it once more an independent nation instead of turning two-thirds of it into a most formidable military instrument for a single power. That would not be viewed with approval."

Then he ended by warning him that the whole of Europe was opposed to his Polish plans as they stood, and no arrangement of any sort would be made while he persisted in them.

The next day Alex paid a social call on Lady Castlereagh, then closeted with her husband for a lengthy discussion.

In a note to Lord Liverpool in London, Castlereagh admitted the interview ended without any change.

"Yes, Alexander stuck to his guns with anger and tenacity, and threatened to use force to reach his goals. So, I admonished it depends upon the temper in which His Imperial Majesty shall meet the questions which more immediately concern his own empire whether the present Congress will prove to be a blessing to mankind, or only exhibit a scene of discordant intrigue, and a lawless scramble for power."

Later, Castlereagh discussed the subject with Darrell and Chad, and told how Alexander's advisers were trying to reason with him, with the result, he removed Pozzo di Borgo, Nesselrode and Stein from his service.

"Yes, his mind is one-tracked on this and seems to be willing to go so far as war to gain his wishes. Well, he is an autocrat, is he not? My observance of his behavior is of a self-centered man."

"Oh yes," said Darrell, "Once he decides, he sticks to it, no matter how difficult it becomes. We must remember, his Grandmother was Catherine The Great, and he is following in her footsteps."

"That is a valid point," said Castlereagh. "In addition, he became a mystic, with his religious advisers filling him with their ideas. Still, he is a relatively young man to have so much power. No wonder it goes to his head."

Talleyrand thought that Britain, Austria, Prussia and France should issue an ultimatum to Russia; so, Castlereagh drew up a memorandum proposing they lay three options before Alexander; but even these men could not agree, so it was dropped, as they realized they could not win through persuasion.

No agreement could be reached as the Congress carried on. Always a new problem came up, putting spokes in the wheels of negotiations.

On 18 October, the anniversary of the Battle of Leipzig, a Festival of Peace was celebrated on The Prater, which was decorated with mounds of captured French cannons and other trophies. The Hauptallee accommodated an altar for assembled monarchs to participate in a Mass, performed by the Archbishop. A military band played and artillery salvos roared as troops paraded in front of the sovereigns. There was a luncheon for 20,000 soldiers and officers, but the elite feasted in Count Razumovsky's castle, and Metternich provided an evening event at his residence.

After he finalized his affair with Wilhelmina; he turned to business. In a note to Hardenberg, he stated that though the hopes of Prussia to incorporate Saxony was a cause of regret for the Emperor of Austria; he would agree to the annexation under certain conditions, hoping they would combine to restrain Russia's ambitions in Poland.

At the ball that evening, Metternich showed Castlereagh the note. The following morning the three met and Hardenberg was in a rage. "We must hold to our objectives, for Prussia's position and desires on Saxony are well-known."

Lord Castlereagh said, "I think we should go ahead with the presentation of the three options to Alexander."

On 23 October, six weeks after their first meeting in Vienna, they had at last achieved a common front, but it was a fragile one.

When Talleyrand arrived at the Hofburg, he was summoned by the Tsar, which did not go unnoticed, as Darrell reported to Castlereagh; who was alarmed and wrote to Wellington in Paris to put pressure on Louis XVIII and his government to rein him in. Alexander reproached him for changing his mind since Paris, and the Minister declared, "France is in favor of an independent Poland, but not under Russian domination."

So Alexander said, "There is no reason for them to be anxious," and added, "In any case, I have 200,000 men in the duchy of Warsaw, and I would like to see anyone try to drive me out for I have given Saxony to Prussia , and Austria consents to it."

Then Talleyrand stated, "Could the consent of that country make them the rightful possessor of that which really belongs to the sovereign?"

Exasperated, Alexander said, "If the King of Saxony will not abdicate, he will be packed off to Russia and may die there; he wouldn't be the first King to do so."

Shocked, Talleyrand said, "Your Majesty will permit me not to believe what he is saying. The Congress was not assembled to witness a violent assault of this kind."

Alexander stormed out to attend a masked Ball at the Countess Schoenborn's residence.

Darrell had been able to get close to one of Hager's informers. Whether the informer knew who he was, he did not know, but here was a chance to get inside information on Austria. The man's name was Karl, and they met at a tavern in the town.

"So, you say the Tsar tricked Prince Metternich? How did he do it?"

"Well, he visited Princess Wilhelmina and used her to find out things about her lover, and he also filled her head with false information. You heard that the affair is over? Can you believe how easily the Tsar finds it to fill his bed each night? Sure, they fall for his charming address, but he always has an agenda of things he wants from them."

" I never thought of that, just thought he liked women, many of them. So, you are saying it is his plot to use them, to bend things his way, even state business?"

"Yes, "said Karl, "he uses his tremendous power to achieve his will."

"And I think he threatened war the other day, because he is determined about Poland and doesn't care how he goes about it. Do you know about that?"

The man looked at him, and said, "Yes, he took steps he should not have. This is a congress for peace. Many plenipotentiaries from many countries are working hard to settle all the issues after the long conflict. The Tsar is trying to manipulate things to his liking."

Darrell said, "There is so much tension—do you think it will go to war again?"

After Karl took a sip of his ale, he said, "My boss does not think so; thinks Alexander is like a child, grasping for toys."

So, they laughed, but found no comedy in it.

No, Castlereagh was not surprised to hear of Alexander's behavior with Wilhelmina over Metternich.

"I believe he will use every opportunity to fulfill his plans, and is not used to being told no, so we have to hold together at this congress to make sure he does not, since it is not in anyone else's interest but his own."

"Well, I heard he is sure he has a divine calling to save the world," said Darrell.

"Yes, I believe that is true, but he cannot see he poses a threat in the eyes of everyone else. There are many frightened people here."

"Most of these people want a lasting peace."

Then Castlereagh said, "Yes, you are right, it is what they want at last."

Later, Chad and Darrell walked along the Fraben, a long open avenue at the heart of the city which was also the principal artery through which everyone would pass. They kept their attention on people of interest, from whom they might gain information.

By the time the Congress officially opened on 1 November, thousands of lookers-on were taking part in the social whirl.

CHAPTER 18

A Threat for Castlereagh

The dark figure moved furtively down the alley, his left arm hung loosely at his side and his leg was stiff, causing an exaggerated limp; he might be anywhere from forty to sixty.

Then he snarled to his companion, "Are ye sure he'll come?"

"Said he'll meet us at the *Corde Haus* on the next street, sir, and we are almost there."

All he got in reply was a grunt, and Ned was concerned that he had put himself in danger by helping Mr. Smith, because hatred shone in his eyes. The man they were meeting seemed a shady character at best, and he wondered if he would ever get out of this situation without harm.

At the cafe, they met Mr. Archer and sat at a table in the corner. Now he appeared nervous, here they were in Vienna, and he still didn't know Smith's plan.

They talked, and he told them a bit about the current situation here, and Ned thought that Archer's experience might even include spying.

Also, he sensed that Smith was a dangerous man, since he definitely wanted revenge, but for what? A lot of thought had gone into this venture as they traveled on the ship from Cork, but Smith was not forthcoming with his plans.

This man Archer looked like a rogue, but in this land of intrigue, who could be trusted?

"What do you want me to do, Smith?"

Then Smith's face hardened more, and his breath caught in his chest as he said, "Revenge! For the murder of my wife and children; for the half-hanging torture that I endured; for transportation to Australia, me, an innocent man! And I want that miserable rat, Castlereagh, to suffer for his betrayal of his fellow Irishmen!"

The tension at the table felt so thick the air fairly sizzled. Ned was in shock, but noticed Archer's reaction to this irate tale—he withdrew from the high drama of it, to put a hold on his emotions; had he suffered torture as well? He did have scars on his face.

"A tall order, sir," said Archer. "Head man, you know—lots of security in place. What do you want done? A scare? A beating? Or killing? That would cost a lot."

"Killing is not enough, he must be made to pay. He must suffer as I and thousands of others did. I want rumors to be spread to the highest places, to humiliate him in the eyes of the world!" The two men remained silent after this onslaught.

Then Archer said, "Oh, spreading them is something you can do yourself, Smith, don't need any help."

So, the young man kept his tongue between his teeth since he did not want to have to do such a thing, it was wrong; even though he suffered abominably. Maybe it happened during the '98 Rebellion sixteen years ago? Many Irishmen were slaughtered at that time, including women and children. But perhaps Castlereagh just followed orders as an officer.

"What's the matter, Archer, don't have the stomach for it? Do you keep connections here that you can spread rumors through?"

"Sure, I do, but it is child's play. What kind are you referring to?"

"That is sodomy!" cried Smith. "It will be humiliating enough to bring him down and ruin him! Maybe even put him in prison; it is a crime."

"Where is the proof? Can't proceed without it."

"I can provide that, even the names of the soldiers involved."

Then Archer sat back and stared at him, turning it over in his mind.

Ned could hardly breathe—he never heard of such a thing. The man still glared at them.

"Look, this proposition is not what I expected, I need time to think it over."

Now Smith was enraged again.

"Think it over and meet us here tomorrow morning if you are still interested," he spat out, as he awkwardly rose and left the room.

They returned to their rooms, and talking was at a minimum because Smith glowered and kept quiet, so Ned was unsure of what to do next.

"Do you mind if I go over to the park for a while, or is there something I can do for you, sir?"

He waved a hand, indicating the door. He was relieved to go out, to get away from the tension. In his five-and-twenty years he had never experienced such a disturbing meeting. For now, he needed to clear his head and think of his situation, wondering if Archer would do the job, because he didn't seem eager—probably just as shocked by what the man said as he was. The charge against Lord Castlereagh was extremely serious, and he wondered if it was true or just a way to ruin a great man. Slander was serious. Mr. Smith would have trouble with the law, possibly transported again.

He wished to get away, but he was committed to his job. And if he were arrested, would he be charged as an accessory? Would they be put in prison?

For now, he could make no plans because he had to wait for the meeting with Archer in the morning to see what was going to happen.

He wandered along and it took him into a handsome boulevard and down to the lake. How wonderful to be outside, feeling the light breeze against his face; and he sat on a bench and watched the ducks turning down to feed off the bottom. That's how he felt, upside down; he settled and pulled his hat over his eyes and tried to relax; sending up a prayer of supplication for his deliverance from this danger.

The morning found them at Corde Haus, waiting. Since his boss had not shared any of his thoughts, he was still clueless. When Archer appeared, he said, "I invited another party to our meeting, and he will be along soon. Are you still sure?"

"Do you mean someone else to do the job?"

As he smiled, he said, "We will discuss it when he arrives."

The young man chatted with Archer about the city and the park he had visited, and was offered suggestions on other attractions that he might want to see in Vienna, which was lovely compared to Cork, and he was amazed at the huge buildings and monuments it contained.

A tall man approached their table, and Mr. Archer rose to meet him.

"Ah, Mr. Pryde, this is Mr. Smith and Ned, I don't know his full name."

"How do you do? The name is not important; he's my assistant on this trip."

"Well, I have told Mr. Pryde some of what you wish done, and asked him if he wished to comply. Since he is aware of the seriousness of your charge, he wants to hear more about it."

"I will only tell you more if you promise to do the job, for I will not tell it for nothing. Are you willing to spread the rumors?"

"Can't make a firm decision without all the facts; there's a big risk involved and I cannot go forward to possible arrest if I don't know it all."

So, Smith glared at him and paused while he made up his mind.

"Yes, I will tell you everything, Pryde, because I want revenge against this man; suffered horrid things for the past sixteen years because of him and men like him. I'll not turn tail because a couple of squeamish men can't take the risk, when I'll pay a large sum for the job."

The telling took some time, while they all sat spellbound as Smith revealed all he knew, and they looked incredulous at the horror of it. Then he relayed the repulsive part about the sodomy with the soldiers, giving names and dates.

So Pryde and Archer considered their decision. If this was anyone but Castlereagh, they would be easier.

"Yes, we will do it. Your story makes us want to find justice for you. Now we will discuss details."

The two men received instructions on what they would consist of and who should be told. A fee was also agreed to.

Poor Ned struggled, wishing he could be back in Cork without all this terrible knowledge. Perhaps Mr. Smith could have requested retribution from Castlereagh for all those years, but he didn't think he would get a chance at that.

To ruin a man's reputation after the years he had served his country as a soldier, statesman, and diplomat was severe. He thought about his options, like telling somebody. Could it be stopped without doing harm? And who would he tell? The police?

Another issue was that Ned had not been paid and his pockets were very thin. No, he could not deny him, for he would forfeit his pay, and would have to disappear to protect himself from Mr. Smith's wrath. So, he faced difficult decisions but didn't know who to turn to.

Smith rested after the trying discussions, but his constitution was not strong since his troubles, and he hoped he would live to see Castlereagh suffer.

The morning came too soon, and Ned saw that the man had not risen, and he expected Mr. Archer this morning. The old man did not appear by mid-morning, so he decided to look in on him, and knocked on the door. There was no response, so he opened it to reveal the old man partly out of the bed, and when he approached him, he saw that the man was dead.

He reviewed his options as he left the room. First, he must contact Archer at all costs to stop the rumors, so he went to the tavern, but did not see him. He asked for directions to his lodgings and went in all haste to find him, but no luck.

Then, back at Corde Haus, he found him, and was relieved. Quickly, he told him what had happened and that Smith was no longer able to pay, so the job should be cancelled.

"I perceive that you are glad to cancel it, young Ned."

"Well, sir, I am fretting about how the ruin of Lord Castlereagh will affect the British work here in Vienna. Much harm would be done to more than His Lordship. In fact, I did not get paid yet and find myself in a precarious position."

He studied the earnest face of this young man, knowing he was not involved in the deal, just an assistant to the old man, but he also knew that the boy would now be stranded in Europe, a bad situation.

"Now it will be necessary for you to report the death to the authorities and I will tell you where to go. There will be arrangements to be made for either burial or return of the body to Ireland, so you may need help there as well. Does he not have any family?"

"No, sir."

Archer gave him the address and sent him on his way after agreeing to meet him this evening at the tavern, so they could review his situation.

Later, Chad told Darrell the news.

"That simplifies everything. Still need you to be the contact with Ned, and we will need to make sure the body is properly handled and that he will be able to return home. But he does not need to know who we are, so we'll still use our cover names when dealing with him."

"Well, I must say I prefer this outcome to arresting that sick old man; must have been half mad with rage."

At the tavern, Archer said, "Ned, what can I help you with? Did he keep some money on hand to handle costs?"

He was glad to talk with someone he now trusted. The police had been difficult, and they had to find an officer who spoke English. A search of

Mr. Smith's papers helped them decide how to proceed, for he had cash and documents in his bags. The documents contained his Irish name and address. Then it was decided to bury him in a local cemetery to avoid the cost of shipping him home, and Ned claimed his wages.

"This is all new to me, and I didn't know what to do next. Thank you for helping me. Now I need to book passage home."

"Yes, I can help you, and I must tell you that you have been a brave lad and gained worldly experience from this, but I think it would be best if you don't tell anyone about the troubles we've had here, especially the things Mr. Smith related to us, since it all may have been a hum anyway."

"Yes, sir, I'd prefer to forget the whole thing, and I'm just glad the plan wasn't carried out."

With a smile, he reached out to shake his hand.

"Conscientious fellow! Not a job I wanted to do either."

Darrell and Chad went back to their routine duties. The disputes taking place were increasing the stress for most of the members, since Poland and Saxony's futures were still the key subjects. Many meetings and written communications failed to resolve the pertinent issues, and any considered minor were put aside for now.

CHAPTER 19

Napoleon Escapes

On 1 February, Wellington came from Paris to take over at the congress, but Castlereagh stayed to help him, since he appreciated Castlereagh's thorough knowledge of what transpired and what positions the countries had taken.

The Tsar visited him on the 2nd, declaring France was in poor shape politically and the army must be riven with deception and unfit. But he soon put him strait, affirming Louis XVIII was strong and the troops in good condition. A dinner was held in his honor that night.

On 13 February, Castlereagh finally went back to London, where he was needed in parliament, and kept in touch with Wellington by letter.

The news of Napoleon's escape from Elba was received early on 7 March. Most people would not believe it.

Wellington received a dispatch from Burghersh, the British minister at Florence; with details of the event, but he was not sure where Napoleon was headed.

That night, the pantomime went on as planned, and Clencarty reported expressions of fear and hope came from the important persons present. The implications were alarming.

By 10 March they learned he had arrived at the south coast of France. Castlereagh wrote to Wellington, "If Bonaparte turns the tide, there is no calculating upon his drive and objectives. If he did seize Paris, he might find in the archives a copy of the secret Anglo-Franco-Austrian agreement against Russia and Prussia."

Everyone was anxious and their worst fears were soon confirmed—Napoleon's Armee welcomed him, many presenting their arms to him as he travelled toward Paris. Many towns cheered in their excitement; since they did not like the King's regime, which had declared him an outlaw.

On 16 March, Castlereagh suggested the Treaty of Chaumont was the only basis on which they could safely proceed, and Wellington began working towards that end. He found that imposing unity on the Allies was not easy. On the first of April at a meeting of the Five, some decisions were made regarding territories.

After excessive wrangling, all the Kings signed separate treaties. Alexander flatly announced he could not make a move until British cash began to flow. The Plenipotentiaries of other powers took the same line, so he assured them the money would be found, haggled with his government in London, and they agreed to pay up to £7 million to prepare to fight Napoleon again.

By 30 March, Napoleon had entered Paris and the King left for Ghent.

At the Tuileries, he began immediately to take his old place and negotiated with the government to recover his position.

Talleyrand was anxious, being a former servant of Napoleon, and chief engineer of the Bourbon restoration. He was now the plenipotentiary for France in Vienna and he had insisted that Napoleon would have no following in France. But that proved false.

Some people blamed Britain for his escape – they were viewed as his policemen on Elba. In actuality, he was sovereign of Elba; orchestrated by Tsar Alexander. The returned émigrés had not been accepting of the King's government and harassed the people in office. Louis was not strong, and had been unable to bring Frenchmen together and heal old wounds. In addition, the military was treated unjustly. Heroes were insulted. "Bring back Napoleon," had been heard.

Soon Easter came and on Maundy Thursday, the entire court assembled in the great hall for the traditional ritual enactment of Christ's washing of the disciples' feet. The Stations of the Cross were observed and a solemn Mass was attended by all the sovereigns and all high officials.

On Holy Saturday, the ministers gathered to review the treaty that had been drawn up; similar to Chaumont, which included France and the second-rank powers, and to sign—a timely move.

Wellington had written to His Lordship that the prevailing feeling in Vienna showed a determination to unite their efforts to support the system established by the Peace of Paris, conscious of its importance.

"All are desirous of bringing the Congress to an early conclusion, so the undivided attention and exertion of all may be directed against the common enemy. I assure you; I am perfectly satisfied with the spirit which prevails here at this occasion."

Wellington left Vienna, after he requested Cathcart take over as head British plenipotentiary.

Few troops occupied Brussels when he arrived, which did not surprise him.

Napoleon was busy making contacts. Tsar Alexander and Emperor Francis conferred about the letters they had received from him, and agreed not to reply to them.

Fouché had approached Wellington secretly, to find out whether Britain would be inclined to accept Napoleon under any conditions, and he also wanted a guarantee he would find asylum in England if he needed to flee Napoleon's vengeance. That remained to be decided in London.

Then Talleyrand found himself in a precarious position because when the King left Paris, the government ceased to function, cutting off his source of income, So Wellington rescued him and advanced £10,000.

Colonel Grant kept his eye on Napoleon's activity, and found he was re-organizing his army with the troops who came back to him in their loyalty. In addition, young men joined him as he traveled to Paris, all untrained and un-equipped. Many of his former soldiers had been mistreated and were prime candidates to join him again. Grant reported that it looked like the little emperor was having success and re-grouping. The biggest question was: when would the battle take place? And where?

Wellington had been disappointed with the meager troops in Brussels. He reviewed again the countryside which he had observed in the area around Waterloo last year. He still thought the terrain would suit his needs for the battle, especially the hills on each side which could be used to hide his troops – one of his favorite schemes. He began contacting high command for officers and their brigades. He set up his office in Brussels and gathered his Aide de Camps. He was good at organization, with his vast experience in India and the Peninsula. Time was the issue.

CHAPTER 20

The Wellington Plot

She waited for him until he left his office in Vienna, and he was pleasantly surprised to see her there. A twinge of excitement shot through him as she smiled, and he was glad for an opportunity to talk with her—his elusive lady.

"Hello, Lady Kerrigan," he said quietly, after he glanced around to find out if anyone was near.

"Hello Mr. Coletrane, I wish for a moment of your time."

"Of course. Let us walk over by the church."

His eyes gave him away as his heart took a leap. What was his green-eyed beauty up to? Must be important for her to approach him in public. As she turned the corner, she slowed her steps and glanced up into his face.

"So sorry to break protocol, but there is some urgent information. The news is, I learned of a plot against Wellington."

Now he struggled for composure.

"Is the source reliable? Why did it come to you?"

Surprised by his response, she felt a little annoyed.

"Well, he is dependable since we are in the same work, and he is aware of my connections here. So, he told me all he knows, which looks serious."

"We need a safe place to discuss this, any suggestion?"

"Yes, I have rooms at the Brau Haus Hotel, and will give you my room number so you can come a little later. Use a different name—Monsieur Du Gay, and I am known here as Madame Forest."

So, he bowed to her and she walked away. On his way to his office, he felt anxious to learn more. He shared the information with Chad before walking to the hotel.

The apartment, beautifully furnished, consisted of a drawing room and bedchamber. He noticed she had ordered coffee and cakes for them, so she sat on a settee with the tray on a table beside her.

How he appreciated the show of domesticity, making her even more attractive. Once food was taken care of, he looked across to meet those striking green eyes.

"Well, I am anxious for your news, Madame."

So, she put down her cup, and met his eyes. A slight blush pinked her cheeks.

"My acquaintance, Paul, came by some shocking information while at a pub last night. After more drinks than was wise, this soldier started bragging, and he revealed that he and his friend were hired by the 'big wheel" to get rid of Wellington before the upcoming battle could happen. For now, they were to continue as soldiers until the crucial moment when the Duke was vulnerable, then shoot him."

Darrell reacted as she expected and said, "That is a dastardly plot, and I am shocked that any of the Duke's men would stoop to such an action as he is much loved by them. Do we have any more, like when and where?"

"Well, I asked Paul to investigate those things, but his informant might not know that part. Are there any other sources for inquiry?"

Mind racing, he searched for other possible people to ask.

"This battle is not far off, so we must hurry. Try to learn which regiment these men belong to, since they may be in sympathy with the French, or just looking for money."

"Men who agree to do such work are usually simple people without much in the way of morals," she said, her eyes sparking.

"Can we meet again tomorrow to compare our findings?"

Laura looked into his blue eyes, and said, "Yes, in the Pleasure Gardens at ten. There is a bench right off to the right of the gate. First, I will contact Paul. Thank you for coming, M. Du Gay."

She was not ready to part yet; too curious about this man—*who was he?*

"Mr. Coletrane, could I ask you a question?"

"Certainly, madame."

She hesitated, looking closely at him. "Where are you from?"

A smile lurked, and the eyebrow rose. "If I tell you, will you tell me where you are from?"

"That is only fair," she said, as she sat down again.

"I was born in London in 1779 to Sir Giles Coletrane and Martha Mannering. My mother died when I was young, and my father still lives at Broom St."

He sat down also – his expectant look indicating it was her turn.

"Well, I was born in Derbyshire in 1780 to Baron Gerald Overton and Miranda Saunders. My parents are both deceased."

"Shall we go further, or is that all you wish to divulge?"

She hesitated, considering the danger of people in their positions not keeping secrets. But there was something about him that made her want to share.

"I have a brother, Richard. I was educated at home by a governess, as most girls were. My brother attended Cambridge."

He nodded, then said, "I attended Harrow and Oxford and I have no siblings—a spoiled only child." His grin made her sure he was teasing.

She delayed her response, then said, "I had a Season in London as expected. That is where I met my husband, Lord Andrew Kerrigan, splendid in his uniform. Who could resist? So, we married the next year when he was on leave from his regiment. He was killed in 1799 in India in the Mysore War."

"I am sorry for your loss, madame. May I ask if you had children?"

A look of sadness crossed her face, then she said, "No."

As Darrell walked back to his office, he had to put all of that away to review later. His mind stirred with the plot disclosure and he took Chad into a room and relayed what he had learned and what he thought of it.

"What a contemptible plot! Will we tell Cathcart now, or tomorrow after we find more details?"

He nodded as he stared intensely out the window, and said, "I think after my morning meeting. For now, what inquiries can we make ourselves?"

Between them, they made a plan of action, and spread out around the city, asking discreet questions of people they knew. Wellington's name was not mentioned—just a high-up military Officer."

In the afternoon, Chad put on his 'every-man' disguise, including an eye patch, and went to many drinking houses to listen for rumors. By late evening, he was at Rop Haus and sat near a rowdy group. The more they drank, the more they bragged of their exploits; often about women. One man was sulking over his ale, a morose expression on his face.

The man was dark haired, unshaven and had shifty eyes, and muttered to his neighbor, "They think those are interesting schemes. Wait till they learn what old Ken is up to; that will make them take notice." His friend, who was close to passing out, slurred, "Wa.sh that? Wa.sh ya up to? Goin' to kill s-somebody?"

Hank glanced at him, not realizing how drunk he was, but he couldn't resist another brag—best make it shocking.

"Yes, our mission is to get the most important guy, so he can't win the battle."

His friend stared at him, and fell off his chair.

Since Chad was close enough to hear and get a better look at Hank, he lingered longer, watching him and trying to find out who he was.

Darrell attended a banquet for the plenipotentiaries and their staffs, with his diplomat disguise changing his appearance enough not to be recognized, and using an English dialect from the north.

As the evening wore on, talk got hotter; some men telling tall tales for a laugh. The table next to Darrell seemed very jolly and it got a bit outrageous. The subject of rumors came up.

A curly-headed chap said, "I heard a funny one today—a plot to kill an important military man. Those Frenchmen won't give up, will they, been beaten; why not take it like men?"

The crowd started breaking up, so Darrell went to the man and said, "Couldn't miss your rumor. Is it possibly true? Do you remember where you heard of it? That's the best one in a long time."

So, he threw back his head and laughed.

The man was pleased by Darrell's reaction.

"Well, I was at a meeting today and a fellow told me in confidence."

"Did you know him? Does he have a position here?"

The man enjoyed his moment, since he wasn't used to people paying attention to him.

"Yes, his name is Claus, and he works for Metternich's group, but he's just an acquaintance,"

"Oh, there was a rich one last week, it was about a clandestine liaison between a well-known official and one of the aristocratic ladies staying here. Wondered what the pillow talk was about."

And they both laughed.

Later they shared their findings in Darrell's chamber. The rumors must bear some substance to be repeated in different places. The debate was whether to tell Cathcart right away, or wait till he talked with Lady K. They decided, after his meeting with her.

He arrived at the bench just as she came slowly down the path, looking at the flowers, and he greeted her with a shy smile in case anyone was watching, as they pretended to be strangers meeting in a park.

"Good morning."

"Good Morning, sir," she said. "Do you mind sharing the bench?"

"Not at all, Madame."

"As you see, I like to start my mornings with a walk in the garden, since it is so peaceful."

Darrell surveyed their surroundings before agreeing.

"Well, it is my first visit here and it was recommended to me, so I am grateful to have come and meet a charming lady."

They chatted about themselves for a few minutes, like strangers would. When the paths were clear, they began to share what they had learned. Since ladies first was the polite way, she disclosed her talk with Paul.

"Yes, he is certain his source was sincere and gave some background information, and it is all about money. The villains are willing to kill their leader for pay!"

"Did he give any details of the task? Before the battle, or during the chaos of the fighting?"

"No, he did not know, except it is to happen in Brussels."

"Here's what my partner and I learned," said Darrell, and he reviewed the bragging conversations.

"That gives more certainty to the plot. Now we must determine time and place," she said.

"Yes, I will be telling Cathcart what we have when I return—I do wish Castlereagh was still here, but he's in London. Can you come with me?"

"It would be too risky to go to his office."

"Well, you could go in disguise," he said, smiling.

"Yes, you are right, I could. What time will we meet him?"

"Once I know his schedule and make the appointment, I will send a message to your hotel by my partner, Rowe."

"All right, I'll look for him."

Then Darrell rose and asked, "Could we stroll in the garden since we just met?" He raised his right eyebrow and had a smirk on his face.

So, she laughed at his antics. "That would be acceptable, sir."

Not taking her arm, he held his hands behind his back as they sauntered along, enjoying the view. How he was drawn to this woman; and hard to play his part in their charade. As they chatted, they shared some experiences they had while on missions.

"I was recruited into the job by my friend, Chad. He had years of experience and said I was needed, imagine! I had been a selfish rogue for so many years that I decided it was my turn to help my country fight this war."

She smiled up to him, then said, "He was right, you are an asset to our government."

"I have heard good things about your service also, my lady. How long have you been doing this?"

"Too long. But I got bored with just helping war widows and children. That sounds terrible, I know, but I needed more of a challenge and I had a friend who recommended me to the Foreign Office. It has been at least four years since I joined, and I hope it has helped the cause."

"That is a long time, and I'm sure we have all benefited from it."

They met with Cathcart in his office at ten, including Chad.

"Now, what is this you have heard?"

"My Lord, we learned of a plot to kill Wellington, and since Lady K first brought the information, she can relay it to you."

She smiled at Darrell, then said, "My associate, Paul, overheard drunken soldiers at a tavern bragging about an upcoming event in Brussels. This fellow

Ken was the head of it, but we are sure there are others above him. The idea is to kill Wellington before he can enter into the battle with Napoleon."

Cathcart calmly sat and listened to her story, and turned to Darrell.

"Yes, Chad and I heard the same rumor, and we feel confident that it is real and that there are others above these men paying for the job."

A lengthy discussion resulted in a plan.

"All right, I want you to go to Brussels and investigate there. If this is true, it must be stopped in time. Use any resources you need to successfully stop it and catch the main plotters. Any suspicions of who might be behind it?"

"No, sir, but we think it goes deep."

"Could it be someone here in Vienna? The soldiers were here and may have been contacted here."

"Well, sir, we will cast out lures to see what we find, and we will put our whole group on it. Lady K, do you have other agents as well?"

"Yes, another besides Paul."

"Perfect, use everyone you can on this as soon as possible," said Cathcart. "Perhaps you should get someone to watch these soldiers to find out when they remove to Brussels."

Detailed plans were made and Darrell contacted Clint and his other man to join them. It was decided to keep Wilfred in Vienna to watch the soldiers.

CHAPTER 21

Brussels in Disguise

The groups travelled by coaches to Brussels, dividing the individuals in two. Since Darrell's group consisted of four men, one had to share Lady K's. As the leaders, she and Darrell spent time bringing their men up to date on the mission. When they stopped to change horses, a shift was made. At luncheon, another switch put Laura and Darrell together with Chad.

"Lady K, you and Chad have the most experience in this business, so we will look to you both for some guidance. Saving Wellington will require cunning and skill. I believe we have a very urgent assignment here; and dangerous," said Darrell.

Chad looked at Lady K. "I have been thinking that it will be necessary to always go in disguise. I'm sure we have all brought at least the basics. What is your opinion, your ladyship?"

She smiled and said, "You are correct, Chad. We will need disguises, since many people will be in Brussels from many places. Numerous people who gather will also be in disguise, so don't expect to recognize anyone not in uniform. I expect a large number of French spies will be trying their best to uncover us, so we must be diligent. We also will need to choose residences to assist in our disguise."

"Have you chosen a residence yet? I would not expect you to stay in a hovel, Laura. Are there any hotels there?"

"Yes, there is a nice little hotel close to Wellington's headquarters that should work for me. I will probably be myself most of the time, just use disguises when necessary. I have worked with Wellington in Paris sometimes. He is a task-master, but will be fair and sometimes harsh. He has a tremendous load on his shoulders—getting ready for the battle. He will be wishing for his old troops, but many are still in America. We must protect him from this plot."

The groups kept shifting coaches so they could all become acquainted by the time they arrived in Brussels. It was decided that Darrell would also stay at the hotel; in disguise all of the time. He was too recognizable to remain himself.

The men set out to search for rooms; then reported their locations.

Darrell met with Wellington and discussed the mission.

"This seems like a fairy tale to me, for someone is always wanting to get rid of me. Do you have anything in particular?"

"No, but several people were overheard bragging in Vienna at one of the taverns, then at a meeting, which pointed to a try to assassinate you, so Cathcart sent us to sort it out and stop it."

"Who is in your group?"

"Well, we joined two groups together for this mission: mine includes Chad Peterman, Clint Warden and Frank Sampson and Lady Kerrigan's Paul Spenser and Wilfred Walters. That gives us seven agents to try to keep you safe."

Wellington was surprised at the number on this one issue.

"So, Cathcart must believe the threat is real. Any details about time and place yet?"

"No, but we think it will be just prior to or just after the battle commences, as their stated objective is to get rid of you so Napoleon can win the battle. And we expect this conspiracy is much larger than this couple of soldiers, who are being paid to do the job, and we want to uncover the head man if we can. We left one agent in Vienna to watch the soldiers."

"Good hunting," he said, ending the meeting.

The next day, Darrell went out riding to observe the land and saw a familiar face—Major Sir Joseph Beverly rode nearby. Since he was in disguise, he identified himself when they met.

"Did Wellington call on you?"

"Yes, he asked me to do some training. These poor boys are raw recruits with no experience," and he indicated a small group, also on horseback.

"They will be in a bad way in the chaos of battle without some idea of what to do. The loud noise alone is enough to terrify."

"Well, they are fortunate to have someone like you to prepare them."

"Time is the problem, Darrell. Don't know if we have a week or a month before it begins—it depends on Napoleon, since we certainly are not taking it to him."

As he nodded his head, he realized that was an important point.

"How do you do with languages, since many of these men do not wear British uniforms."

"Tried to learn the basic words for orders in several tongues and hope I will not make a mistake., because it could cause serious problems in the field."

"Yes, and I must tell you that I am here undercover, so will be lying low, can be reached through Wellington's office, but only if needed. Some intrigue is going on which we are trying to crush, so wish us luck."

Sir Joseph saluted and wheeled his horse away, favoring his left arm a bit, and Darrell remembered his long recovery back in '11 after Badajos; and here he was, getting right into the thick of it again.

He couldn't sleep, so finally he got up; an insistent idea lodged in his mind. Then he took some charcoal from the cold fireplace and blackened his face a bit, and dressed as a workman; put on a padded vest to indicate a stoop, a long dark brown coat, a slouch hat, and gloves. He remembered not to wear shiny boots.

So, he walked along an alley to a street where a tavern was open and stood back in the shadows while patrons came and went. The windows were too dirty to see inside, but when someone came out, he got a glimpse of a table-full of men. One of them was laughing in a familiar way—it reminded him of Wally Finchly! Was he working here too? The next time the door opened, he got a better view, at least two of them were soldiers. Pulling back, he thought of what to do. Was he on the same case? For the Admiralty? But it didn't make sense. The navy wasn't involved.

He decided to wait for the other men to leave—they were quite drunk, and they staggered up the street. Then he heard a name, "Ken" and he followed them until they entered a rooming house. While he walked back to his hotel, he was turning this new information over in his mind, because he couldn't forget Wally. Why was he here? He didn't like it; felt sinister. He thought to ask Weatherbee about it; went back to his room and wrote a letter.

"Dear Francis,

Writing to ask you a question. Am on a mission in Brussels and just saw our old partner meeting with my suspects. Is he on a case here? Didn't seem right they would send him on this, which has no effect on the Navy. Please reply soonest. Thank you, old friend. DC

The sunrise was close when he fell into a troubled sleep. When he went to breakfast, he found Lady K there, showing her sunny face, happy as usual for a new day.

"Oh, you look rather drawn; did you not sleep?"

"Yes, but not for long. When I followed an idea, I made a startling discovery. The soldiers were in a tavern; one was Ken, and they met with an old friend of mine, who used to be with the Admiralty. Why would they send a man here on this mission?"

She looked surprised and said, "No, it doesn't sound right. What should we do?"

"Well, I wrote a letter to an acquaintance to find out. Trouble is, the mail will be slow."

Then they both sipped their coffee, eyes meeting over the rims of the cups.

"The only other course is to try to follow this person to find out what he's up to. Do you know any of his friends?"

The only one Darrell came up with was George Freeman, in Warminster, where they met from Bath, and he told her of the connection.

"I think I will report this to Cathcart as well as Castlereagh, since they might have some inside information. The other thing is to keep an eye out each night to see if they meet again."

"No, you can't go every night without sleep; can we take turns and let Chad help us?"

"That's a good idea; the villains will not be as suspicious; and he may learn some of their plans. Thank you, two heads can be better than one." And he paused a moment to admire her green eyes, letting a warm smile curve his lips.

The appointment with the Duke was at ten, so he wore his normal disguise. Bustle at headquarters meant he must wait his turn. The Duke was in an agitated mood over something to do with the Prince of Orange, but he turned to him and said, "Follow me."

And they went into a small room with one window.

"Any news?"

"Yes, I observed a meeting late last night that troubles me."

Then he relayed the information and the oddity of Wally's presence.

"I wrote to a friend at the Admiralty to check on why Wally is here, and I also sent letters to Cathcart and Castlereagh."

The Duke sat back, thinking this over.

Then he said, "No, it will take too long, any other options?"

"Yes, I will send my partner tonight since he is good at fitting in at taverns and may hear their conversation."

"OK, let's try that. Let's get information on when they will attack. The other option is to arrest this lot now and not wait for them to strike."

This surprised Darrell.

"Well, your Grace, the drawback is lack of actual proof; since they could say they just ranted while in their cups."

"OK, we'll do it your way."

When he was excused, he went to talk with Chad, telling him of the meeting, and asked him to cover that tavern tonight. "We need to consider when to take these two soldiers in. It doesn't seem to be urgent at the moment." Chad agreed, but he would keep them in view, along with Wally; if he meets with them again.

He told Laura, and she said she would go to another tavern dressed as a man to see if they might be changing sites.

"That is too risky, my lady. Let me do it."

"In the past, I did it often, so don't worry about me."

"At least let me walk with you. I will be in disguise too."

And she looked at him for a few minutes before agreeing.

The tavern she chose was in a better district and even offered gambling. A back room was set up and a waiter kept everyone's glass filled. As she entered the room, all heads turned, but so many people came to Brussels these days it was not unusual for a new face, and she looked rather nondescript in her man's clothing.

She played carefully at first, to let the other men get used to her. The next round started, so she played aggressively, and one man confronted her.

"Here now, let's see your money, my lad, how do we know you can stand a loss?"

Then Joe looked him in the eye as she took her purse out and spread her coin.

"Is that good enough for you, My Lord?"

The red-haired man across from her sneered; another one laughed and winked at him.

"What do you say, is he in?"

Angry at being shown up, he agreed.

After an hour of hard play, several of the men left the table. The redhead and James were still in, as well as three others.

As they proceeded, some of them relaxed enough to talk quietly with each other. James said, "Are you meeting him tonight?"

Red gave him a dirty look, but said, "Yes, at 10 at the regular place." And signaled with his hand to shush him.

After a while, Joe seemed to run out of luck and left the tavern.

She stayed outside and watched him leave and go to the next alley, where he turned south. She walked in the shadows, keeping him in sight. Also, it was very quiet, so she was careful not to make a sound. After turning several corners, he came into a well-lit street with large, stylish houses.

Then she sank back by some shrubs. The doorbell was answered swiftly by a butler, letting Red enter, and she took note of the address, so they could find out who owned it. This was a new angle for them to follow—taking them into higher society. Perhaps they would find the leader here.

Darrell had spent part of the day walking the streets of Brussels, keeping an eye out for Wally, but no luck, and he wondered what he would do if they ran into each other, because he didn't want to believe he might be involved in this plot.

Then he met with the other members of their team, informing them of the proceedings. They had been assigned territories, but had no news. Maybe he would have them cover the taverns next; these soldiers liked their ale. Naturally, he worried about Lady K going out alone. He smiled at the image she made, dressed as a man. Actually, she did an excellent job of acting like one.

When she got back to the hotel later, he was relieved, greeting her warmly.

"How did it go?"

Removing her head-gear and jacket, she said, "It went well, and I think I found some new information which could be helpful."

She told him what happened, including the house location.

"Now we need to inquire as to who lives at that house, Darrell, since it could even be the leader if we are lucky. The man with red hair went to meet him at 10, and I was there."

"This is great, Laura, you did well, and we will find out whose house it is first thing in the morning. Did any of the men look familiar?"

"Yes, I remembered a red-haired man in Vienna; this must be the same one." As they sat over coffee and discussed it all, each admired the other's skill in their work.

"We can set up a surveillance at the house right away, and I will take the first shift early this morning. Can you line up Chad to relieve me? Then I will find out who lives there."

He was in place at Rue de Brabat by 5 o'clock in the morning, sheltering in the same shrubs that she used. By 9, Chad came, so he went to headquarters.

When Wellington was not in, he talked with Marsh, but could not find anyone with knowledge of the house. So many of the houses had been rented to the mass of people who gathered here, wishing to be near their loved ones in the army, it would be a difficult task.

Paul came to relieve Chad, so he took a chance to investigate the rear of the house, which had a mews. A groom was working there and struck up a conversation, but he was not able to tell him much, just mentioned the "Toffs" who came by with their expensive livery—some of them French, and he was enjoying his work and receiving good tips.

Frantic to find out who was in the house, Darrell wondered; maybe Wally? But the surveillance was not profitable. He must remember they would all be in disguise also.

Watching at the taverns turned up very little, although Ken was seen again. Wilfred was now on duty in Brussels, so he followed him when he left, but he went back to the house they had discovered the first night. Maybe they should keep an eye on the house; so, it was done.

The days flew by, and they were not progressing much, so Darrell decided they needed to meet again, and set up one in the Forest of Soignes, away from any activity. All seven agents attended and they brainstormed the situation. Time was not on their side, but Lady K heard that Napoleon was apparently still in Paris, meeting with the Legislature to shore up his position.

Each made an up-to-date report, but clues did not fit together to give a picture.

"Well, we are under great pressure to solve this mystery, my friends, and it is urgent that we do so before they carry out their plan; for we cannot allow anyone to assassinate him right under our noses."

Then they all squirmed a bit, realizing again how desperate the situation was. There were a couple of suggestions, but they were not thought helpful.

"Finding out who is behind these soldiers is paramount," said Darrell. "No, we don't even know who is to do the actual job, whether it is those who sold themselves to some mysterious fellow."

Everyone appeared sullen, as though they had been reprimanded.

Chad asked, "When will we arrest the soldiers? They are not hiding out, are they?"

After some thought, Darrell said, "Perhaps we should, but the time may not be right. When we do, I think we will move them out of town, out of reach of their leaders."

Noticing the worry on their faces, he said, "Look, you have all been very diligent in your work, and we appreciate it, but we must think bigger. Let's say there is a consortium of Frenchmen who want above all to remove the Duke before a battle begins—who might want to do that? Fouché? de Maitree? Even Talleyrand? If this is a French plot, as we suspect, any of them might be in on it.

Consider the result if they take him out and win. The Emperor will go back to trying to take over all of Europe and maybe England. Do we want him to rule our homeland? No. So let's all think big, with high-ranking plotters leading the action. Even if you come up with outlandish ideas, please share them with all of us, for it might fit in with something we learned."

When Darrell and Laura reviewed the meeting, he said, "How I wish I could find Wally Finchly here in Brussels, so I could learn if he is involved for sure. We could try to find out who he is working for. Perhaps someone in France is blackmailing him to make him act for them. Yes, it is a weak clue having seen him at the tavern, but it is just one thing which might develop into more."

The surveillance of the house continued.

Wally was in a heavy disguise as he walked by the park, since he had to meet Mr. X soon, he wasn't happy. Ever since the beginning when Sorel told him of the plot, he floundered, he did not want to be in this!

When he met the soldiers at the tavern, he established their part, and they would be paid well for the shooting. If the Duke were gone, the plan was that Napoleon would win the upcoming battle.

When he reached Rue de Brabat, he went into the house, but had to cool his heels in the hall until the man arrived. As he fidgeted with his ring, he thought of his dead wife. If she knew what he had become, she would have tried to save him. Oh, he missed her so.

The door opened and a man entered; obviously in disguise also, and motioned Wally to follow him into the library.

"Well, do you have those blasted soldiers all lined up? Do they know when the deed is to be done?"

"Yes, they are, sir, but have not been given the details yet."

"Just as well, they might spill it when in their cups. We'll be sure they die after it's finished, I have Canter for that. But I want you to be on guard for any spies; the place is crawling with them. Expect them to be from any country, since they all have a stake in this. Just be sure you are not arrested before we complete our plans. Remember the price you would have to pay if caught."

He sat stiffly in his chair, because he knew well what he meant. They covered more details before he was sent away. When he left the house, he did not see the man watching from the stables. He headed back to the park, and felt uneasy, but did not notice anyone behind him, so went to his rented rooms to calm down.

Paul and Clint went to Ken's lodgings—they hoped to find both soldiers there, because it was time to move them north. They were surprised when the men came in. Ken had answered the knock, but did not know them. They still felt unsure of their job and they had become suspicious of their futures with the plotters, so they willingly listened to these men and how they wanted to help.

Paul said, "We are sure they plan to kill you both when the job is done—these are cold-hearted villains. Do you agree to come with us?"

The men huddled for a minute, and agreed to come. "We have worried because if Napoleon wins this war, he will take control of Europe and probably invade England. We made rash decisions when we agreed to it and we're sorry."

"Pack your things you want. We will go north and find a place for you to be safe. You will be set up in lodgings with some money to live on, and some new clothes. It will be up to you to stay secret.

Since Chad never met Wally Finchly, he did not recognize him, but he noted the address and went to find Darrell.

"The fellows met, and one left after a while. So, I followed him to a house; and I can take you there."

"Let us go immediately."

They approached stealthily, and knocked on the door. A woman answered. "What do you want?"

Chad asked for the fellow who came in earlier; and gave a slight description.

"Think he's an old friend of mine and want to see him again."

She relented, led them into the hall, and went up the stairs grumbling. He sat down, but Darrell stood back by the coat rack.

A man came downstairs to Chad; not recognizing him. As he came closer, he said, "Yes, what do you want?"

"Saw you earlier today and thought I knew you. Is your name Finchly?"

He almost turned and ran, but kept himself in place. Then he noticed the second fellow, who reminded him of someone.

Darrell stepped out and reached out his hand.

"Hello, Wally."

By instinct, he took his hand, then seemed to want to run; but he held him tightly, putting his other hand on his arm.

"Look, I need to talk with you. Can you come with me?"

He now had a dilemma; he had just been thinking of going to his old friend, and here he was. Yes, he will be going against orders if he goes with him, but if he does not, he is sure Darrell will not give up, so he took a deep breath and nodded his head.

Then Darrell handed him a coat from the rack, and they left.

As they took him to Chad's rooms, he was not his normal jovial self, but appeared to be worried, so they gave him details of the meeting at the tavern and when he met with someone at Rue de Brabat earlier.

"We are working on this, so what can you tell us about where and when? We will protect you against your other plotters."

"The funny thing is, just this morning I wanted to find you and let you stop this dastardly plot, because I can't abide what the results will be if the French win."

Both Darrell and Chad raised their eyebrows in surprise. They began to go over all he knew, including the people involved.

"But I must tell you something else, if they catch me after this, they will tell the world of my indiscretions and I will be charged with treason and hung."

Darrell was surprised, but kept his head.

"Well, we will send you out of Brussels, Wally, to a secure place until this is over."

Soon, they offered him some hot tea and biscuits, and proceeded with the questioning. After learning the plans of the plotters, they asked who was controlling him.

He gave them the names of the group, and they were not surprised at most of them, except for Captain Jean de Maitree.

"I haven't heard the Captain's name before. How is he involved?"

"Oh, he is the brother of the Comte, and he is the one who first black-mailed me for a fatal error I made in the past. The other is deep into espionage and has used it against me for years."

"So, who is the kingpin?"

And he mumbled, "Fouché". Then they looked at each other, it was just as they thought.

"Well, I am so sorry you fell into the hands of such dangerous, ruthless people, Wally. No matter what error you made, what they did to you is deplorable."

Chad stayed with him in the safe house, and Darrell returned to headquarters.

Darrell had to wait a long time for the Duke to be free, so he went over all he had learned. Perhaps this explained a lot. Maybe it was Wally's presence in Bath that caused his uneasiness—his feeling of becoming trapped. Possibly it was not Smithson.

They made plans that Wally would go north to Ghent, where he would be out of contact with the plotters, then moved to Amsterdam and into hiding until this was over.

When Darrell offered to confront Martineau after he was safely away, since he would relish the opportunity and had a score to settle; Wellington told him to set personal vendettas aside for now, and he agreed.

"Let us consider how to go forward with this, since you and your group can now seek as much information on these plotters as possible, and we don't want them to replace the two soldiers with others. Are you sure the first two are safe?"

"Yes, we are moving them north, away from the military presence, and we have provided them with money, clothing and new disguises, so they have protection as long as they don't panic and run. Also, I must tell you, your grace, all three of the people we caught said the same thing: that they couldn't abide the possibility of Napoleon winning and invading England, but two succumbed to the offer of money."

"Humph, what good is that when your country is overrun?"

Next, he sought out Laura and told her all the news, and she was relieved.

"Excellent Darrell, your team did well. Now how will we handle the other plotters, since they could find replacements for those who were caught."

"That is a real possibility, so I think the next step is to find one of them, Martineau, for instance, and get the truth out of him—I would enjoy a round with him."

"Perhaps we should go higher, to de Maitree, since he has been involved in plots we know of and heaven knows how many others. Do you think you could recognize him from Rouen?"

"Yes, unless he is in disguise, but he might be staying safe in France and letting his underlings take the risks here because that appears to be how he operated in the past. Next, we must find out where he lives, maybe in Paris."

When Darrell considered the possibility, he had a thought. Wellington was Ambassador to Paris before he came to Vienna.

"So, I heard he had entertainments there, perhaps de Maitree was a guest?"

"Wouldn't it be a strange coincidence if he already met him? The Duke is a very affable fellow. Should we ask him?"

"Well, I think that is something for you to handle, we know he appreciates a pretty face."

She laughed and said, "I will go directly for an audience."

The disguise she chose was of a high society lady, to help get into the Duke's office.

Darrell accompanied her to headquarters, then took a walk in the park across the street, as he needed to think of the possibilities and determine who to send north with the soldiers and Wally, because he had promised to keep them safe and must do so. He found a bench and sat there, waiting for Laura to appear, and he relaxed in the sunshine. When she came out of the building, he slowly walked to the corner. Then she went down another street for a few blocks before joining up with him.

"How did you do?"

She smiled her coquettish smile and said, "Success, my lord."

Then they separated again, rejoining at the hotel.

"The Duke was surprised we were looking for de Maitree. Yes, he had met him, but did not know where he lived. So, he wondered whether Charles Stewart might, since he was a social butterfly there."

"Would you go to Paris, Laura? Take Paul Spencer with you, since I must stay here to cover the safety of our snared plotters. As far as we know now, the plot is on hold until they figure out who they've lost and try to replace them."

"Of course, I will be glad of a trip to Paris again—although there will be no parties unless required to catch our target."

Darrell laughed. "Oh, you know you will find a way to enter society again and I can't blame you, my dear. Enjoy, but keep on guard as usual, and I will miss you."

"Yes, I will meet with Paul and make arrangements, and I happen to have some friends there, so may be able to lodge with them. Please be careful and refrain from any boxing bouts."

Paul agreed to go to Paris and left Clint in charge of the soldiers.

"The men are at Clint's rooms, waiting for instructions, "said Paul. "It was no trouble getting them to agree, since they were suspicious of the plotters plans. We gave them some decent clothes and they are ready."

"Good job, Paul. Now you accompany Lady K, and be sure to take care of her."

Paul hid his grin, then went to the hotel.

Clint agreed to take the soldiers, and Wilfred would take Wally further north.

Darrell called a meeting, so Chad and Frank came together to discuss their new situation.

CHAPTER 22
The Search Goes On

Darrell spent time making plans. *Now we have more information in our hands, we may set up blocks to stop the plot,* he thought. But he worried about sending Laura to Paris at a time of turmoil and prayed she would find success and safety.

When Chad came, they sat down to plan together.

"Now that we removed the three operatives, we can concentrate on the conspirators. At least we have their names, and we need to figure out how to cripple their plans. Let us hope Lady K will find de Maitree in Paris. I gave her his general description, and his arrogance will stand out."

The location of the brother was unknown, but he probably lived in France, and they wondered if the family lands had been returned, considering their work for Napoleon's benefit. The question was; did Napoleon know what they did? Fouché was always using the current situation for himself, showing no loyalty to anyone.

"The best thing to do is search for details of the shipping empire; since he used Wally to further his competitive business, he must be known in that circle. Wonder if he's tied up with Eynard in any way? Perhaps it is the reason Eynard holds so tight to his information and the strange behavior. Maybe they knew us at the Convention and tried to avoid us."

"It would not surprise me. Didn't you have a robbery in your hotel room?"

"Yes, and by professionals, since they stole our notes while we slept."

"So, if they figured out who you and Clint were, do they also know you are here?"

How alarming. Perhaps he should get another agent to take over this job, as he did not want to cause further risk for the Duke. Now he worried if Laura's association with him would bring her harm. Should he go to Wellington with these thoughts, or just alter his location and disguise? How to warn Laura?

Then he talked this over in depth with Chad—looking at all the possibilities; and felt their group should change locations and modify their disguises. Darrell collected Frank and they went to meet in the forest again.

The sun was not shining, so it was rather dark among the tall birch trees, but they kept alert for any disturbance.

After Darrell revealed the concerns he and Chad uncovered, he asked, "Did we look any different when we arrived?"

"Yes, you did, but I knew you both," said Frank.

"Well, we are all in danger here, and we still must complete this job and save Wellington; so, we must help each other make changes, not only to our appearance, but to our residences as well."

"Seems to me we should use padding to alter our shapes. Also, change hats often. There is a rag-picker's shop in Brussels which should provide us with different clothing." Darrell remembered Paris, how they had to deepen their disguises. It might work here as well.

So, they talked about possible lodgings; the hotel was out and rooms in dilapidated buildings were in.

The next question was, should they lodge in new neighborhoods?

"We don't know how long before the French come north, but it may not be long, so we must reside in terrible conditions for now."

Then they all agreed, but it would be hard being separate, so perhaps they should plan a meeting place. Darrell emphasized the danger again, so they would all take this seriously. Also, they set a schedule for visits to the rag-picker's shop.

What would they do in an emergency? Well, he would inform them of his rooms after choosing them, and they scheduled a gathering for the next day.

The store was well-stocked with poor clothing, but Chad had the extra problem of his facial scars to contend with, so he found a floppy hat with a wide brim which would hide his face. Then he decided a cane would be useful, and he selected a rooming house not too far from the center of town which would save him some steps.

They agreed to continue their observations at the taverns. New soldiers hired for the job might be excited and talkative.

So, Darrell removed his belongings from the hotel, mentioning a trip to Ghent, and found a horrible room in a mean house as a further disguise.

The next day they met again in the forest, reported success in their lodgings and admired their new disguises.

"This should help confuse anyone who is watching us," said Darrell.

Talking over their schedules, they left separately, in different directions.

The first night at a tavern did not provide much. The men imbibing mostly bragged about women. The next night, Darrell went to another, where he did overhear a fight between two men. At first, it seemed to be over a woman, but soon it got down to jobs; they were nervous about what they agreed to do, but after several more minutes of dispute, it was clearly not an assassination that interested them.

The other agents reported similar experiences, so it appeared unlikely they had uncovered the new assassins. Perhaps they would be brought in from another area at the fateful time.

When Darrell met with Wellington away from his headquarters, he laughed at Darrell's new get-up.

"Yes, we made drastic changes, your grace, as well as locations, and we hope to be invisible. Do you have any news for me?"

"Well, I did hear from Paris—Lady K is fitting in. We haven't heard if she has located the Frenchman yet, but Charles is keeping an eye on her."

"We realized what great danger we are all in, thence the changes in our disguises; and I was wondering if we could use military ones to get in among the soldiers. Would it be possible?"

"Yes, but you would need to act the part, with maneuvers and training. Since we have so many untried troops you could do all right. Tell me if you decide to do it, so I can direct you to the right people."

"I will tell you tomorrow, your grace."

Darrell wished Chad was in better shape since he had military experience, but he would not put him in such a position, so he asked Frank.

"Well, we may be able to place one of us into a unit in training. The purpose would be to see if any of the men might be replacements for Ken and Gerry, and assume the plotters will try to use other soldiers now, after the first disappeared. What do you think?"

Frank looked surprised, but he was rather athletic and a good shot, so he was willing to do it.

"Could have a go. Where and when would I join the unit?"

"First I must arrange it with the Duke. Since he has so many raw troops coming in, he thinks he could slip us in. The worry is that anyone who had agreed to do the deed would hardly talk openly about it, more likely brag while in his cups."

"Would you rather we spend more time in the taverns?"

"Yes, I guess we would have a better chance, and we will spread out over several of them. Which one will you cover tonight?"

Next, he reported their decision back to Headquarters. Stopping by the hotel to check for mail, he felt worried about Laura's position in Paris, but she would do a superb job as usual. Then he decided to search for Major Beverly.

He looked so imperial astride his war horse, he smiled in appreciation, and waited until the troop was dismissed before approaching. The disguise would confuse him, so he made a movement, and came over. After greetings, he cautioned him of his clandestine situation, he walked away from the others, and pretended to be begging from the major, and asked if he had seen any soldiers acting shifty or stealthy which might indicate they had a secret?

"Do you mean because of the plot?"

"Yes, we uncovered two soldiers, and they are safely out of the area, but we think they will be replaced with others."

"This is unbelievable. Do you know the plotters?"

"Yes, but no proof for an arrest, and we are covering all the angles—here and in Paris."

"Then I will keep an eye out for anything unusual. By the way, you make a good vagrant!"

They hid their laughter and parted after saying he could be reached through headquarters; the Duke only.

There was a soup-kitchen for soldiers and vagrants, so Darrell entered, got his bowl of soup and sat at one of the long tables, listening to the conversations while slurping the hot liquid. It was a thin, greasy mixture but a chunk of dry bread helped get it down. As he finished, he saw an earnest conversation between two soldiers, who were very young and arguing. One of them urged the other to take part in something, so when they left, he followed them.

They continued their discussion down the street. The first was gesturing wildly to the other, but was not winning the argument. So, he stayed with them until they turned toward the exercise field where troops trained.

That night, he went to the tavern near there and saw them again. After a few drinks, they started again, so he strained to hear names, and finally, the aggressor called the other "Bruce.

The boy was not happy and looked to see if anyone noticed. "Look Tom, don't shout my name about."

"Well, I'm sorry, I guess I got carried away, are you interested or not, because I have to find someone else and it's a lot of money, doesn't it interest you?"

"No, it wouldn't matter if it was twice as much, I am not going to do it." Bruce glared at him, and slammed out the door.

As he followed him, thinking he had been right—they would replace the first two, he wondered what they would do if no one accepted, probably make Wally do it. What about this guy Canter? After Bruce entered a tenement lodging, he headed back to his own place.

CHAPTER 23

Lady K in Paris

Lady K stood in the receiving line for a ball at the Embassy, escorted by an old friend, Lord Jackson. She had worked hard to obtain the invitation, so she might observe the elite of Paris. After several days, she still had not obtained the information she sought and time was running short as she tried to learn about Napoleon's plans to go north, but he was using his troops within France now, getting them ready for the big battle with Wellington.

Lord Jackson took her out on the dance floor for a minuet, and they made a handsome couple. Also, she was keeping an eye out for de Maitree; remembering his description. The enjoyment was evident on her face for she had always loved to dance. When they came off the dance floor, she noticed a knot of men by the refreshment table, in earnest conversation.

So, she mentioned how dry she was after the dance, and Jackson led her to the tables, where she overheard some comments.

"What do you mean, you lost your men?"

The other fellow was rather frightened and replied, "They just disappeared! Can't find them, and we're looking for replacements now."

"'Well you had better hurry; it won't be long now."

"'There was another man that went missing about the same time. Perhaps he took the other two away."

So, she sipped her lemonade slowly to stay near them and carefully observed the men for whether she had seen any of them before. One was familiar, but she didn't remember where she had seen him, so she walked away with Jackson before she became obvious.

New arrivals came to Paris often, but there was a couple who didn't look French, and her friend did not know them either. When she got a chance, she approached the host, and inquired.

"Tell me Charles, who are those rather plain-looking people?"

Then he followed her gaze, and laughed at her.

"Well, Lady Kerrigan, that is none other than John Quincy Adams and his wife, who are American, of course. He was in charge of settling the Treaty of Ghent. And I also learned he will be the next American Ambassador to England."

"Thank you for your superior knowledge—I am among the distinguished at this event, but who are some of the French dignitaries?"

So, he pointed out several to her, but not de Maitree. Then he asked her for a waltz, and they went sweeping around the floor; thinking him a charming rogue, a handsome Irishman with a reputation. She always enjoyed dancing with him when the opportunity arose.

Next, she wrote a note in code for Darrell and sent it with Paul to Brussels for she didn't trust the mail. If he is stopped and searched on his travels, he would be arrested. French spies were everywhere, particularly at the borders. It was a great risk.

Glad of news from Laura, he thought there was nothing significant. Perhaps de Maitree was here now, and would be distressed for losing some of his men. He took Paul into his confidence about the current situation, as he would also need to deepen his disguise and seek other rooms, but he offered him lodging for the night. The next day he received a letter, and took it into the park. It was from Weatherbee.

"Hello, I was surprised by your inquiry. True, the Admiralty did not send anyone, so I can't think why W would be there. Please be careful; it may be a bad sign. I would trust him with my life, but this intrigue is more dangerous than any I have been in. Best wishes always, Francis."

As he sat on the bench, he realized his suspicion had been correct, but now Wally had been removed from the scene, and he felt sorry for his old friend who was caught up in a terrible conspiracy. Wilfred had sent word that his new lodgings should keep him safe in Amsterdam, so he went to his meager room.

He dressed for the night's observance, then put on extra clothing to look heavier and played a poor derelict. Then he found a spot in a tavern, and scanned the room as though looking for a waiter. There were tables with the usual people of the night, plus one back in a corner at which two soldiers sat. His senses tingled, maybe... As he got up, he tripped and fell toward their table, hearing, "I don't care what we have to do, I need the money!"

The short one jumped to avoid the fallen man.

"Hey, watch where you're going!"

"S-s-sorry, sir-r-r," he slurred.

The soldiers glared at him, but didn't help him up in all his dirt.

He took his time struggling to rise, slipping back several times, observing their faces, noting their uniforms, and then followed them. They were still arguing as they arrived at their rooming house, and Darrell made note of the house location. Possibly they were the ones for the job. As he thought about it on the way back to his room, he realized it was strange the plotters kept trying to find replacements since each time they disclosed the job, they were taking a big chance, any of these soldiers may reveal this to their officers.

Lady K decided to see what she could find out about Fouché while in Paris, since he was apparently the one behind the assassination plan. Then she talked with Stewart, who said he was still involved with the low schemes he usually dealt in.

"But Charles, there is a rumor he is backing a dastardly plot."

"Oh yes, he is always engaged with the most revolting plots, my dear. Even heard he stashed a fortune away from his dirty deeds. Remember, Lady K, he has no morals, so plays both sides—a scoundrel who it is wise to avoid."

"That is terrible; how does he get away with it?"

Charles laughed. "You see, he has a stockpile of information on everyone and does not hesitate to use it for his own benefit. Stay away from him at all costs." Then she made some inquiries about Captain de Maitree, as well as the Eynard group, but no success. When she thought of Darrell and the others working so hard in Brussels, she decided to return.

After making an appearance at her hotel, she went to headquarters, which was a hub of activity, some of it rather frantic. She waited for the Duke, not knowing where he was, nor the other agents, and watched the antics of some Staff members who made an effort to be helpful. Finally, Marsh came to take her to Wellington.

She greeted him fondly, and made a succinct report of the happenings in Paris.

"The word is "soon", but no firm plans, your grace, since he is still preparing his troops."

"That is what colonel Grant told me yesterday, so you are on top of it, my dear girl. Did you find anything else of interest?"

"Well, I did some research on two of the main plotters, with no result. Perhaps they are in Brussels by now."

"Yes, we are trying everything we can to find them."

"Can I leave a message here for Mr. Coletrane, your grace?"

"Of course. Give it to Marsh."

Darrell sent a note to her of a gathering in the evening, so she made a thorough job of disguising herself.

The meeting was at a new place, which she found easily, and she was happy to see him again, even in his superb masquerade. But he controlled his greeting, keeping to business.

"Any news for us?"

"Yes, but not as much as I had hoped, and I already advised the Duke."

So, she told them what had happened in Paris.

"I even tried to find out something about Fouché and de Maitree, but no success to speak of, so I believe they must be in Brussels."

"That is interesting," said Darrell. "Since we thought they would stay away from here on threat of discovery. Did you learn anything about them?"

"No, I was unable to find that kind of information. Remember, I appeared as myself at the social events, so no one offered me political or military news."

They talked over every little thing which might be a clue; including some sightings of soldiers who were discussing work for pay, and told of the last two he saw and how they argued.

"And, what will we do next?" asked Paul. They looked at each other, searching for anything to take action on, but no one had any ideas.

"Well, we seem to be at a stand-still, don't we? The changed disguises may not be beneficial. Any rumors? Any arguments? Or anyone looking excited at a proposed profit?"

No one offered anything worthwhile.

"Well, we need to re-evaluate our schemes. I know it is frustrating, but we cannot give up, maybe we are not looking in the right places. Perhaps the taverns can be dropped, and we can find out better ones."

Frank said, "There will be a "Troop Review" tomorrow in the Allée Verte. Let us all put on respectable disguises and attend, as it will be a huge event and could even be a possible place for an assassination. We can either ride there or hire some carriages and maybe go in pairs. What do you think?"

"Yes Frank, it would allow us to mingle with the people and keep an eye on the Duke," said Lady K.

"Perhaps we will overhear gossip from the audience which will be of help, or we may see someone who could be our target."

They made the plans and departed, as they would each have to use another disguise so they could mingle with the crowds.

As Darrell and Laura lingered behind the others, he said, "Happy to see you back my dear, I missed you." She smiled, thanking him for his kind words.

"Yes, I am disappointed we are at a stand, for I know how hard you all have worked."

"We have tried every way to solve this dilemma. It was lucky to remove the two soldiers and Wally away to safety. Now we must get some proof."

"I have to decide whether to go to this Review as myself. If I do, I can't accompany you."

Darrell looked into her eyes, seeing almost a pleading look.

"Well, my dear, why don't you go as yourself and I will use a disguise and attend you? I could be your driver, for I'm too large to be a tiger, you know."

They both laughed at the thought.

"Well, I would prefer you go as you also, but I understand it would be a risk, since too many people know you."

"I will drive. At least I can keep an eye on the crowd and hopefully protect you."

"Oh, I will be so glad when this is over, Darrell, so we can resume our friendship as we want."

He smiled his brilliant smile, raising that right eyebrow.

"Now you take my breath away, madame, giving thought to the possibilities."

And she lowered her head to hide her grin.

"Don't put me to the blush, sir."

"No, I will never dishonor you, my dear, and will just have to be patient."

She looked up into his eyes before going to the hotel.

The morning was perfect for being out-of-doors, and Darrell picked up Laura at her lodgings, dressed in a fetching dress and wide hat. They chose a spot among the other carriages, so they could hear nearby conversations. But he did not talk at all since it would not be correct for a driver to converse with the Lady. He had learned at headquarters the review included not only the Picton regiment, but also the Reserve of the Army, including English, Scottish and Hanoverian units quartered in and around Brussels. The crowd was excited at the potential enjoyment in store, some gathered into groups and shouting for it to begin.

First, Thomas Picton's 5th Division marched by the stand, impressing all who saw them. The Duke called them crack troops and the crowd felt more secure seeing them as their protectors. Someone heard him say, "some of our best," regarding the group of men. Next came James Kempt's four proud regiments: the 32nd, the Slashers, the Cameron Highlanders, and the 1st battalion of the 95th Riflemen in their dark green uniforms and jaunty caps.

A highland brigade under Denis Pack, moved the Belgians to cheer, for the Kilt never lost its fascination; and next the English 9th regiment.

The Royal Scots went by with their pipes playing, followed by Macara and his 42nd Highlanders, and the handsome John Cameron led the 92nd: The Gay Gordons.

The crowd broke into cheers repeatedly, and hats were waved and handkerchiefs fluttered.

The last of the kilts and tall caps with their nodding plumes had gone by, and some thought the best of the review was over, as it seemed Colonel von Vincke's Hanoverians excited little enthusiasm, but then, as they marched past, the Duke said in his terse fashion: "Those are good troops, too; or they will be when I get better officers into them."

The crowd gathered in small groups to discuss it, impressed with all the military might, but it was not possible to join a group of carriages, so Darrell worked his out of the crowd.

When they were back on the road, Laura looked at him and said, "That was very moving, was it not? Those Scottish regiments put on quite a show, for I always love the skirl of the pipes, don't you?"

"Yes, it always moves my soul. It is like it comes down to us from eternity, and you don't even have to have their blood in your veins to feel it."

Then they traveled in silence until the road cleared.

"Well, I will be going to Ghent today, and coming back as myself, as I think it is time to try something new, don't you? Do you think I should return here?"

"Yes, it is what I anticipated, so we can attend the social events in Brussels and be close to society. We will have to make plans of how best to take advantage of this new status."

Darrell studied this beautiful woman who had become so dear to him. He tried to envision the future; hoping she would be part of it. Her striking green eyes had captured him from the first glance. He pictured them dancing a waltz at a fashionable Ball. Then he shook it off and brought himself back to reality – the reality of impending war.

CHAPTER 24

Darrell at the Ball

The afternoon found Darrell in Ghent, where he went to a tailor shop and bought evening dress; since he hoped he would be going to a ball. The town was crowded with men in uniform and visitors from England, hoping to spend some time with their military men before the big battle. He noticed the huge cathedral which had a steeple souring into the sky, but had no time to visit.

Back in Brussels, he checked in at the hotel as himself, using his own name for a change. Next, he visited headquarters to talk with the Duke.

"Your grace, I need to get your direction on some entertainments I can attend as myself. Do you think I should stay away from Lady K?"

Then Wellington actually grinned.

"Yes, I think it would be better, since she came here often as herself and you did not, and I will introduce you to a few people. Where did you come from?"

"Went to Ghent today, but I could have stayed for a while, or just arrived from anywhere."

The Duke studied him for a couple minutes before answering, admiring this handsome man. "Let's say you came from England, since you have not been yourself here. Why did you come, do you think?"

He laughed, enjoying the levity.

"Well, I came to see my old friend, Joseph Beverly, who is here working for you, your Grace."

"That will do, but I didn't know you knew him."

"Yes, we went to school together and when he was injured in the Peninsula, he went to Kent to recover."

"One never knows where one will meet someone from our past. So, you can attend a soirée tonight at Anderson's, I'll arrive at 10."

Smiling as he left headquarters, he had to remember to be himself instead of acting like a spy in costume. *Stay in character—as himself!* He couldn't remember when he last did so. One had to always be on guard.

Darrell saw several people from London, and it felt good to be able to talk with old friends. So, he told Oliver Kershaw about his trip from England and his short stay at Ghent, and they had some laughs over experiences in London during Darrell's roguish days. But he did not recognize any of the plotters, and thought if he did, he might give himself away with surprise. Soon he decided this was not the right event and wondered if any Frenchmen held social events. Wellington would know, so he waited until after 10 for him. When the Duke was available, he gave his report and asked his question.

"Well, I can't say I am familiar with any Frenchman giving a party, so I think they are keeping out of the limelight."

A while later, he slipped out.

The next day, he wrote a short letter to Wilfred, asking him to question Wally about the habits of the plotters, might they be in Brussels, or in society? Anything to help identify them would be useful.

Rumors circulated in regard to the French Armée—it was reported they were ready to march north.

Wellington reviewed his army's positions. In fact, the troops of the battalions and regiments were spread across nearly 100 miles of Belgium in total. Also, he had concern about the Prussians under Blücher; too distant for ease of communications, and he was aware of Napoleon's favorite scheme, divide and conquer. Yes, he wished he had more seasoned men and officers, but what they had would do their best. Experience in past battles caused a sorrow for the loss of life of many of his men under fire, but that was the price that must be paid to be successful.

Lady K greeted Darrell with pleasure, because they both could act themselves. She made a fuss at the hotel and greeted him as though they hadn't seen each other in years. He used his debonair charm to almost bowl her over. Even under the extreme pressure of their mission, she could appreciate his magnificence. Then she looked forward to the end of this war at last. He brought her up to date regarding his travels and meeting with the Duke.

The Duchess of Richmond was famous for her social events, so when she asked the Duke, he said, "Throw a Ball on the 15th to raise everyone's spirits."

Delighted, she made all the arrangements for a splendid event. The guest-list was all-encompassing and decorations spectacular. As the guests arrived, she was happy to see all the ladies dressed in their best and the gentlemen either in military uniforms or the finest evening dress.

When she received a note from Wellington saying he would be late, she had the dancing go on without him.

Then rumors circulated that the French had arrived at the border, where there were some skirmishes of men at outposts at Charleroi and the fighting would probably start on the morrow. Ladies looked at their men with melancholy, knowing this might be their last evening, but everyone kept on dancing.

After much planning, Darrell spread his agents out to watch for suspicious activity, and Laura danced a waltz with him.

"Oh, you look ravishing, my lady," he said with a seductive smile.

"Thank you, sir, as do you," looking into his face and locking on to his blue eyes."

But then they watched closely for any sign of weapons. The soldiers would be wearing small swords or pistols, so they concentrated on men not in uniform. A gun usually left a bulge under a dressy coat. Most wore dancing shoes, and couldn't hide a weapon in them.

Later, word came that the Duke was arriving, and Darrell left Laura with an officer she remembered and went toward the entry. Now he hoped his men covered the two who were there to shoot the duke. His mind was racing, reviewing all their preparations. There was laughter among the Duke's entourage as they approached the last steps, and Darrell's eyes swept around, noticing the ugly expression on a man's face, a man who had a gun—who was raising his hand—and he threw himself down the steps toward the Duke.

CHAPTER 25

Chad seemed still in shock as he talked with Paul.

"Darrell took a bullet in the shoulder."

"What? How did it happen? Is the Duke OK?"

"Yes, he was not hurt, but if our friend had not thrown himself in front of him, Wellington would be dead."

"How is Darrell?"

"He was lucky. He lunged off the steps to block the Duke from the shooter and the bullet struck his shoulder."

"Did they arrest the villain?"

"Clint chased him and several officers blocked his escape."

"Do you know who he is? One of the leaders of the plot?"

"Well, I believe he is Martineau, but he wore a disguise, so I am not sure yet."

"What happened to the turn-coats? Were they arrested?"

"A long story, Paul; will tell you later. Now I want to check on how badly Darrell is hurt." So, he went to Richmond's library where a doctor treated Darrell's injury. Some officers were in attendance also, blocking the way. Darrell's face was ashen; looked terrible, and Chad worried; then he finally pushed his way to the surgeon.

"This is my partner, sir, can you tell me how he is?"

The poor man turned with a harassed look, trying to tend his patient.

"Too soon to tell, but since I surmise no vital organs are injured, I believe he has a fair chance of recovery. Too early to tell—loss of blood may be the worst problem."

The Duke stood to the side, talking with Richmond and several officers. His mind was still concentrated on the preparations for the battle ahead, but awaited news on Darrell's condition.

Then he said, "Gentlemen, I think we should join the ball now, so people will not be worried, because they might think it is myself who is injured, and we must keep up their spirits so there will be no panic."

With these pithy words, he removed to the dance floor and selected a lovely lady for a waltz. He was observed to be at his social best, disproving the rumor he was hurt.

After the doctor did what he could, they moved Darrell to a guest room with Chad by his side; alarmed by his pallor. Some visions of his own traumatic injuries in Paris kept floating through his head, so he sent up prayers that his friend would recover, but he will likely suffer from fevers during his convalescence.

Lady K danced and played the part expected of her, all the while thinking of her dear Darrell lying ill upstairs, then prayed he would rebound from the bullet—it was mostly his right shoulder that was damaged, and she knew he was a strong, healthy man and had a good chance. So, she followed the Duke's example and acted gay and unconcerned. What would tomorrow bring?

As the evening wore on, the Duke gave orders to his head officers who were attending, and sent messages by his Aides de Camp to the others. Later, he met with Richmond in his study.

"Do you have a map of this area?"

"Yes, I do."

He took it from the desk drawer, spread it out and Wellington studied it for a few moments before exclaiming, "Those crossroads are crucial to movement here. If the French have taken control of them, we are in trouble. He stole a march on me; I've lost 24 hours!"

Then he rushed out to confer with his senior officers again, informing them of this news.

CHAPTER 26

The Battle of Waterloo

No, Darrell was not used to being called a hero, as he simply reacted to the circumstances and did his job. Also, his muscular physique saved him further injuries, but loss of blood did the most harm and caused his fevers.

He still stayed at the Richmond's Home. By the time he was able to be removed, no space remained for him anywhere, because wounded soldiers flooded the town after the ferocious battle.

As he reclined on his pillows, reading a book, a visitor came in; someone he never expected. Lord Smithson sauntered into the room in all his dark complexion and brusque voice.

"Well, Darrell, had to come and see the hero who saved the Duke."

Darrell laid the book aside and rose to a sitting position, so he could shake the proffered hand of his nemesis with his left hand.

"This is a surprise; never expected to see you."

"Heard of your chivalry at the crucial hour—well done old friend."

Smithson actually smiled.

"Just doing my job, as anyone would do. And I learned you worked for the Foreign Office as well. Where did your duties take you?"

He recovered from his surprise and said, "Mostly in France, but sometimes further afield."

"Surprisingly, they did not tell me much about you there, and I suspected you of being a double agent. Were you?"

He took a step back at this aggressive question, and his anger showed.

"Yes, I took on assignments not known at the Foreign Office because they thought since I had been out of England for years, I could fit the job better and not be recognized."

"Do you remember Chad Peterman from Harrow? Well, he brought me into the office. Did you know he was arrested in Paris and tortured severely?"

He almost stepped back again from the expression on Darrell's face.

"Yes, I knew. At one point, Fouché insisted I attend a torture session—so gruesome, but my role was for the French. How is he now?"

His eyes snapped, and he said, "After a long time of excruciating suffering, he recovered sufficiently to go back to work."

"Look, I was bound by my position, and certainly did not enjoy the occasions when my English brothers were mistreated."

Darrell turned his gaze away, a look of disgust on his face.

Silence prevailed for a while as each grasped these disclosures.

Then he asked, "Did you get involved in the House Party near Bath where a French Plot to blow up the Admiralty Mess transpired? Did you ever attend Allen Court?"

"Is it necessary to review it all? I was on assignment, just like you." Then he turned his head to glance outside to calm himself.

"All right that's acknowledged, but there is one thing I want, Smithson; did you try to trap me into a charge of treason?"

Now he looked surprised again, and turning toward the window, he said, "A couple of the leaders thought it might be entertaining to cause you some trouble."

"Why me?"

"Because you did too good a job, and they feared you would ruin their plans."

Now Darrell simmered, but kept control.

"One more question; where are de Maitree and his brother now?"

Now Smithson got angry at this grilling.

"How would I know? Haven't seen them for months. I resigned from the Foreign Office now that the war has been won."

"Well, they were behind the plot to kill Wellington—weren't you also?"

Smithson knew this was the key issue, and he must handle it carefully. So, he pulled up a chair and sat there considering his words.

"Yes, I needed to play the part they required so as not to show them the truth. And I had to help them with their schemes as well as try to protect England."

"So, that's a yes," said Darrell.

"Yes, I was on a tightrope for several years—not an easy assignment. Thank God you saved Wellington. When Martineau took that shot, my heart stopped, because I did not want the French to win.... ever.

"I'm tired now so you must go. Maybe one day we can have another discussion. I appreciate that you came, William."

When Laura came later in the day, she was astounded to hear about Smithson's visit.

"Oh, Darrell, you learned what you wanted so much to know. "

So, he lay still, studying those gorgeous green eyes for he had so much to be thankful for.

"Yes, I feel better; clearing the air. A lot of my suspicions proved true, but some did not, so I guess it all comes down to the fact that those I worked for also employed him in a more clandestine position, but I could not do what he did. He was always a vindictive person, even in his youth, and his parents did him no favors. Now I hope he can go forward into a better future."

"You are very generous my dear. And I have some news—your old room at the hotel is available, so I booked it for you. A few more weeks of rest will do wonders, and I will take special care of you, my love." Then she kissed his cheek before she read to him.

Soon, Chad decided it must be time to tell him about the great battle which was fought while he was unconscious.

"Well, Darrell, I have been hesitant to tell you the details of the fight while you were so ill. Would you like to know about it?"

He nodded his head. He had heard bits and pieces of it already, but Chad would put it all into perspective.

"There is an interesting story that came out of the battle for the Chateau and farms at Hougoumont. Napoleon's brother, Jerome, wanted to capture it for his own glory, and he called for an attack against orders. Napoleon was waiting for the ground to dry after the heavy rains, and ordered General Reille to threaten—not attack the chateau. He did not want a major brawl to use up too many French troops. The main effort would be against Wellington's left and center, not his right.

Jerome's troops pushed the defenders out of the Oak woods and now faced the fortress. As they emerged, they were faced by this formidable range of walls and buildings. Over 9,000 French tried to evict the 1,200 defenders.

Wellington sent more troops, but the struggle was fierce and unrelenting. After hours of fighting on the 18th, MacDonald found that the main gate was open and the French were rushing in. A stiff battle achieved the closing, and the French who had gotten inside were killed. Next, cannons were brought up, the house was set on fire, and shells continued to be lobbed over the high walls. The main house and barn burned along with wounded men and horses within.

Jerome's attack used up inordinate numbers of French infantry."

Chad paused to see if Darrell had comments, but he was just imagining the horrific scene.

"Napoleon struck at Charleroi during the Ball. The Allies were almost caught unprepared the first day. The next morning, Wellington sent three more battalions to the Bossu Wood area. One was the 69th. They formed squares, but Slender Billy ordered some into line. The 69th was vulnerable to the attack of French cavalry, who destroyed them and captured their colors. This was the high point of the battle for the French. Only a few of the men managed to join another square.

Wellington had won the battle his troops were in; so, he held the crossroads and denied Ney from swinging eastwards to fall on the flank of the Prussians.

The Prussians retreated from Ligny, badly mauled, and the British from Quatre Bras. Rain came down in torrents, affecting everything. After defeating that army and holding The Duke in secondary battles south of Waterloo on June 16, Napoleon's Marshals, including Ney, failed to attack and annihilate either army while they remained separated. Grouchy, with nearly one-third of the French troops, led a dilatory pursuit of Blücher. By the 18th, he was still tied down at Wavre by part of the Prussians' rear guard, while the major force had rejoined Wellington to turn the tide of battle at Waterloo.

Napoleon made a huge blunder in delaying the opening of his attack on The Duke from morning until midday on the 18th; to allow the ground to dry. This delay gave the Prussians troops the time they needed to reach the battlefield and bring support to Wellington as Blucher had promised.

The four prime French attacks against Wellington's army prior to 6 PM on June 18 all failed in their object to decisively weaken the allied center to permit a breakthrough; because they lacked coordination between cavalry and infantry. Meanwhile, a secondary battle developed in which they were on the defensive against thirty thousand Prussian troops under Bulow. The Prussians put pressure on Ney's eastern flank, so Napoleon was forced to shift a corps under Mouton, and to move several Imperial Guard battalions from his main fight against Wellington.

Finally, at 6 pm Ney employed his infantry, cavalry and artillery in a coordinated attack and captured La Haye Sainte, a farmhouse in the line. The French began blasting holes in the Allied center.

The decisive hour had arrived.

Wellington's heavy losses left him vulnerable to any intensification of the fight. Ney's request for infantry reinforcements was refused because Napoleon was preoccupied with the Prussian attack. Only after 7 pm when his flank was secured, did he release several battalions of the Imperial Guard to Ney, but by then Wellington had reorganized his defenses. Then Ney led part of his troops and other units in the final assault on the Allies.

The firepower of the Allied infantry shattered the tightly packed troops. The repulse of them at 8 pm was followed by the beginning of the general advance and further attacks in the east and it threw the French army into a panic and a disorganized retreat began."

Darrell was astounded by this tale, grateful of the outcome.

"Since Wellington said it was "a close-run thing," I guess it's true. The troops must have been handicapped by all that rain."

"Yes, it was unrelenting and created a tremendous hardship on everyone. The ground became a muddy bog. No campfires could be used to warm food while it rained so hard, in fact, many did not have any food at all, but they carried on in their discomfort and fought like tigers."

"This ended the One Hundred Days of Napoleon's freedom, but it appears to me Napoleon's abilities had diminished, for it was unusual for him to make such disastrous mistakes. Thank god he did," said Darrell.

"Between Wellington and Blücher, they out-generaled him."

"What about casualties?"

"The loss of lives on all sides is astounding, and with the deep mud, many injured men on both sides perished during the night. The whole town became a hospital—wounded were taken into almost every home or building and the women-folk worked around the clock at times to help the doctors and care for the wounded. It was a huge benevolent effort, Darrell. But we lost some of our most valiant leaders in battle, including Picton, and Brunswick."

"Someone said, "War is hell," and I tend to believe it. Thank God we beat Napoleon, and he is now in exile on St. Helena's Island."

Chad sat with him for a while and they hashed over some of the great risks taken by the Allied troops. Even though neither of them was able to fight, they were grateful for those who did.

Darrell appreciated Laura's good care of him. He could feel the love growing between them and hoped they would have a future together, but was cautious of what he could say to her. He felt he should be fully recovered before broaching the subject of marriage.

As Darrell improved, their conversations sometimes went to their experiences. One day she recalled a time in Paris when she narrowly avoided death.

"When I was new to the job, my lack of experience nearly caused me great harm."

"What happened, Laura, did someone let you down?"

"I was partnering with Anthony Young, trying to infiltrate a group of French revolutionaries. Our orders were to find out where the leader was hiding. He had been undermining our operation, but couldn't uncover us to the government, because they were looking for him. We laid a trap for him, but he saw through it."

"Was he caught?"

"No, but he continued to try to cause us trouble. One day, I went to the park to see who was gathering there. I was in disguise as a man that time and hoped it would protect me. There was a group over by a stand of trees who looked rather aggressive—shouting insults to people. I avoided contact, but someone came up behind me and grabbed my arms. My partner was not approached, so he avoided the fracas. He stood by while I was roughed up and questioned. They found my pistol in my boot. Now I was sure they would kill me.

"Why are you carrying a gun, my lad? Who are you going to shoot, huh? Are you going to shoot me?"

"Anthony looked unsure of what to do and stayed still. I knew he was armed also, but he didn't do anything. I was terrified that they would find out I was a woman. A policeman approached and questioned about the gun, thinking it was the tough guy's, but another pointed to me.

"Officer, the man is right, it's my gun. I'm sorry I forgot it was in my boot."

The policeman evaluated the situation, which seemed about to explode, and decided to remove me and the gun from the scene.

"You just come with me, mister, with your gun. We'll go down to the station and see what we find."

So, he took the gun away from the man and removed me – to safety, I hoped."

"What did Anthony do? Did he go with you or stay clear? Was he afraid?"

"He followed at a distance as I walked with the officer, to see where I would be taken. Remember, we were both undercover and should not reveal who we were, but I had to make a decision. In the heat of the moment I told the officer that I worked for the government in hushed tones, and he played along with me.

He got me into his office and said, "I understand you are in a difficult position and will cover for you. I'll put you in a cell until the gang leaves."

"I was very lucky, Darrell—I could have been killed, but I was diligent to avoid such a situation after that."

Darrell held her hand, raising it to his lips. "My dear, I hope you will never be in such danger again. We will be able to live a normal life now."

Laura's love grew daily during the long convalesce, aware that his feelings were growing in the same manner. It was the eyes. Their distinctive eyes would lock often to radiate their love and endear each other. It was like word-less communication—straight to the heart. She wondered how long he would wait to propose, wishing he could say the words now, but understood why he delayed. She realized how lowering it would be to ask the question when he was still lying on his back and was feeling weak.

Now that he was up and getting around, he felt more secure in his love. He must exercise relentlessly to regain his strength. He had regained the full use of his right arm and now had to become his old self with all his strength regained.

Laura received another letter from her family. Her uncle Charles was inviting her to come north for a visit. She hadn't seen them for years, so agreed. She talked it over with Darrell and he encouraged her to go. She was sorry to leave him, but he had others who were helping take care of him. He would miss her terribly, but knew she needed her family after these years of war. So, they had a fond farewell, with promises for when she came back.

They would both count the days before they would be reunited and perhaps wed.

CHAPTER 27

The Wedding

It was a great day when Darrell returned to Broom Street and saw his father. They had an emotional reunion; pleased with the outcome of his efforts.

"Well, they tell me you are a hero, son, and I am most proud of what you did."

"I told many people—I just did my job, Father. Such an amazing experience being in the middle of the Congress and helping Castlereagh—especially with my friend Chad, because he did as much as I did during all those months, and he is my hero."

Sir Giles accepted this, but still felt much pride in his son, who overcame his past and shone in the spotlight of his service.

They sat with their port and reminisced.

"Do you think you will settle down now? Will you stay with the Foreign Office, Darrell?"

"No, I don't think so. Made some other plans I need to tell you about, because I found the woman I wish to marry, Father. She was in the same work as I, and we became close. In fact, if she agrees, I expect to. Her name is Lady Laura Kerrigan and is a widow."

Sir Giles's eyes crinkled at the corners. Now his son found the woman he had been looking for.

"Well, I am delighted, and hope I can meet her soon."

"She is visiting some relatives up north now, but when she comes back, you will see her. I could spend hours bragging about her, but I will let you fall under her spell for yourself. One thing you should know—she has the most gorgeous green eyes which shine with love."

Even though he missed her, he appreciated that her uncle invited her to visit, to remove her from the intrigues and the wars for a while; because her bravery was as boundless as her heart was tender.

So, his prayers were answered, and he had found his match at last.

When Mr. Bart sent a note to come in, he laughed with Trent while he donned his usual disguise for foreign office visits—a satire of their association, which was accepted as a joke by Bart.

"How is your shoulder, Darrell?"

"Still feels stiff, but improving."

"When the news of your bravery reached us, we were not surprised, and quite proud."

"Well, I was so intent on protecting him, I automatically dove at him. Thank god it worked."

"It doesn't bear thinking of the alternative, does it?"

"We had our work cut out for us, but our team did their best. If you could have seen some of the disgusting disguises we wore, and the lodgings— you would be shocked. Major Beverly even told me I made a good vagrant!"

They laughed heartily until Mr. Bart said, "Do you have plans for your future, Darrell?"

"Yes sir, the first is to end my employment, second, to get married." Then Bart's eyes widened, and he extended his hand.

"Oh! May I ask who she is?"

"Actually, you probably know her—Lady K."

A satisfied look came upon Bart's face, and he said, "A perfect match!"

Soon he received a letter from Laura.

"My dearest love, I miss you and long to come, but Uncle says I must stay a little longer, so I bartered for another week. It is wonderful to be with family again, I must admit, but it is you I long for.

I hope your arm is healing well and the pain lessening. I look forward to my return, my darling. I have been making lists for the future and you are at the top.

All my love, Laura."

Emotions chocked him and his eyes were misty as he read, then held the letter to his heart.

When Laura returned, Darrell invited her to dinner at Broom Street.

"Father, I would like you to meet Lady Laura Kerrigan, and Laura, this is Sir Giles Coletrane."

She curtsied to him as she held his hand. He was elated to meet Darrell's prospective bride. He bowed as best he could and smiled.

"I am so glad to finally meet you, Lady Kerrigan, since I have heard much of you. Welcome to our home, my dear."

"The pleasure is mine also, Sir Coletrane. Your son has swept me off my feet with his charm, so I expect he got that from you."

"I am bursting with pride over his heroism and service. But also, with his choice."

She smiled as she looked at Darrell, but he was not embarrassed by his father's words. She felt safe in this home, with these men. Then they were called for dinner. It was a happy meal, with lots of laughing. She was engulfed with love.

Darrell took her to the Drawing Room when his father retired. He had things to discuss with her. He seated her on the sofa, then knelt on one knee before her. She giggled. He took her hand in his, then said, "My darling

Laura, will you do me the honor of giving me your hand in marriage? You already know of my deep love for you."

She did not simper, but kept her eyes on his—her wonderful friend who soon would be her husband. "Yes," she said, still holding their gaze.

He couldn't help himself—he pulled her up onto her feet and they shared a searing kiss and embrace. Then they laughed joyously.

They had plans to make, so he poured brandy and they each shared their thoughts about the wedding. She had drawn up her list, and he had a vision of his own. After all that was shared, they settled on the perfect wedding at St. Georges, Hanover Square.

"Laura, my love, I have dreamed for years of being married in that church. I have attended many weddings of family and friends there already."

So, they chose what was most important to them and set a date, 16 September, which was a month later, so the bans could be read.

"I can't wait to make you mine, Laura." And she agreed; feeling the same.

The sun shone brightly on 16 September 1815, spotlighting the famous church. Darrell's feelings almost overcame him as he waited for his bride with Chad, looking proud of being the Best Man. The music from the huge pipe organ almost shook the rafters of his favorite—St. George's, in the heart of London.

The church was full of well-wishers as well as those who just came to see this event.

The congregation stood as Lady Kerrigan arrived at the massive front doors, then she came in on the arm of her Uncle Charles, who looked proud.

The organist played the wedding march as the most beautiful bride came to join her fiancé at the altar. The vicar was accompanied by the Bishop, looking happy; for he knew her since her birth.

Yes, Darrell came early to soak up the ambiance of this magnificent church. As he stood watching his bride's progress down the wide isle, he raised up a prayer of gratitude to the Lord—his dream was coming true.

The Bride's exquisite dress; a soft rose color and the matching pink roses with trailing white ribbons she carried, made her breathtaking. She met her intended's eyes as she approached, and they locked—green and blue— lost in their joy.

Yes, Darrell tried to listen to the vicar's words, but he was captivated by the reality of this blessing, to be joining with Laura for the rest of their lives. He stood there gazing, and had to be reminded to repeat his vows.

Laura's happiness overwhelmed her, and she also missed some cues, but it didn't matter—her dream came true at last.

The wedding breakfast was held at Broom Street; where all their families and friends gathered to celebrate this beautiful couple. It had to be acknowledged, since many were overcome by their beauty and grace. Sir Giles was placed in a large armchair at the head of the table. Mr. and Mrs. Darrell Coletrane were on his right and he was thrilled for them. He thought of it as a match made in heaven and wished them many years of bliss. Sir Hector Beckworthy and his wife were happy for him, and delighted to add Laura to their family. Captain and Mrs. Mark Littleton were also pleased to see Darrell settle at last, and with such a beautiful bride!

A glorious day for all, and the many hugs and well wishes continued until the couple left the house—they had a schedule to keep. Then they sailed away on a very long honeymoon.

EPILOGUE

Wally Finchly was punished for his part in helping the French: his blackmailers. After consideration and Weatherbee's backing, he was discharged from the navy. He later took his children and removed to America to re-start his life.

Chad's future looked bright, with a career at the Foreign Office. The next year, he married a lovely girl and settled down.

Clint joined the Metropolitan Police in their headquarters to organize their records.

Bernice and her hero lived happily together, doing good works.

After a thorough investigation, Humphrey Beales was arrested for manslaughter in killing his wife and was put in prison. The Breach of Promise charge had been thrown out of court.

They investigated the Drummond's deaths and found the persons who tampered with their carriage. Those same men were trying to get money through the son, who didn't have any knowledge of it. So, they killed him and threw his body into the Thames. They got the gallows.

Smithson went to his Estate, learning the skills of being a landowner. He married a sophisticated lady who had also traveled widely, and he finally found peace.

Mr. Semple spent the next years expanding his agriculture business—becoming almost as well-known as Coke in animal husbandry and land improvements. He continued to care about those in difficulty; and helped find work for many of the soldiers after the war.

Sir Louder turned West in his shipping business to America and the Bahamas. He never married.

THE END.

ACKNOWLEDGEMENT OF RESOURCES FOR HISTORY.

Books:

History of England (Napoleonic Era) - H. E. Hunt

A History of England and the British Empire - 1953

Kings & Queens of Britain - Phillips

Rites of Peace - 2007 - Zamoyski

Waterloo - 2014 - Cornwell

Internet:

The Foreign Policy of Castlereagh 1812-1815 files.

Wikipedia: Congress of Vienna - Major players and the process, and The Battle of Waterloo

www.britannica.com: Congress of Vienna and Waterloo: Wellington and Napoleon

www.History.com

DVD:

Napoleon, An Epic Life - producers: Guerin and Depardieu - AAE drama.

Teaching and Student Achievement

*Report of First-Year Findings
from the 'Mosaic' Study of
Systemic Initiatives
in Mathematics and Science*

Stephen Klein, Laura Hamilton,
Daniel McCaffrey, Brian Stecher,
Abby Robyn, Delia Burroughs

RAND
EDUCATION

The research described in this report was supported by the National Science Foundation, grant number ESI-96-15809.

ISBN: 0-8330-2879-0

Building on more than 25 years of research and evaluation work, RAND Education has as its mission the improvement of educational policy and practice in formal and informal settings from early childhood on.

RAND is a nonprofit institution that helps improve policy and decisionmaking through research and analysis. RAND® is a registered trademark. RAND's publications do not necessarily reflect the opinions or policies of its research sponsors.

Published 2000 by RAND
1700 Main Street, P.O. Box 2138, Santa Monica, CA 90407-2138
1333 H St., N.W., Washington, D.C. 20005-4707
RAND URL: http://www.rand.org/
To order RAND documents or to obtain additional information,
contact Distribution Services: Telephone: (310) 451-7002;
Fax: (310) 451-6915; Internet: order@rand.org

During the 1990s, the National Science Foundation (NSF) funded a number of large-scale initiatives designed to change the way mathematics and science are taught in schools. These efforts, called Systemic Initiatives (SIs), shared a common emphasis on aligning all aspects of the educational system in support of ambitious curriculum and performance standards. Particular emphasis was placed on teacher training and professional development to promote changes in instructional practice that would enable students to achieve the new standards.

Funds were given to states, to urban school districts, and to consortia of districts to implement reforms consistent with NSF's purposes. Sites had considerable flexibility in designing their programs, and they adopted very different strategies for promoting reform. As a result, initial research on the SIs focused on the complex process of development and implementation. Although individual sites gathered information, after five years of funding, NSF had no broad picture of the effects of the reform on student achievement.

In 1996, NSF provided funds to RAND to investigate the relationships between student achievement in mathematics and science and the use of instructional practices that are consistent with systemic reforms. The study, called the Mosaic project, was conducted in two waves: A set of six sites (including both states and urban districts) that were implementing systemic reforms was studied during the 1996–97 school year, and a similar set of six sites was studied during the 1997–98 school year. The same basic analytic design was replicated at each site, and the study draws much of its power and generalizability from this replication.

This report presents results for the first wave of the study. The results should be of interest to educational policymakers at all levels of government, as well as to program developers and school administrators interested in mathematics and science education.

CONTENTS

FIGURES

TABLES

During the 1990s, the National Science Foundation (NSF) supported the efforts of several states and large school districts to change the way mathematics and science were taught. These programs, called Systemic Initiatives (SIs), emphasized aligning all aspects of the educational system with ambitious curriculum and performance standards. The funded sites had considerable flexibility in designing their programs, and they used many different strategies to promote reform. However, extensive in-service training for teachers was often the centerpiece of their efforts.

In 1996, NSF awarded RAND a grant to investigate a key assumption underlying the SI program, namely, that greater use of instructional practices that are aligned with the reform would lead to improved student achievement in mathematics and science. To carry out this research, RAND and NSF collaborated in identifying 11 SI sites across the country that were emphasizing reforms in mathematics, science, or both. Data were collected at the following six sites in the first year: Fresno, CA; San Francisco, CA; Connecticut; Louisiana; Columbus, OH; and the combination of El Paso, Socorro, and Ysleta, TX.

RESEARCH DESIGN

The same basic research design was used at all sites. This design had the following three major components: (1) a measure of instructional practices, (2) assessment of student achievement, and (3) an analysis of the strength of the relationship between instructional practices and student achievement after controlling for student background characteristics.

The teacher questionnaire used to measure instructional practice was administered to a large sample of the teachers at each site who taught mathematics and/or science at the grade level being studied at that site. The questionnaire asked teachers about the frequency with which they used various types of reform and traditional instructional practices. For example, it asked how often the students conducted their own science experiments (reform) versus listening to the teacher lecture (traditional). Horizon Research, Inc. (HRI), under a subcontract from RAND, had primary responsibility for designing and validating this questionnaire.

The student assessment component involved administering tests in mathematics and/or science to a large sample of students at each site's targeted grade level. To conserve resources and reduce the testing burden on students and teachers, scores from existing statewide or districtwide assessment programs were used when such scores were available. We augmented these "local" measures with tests administered by RAND staff and consultants. Students at all but one site took both a multiple-choice and an open-response test in the subject(s) assessed at their school. Consequently, the specific tests used at each site differed.

The third research design component common to all sites involved the statistical methods used to analyze the data. The relationship between instructional practices and student achievement was examined, after controlling for relevant student background characteristics (such as prior-year test scores and whether the student was in a free or reduced-price lunch program). However, the specific control variables differed somewhat across sites (e.g., not all sites had test scores from a prior year). The analyses also controlled for the "nesting" of students within classrooms. Taken together, these controls helped to isolate and measure the relationships between use of the instructional practices and student achievement.

Table S.1 shows the grade level and subject(s) studied at each first-year site and the number of schools, teachers, and students that participated in the study.

TEACHER QUESTIONNAIRE DATA

Analyses of the teacher questionnaire revealed that the frequency with which a teacher used the reform practices was generally un-

Table S.1

Details on Participating Sites

Site	Grade	Subject	Number of Schools[a]	Number of Teachers	Number of Students (varied by test in some sites)
1	3rd	Math	17	46	804
2	5th	Math	20	100	1,651–1,686
2	5th	Science	20	99	1,639–1,662
3	5th	Math	18	73	1,366–1,451
3	5th	Science	20	74	1,367–1,438
4	5th	Science	19	45	909–932
5	7th	Math	17	48	2,937–3,018
5	7th	Science	19	33	2,047–2,079
6	7th	Math	25	57	3,237
6	7th	Science	25	52	3,279

[a]Some schools at each site are included in both the mathematics and science samples.

related to the frequency with which that teacher used traditional practices. For example, some of the teachers who used the reform practices relatively frequently also used traditional practices frequently, while other frequent users of the reform practices used the traditional practices only rarely. Thus, the two aspects of practice were not opposite ends of a single dimension.

The analyses also showed substantial variability in instructional practices within schools, regardless of the degree of implementation of the reform program. There are many plausible explanations for this finding—for example, not all teachers were trained in the same way or at the same time—but examining the source of this relatively large within-school variation in instructional practices was beyond the scope of our study.

STUDENT ACHIEVEMENT

After controlling for student background characteristics, we found a generally weak but positive relationship between the frequency with which a teacher used the reform practices and student achievement. This relationship was somewhat stronger when achievement was measured with open-response tests than with multiple-choice tests. The use of traditional practices was generally unrelated to achievement. The foregoing trends held for both mathematics and science; and they were generally consistent across the six sites, i.e., in most cases, the pooled results across sites were not driven by the data at one or two sites.

Table S.2 illustrates these trends by contrasting the standardized regression coefficients for the relationship between student achievement and the teacher-reported frequency of using reform and traditional instructional practices. These trends are also illustrated by Figures S.1 and S.2, which show the pooled (across-site) effect sizes (i.e., the increase in student achievement, as measured in standard-deviation units, that corresponds to a one-standard-deviation increase on the instructional-practices scale).

DISCUSSION AND CONCLUSIONS

Taken together, the data in Table S.2, the results in Figures S.1 and S.2, and the consistency of findings across sites provide some (albeit weak) support for the hypothesis that the reform practices are associated with improved student achievement in both mathematics and science. However, as with most large-scale field studies, there are many factors that may have artificially increased or decreased the observed effect sizes.

Table S.2

Standardized Regression Coefficients from Pooled Analyses of the Relationship Between Instructional Practices and Student Achievement

Instructional Practices	Mathematics		Science	
	Multiple-Choice	Open-Response	Multiple-Choice	Open-Response
Reform	0.030	0.053[a]	0.045[a]	0.079[a]
Traditional	0.001	−0.025	0.006	−0.018

[a]Statistically significant relationship ($p < 0.05$).

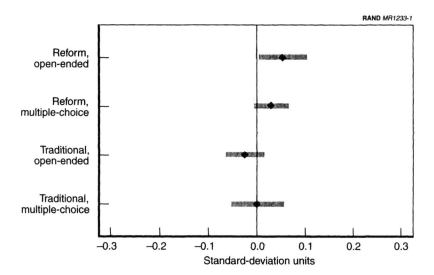

Figure S.1—Pooled Results from Mathematics Analyses

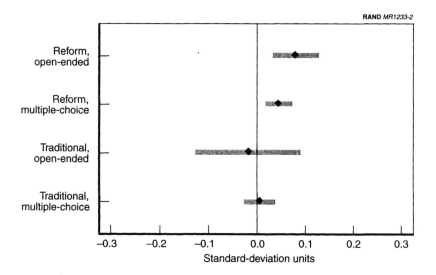

Figure S.2—Pooled Results from Science Analyses

The following examples illustrate the problem: Teachers may not always have provided accurate reports of the extent to which they used various instructional practices, and some may not have become proficient in the use of the reform practices at the time the data were collected. The tests used to measure student achievement may not have been aligned especially well with the reform curriculum. Students whose teachers use the reform practices relatively frequently may differ from other students for reasons that are unrelated to the use of the reform practices per se. Finally, students may have to experience the reform practices for more than one year in order for these practices to have a significant impact on achievement. Nevertheless, the consistency of results across sites, despite the differences among sites (e.g., in the grade levels, control variables, and tests used), is encouraging. Data from the second year of the study will provide additional evidence to aid in the interpretation of these findings.

The Mosaic project was supported by the National Science Foundation, Division of Elementary, Secondary, and Informal Education, under grant ESI-96-15809. The project would not have been successful without the cooperation and support of key individuals at each of the participating sites. The first-year sites included State Systemic Initiatives (SSIs) in Connecticut and Louisiana; Urban Systemic Initiatives (USIs) in Columbus, Ohio, and San Francisco, California; and Local Systemic Change (LSC) projects in Fresno, California, and El Paso, Socorro, and Ysleta, Texas. We are indebted to the individual leaders of the reform program at each of these sites, as well as to the regular state and district administrations. The list of those who contributed directly to this project includes the following individuals:

Fresno, California

Charles E. McCully, Superintendent
Georgina Takemoto, PI, Assistant Superintendent
Robert Grobe, Administrative Analyst
Paul Messenhiemer, Data Systems
Linda Ball, USI, LSC
Bob Harringon, Assistant Superintendent for Research and Evaluation

San Francisco, California

Waldemar Rojas, Superintendent
Maria Santos, Associate Superintendent
Pat Anderson, Supervisor, Testing and Evaluation

Sandra Lam, Program Director
Carmelo Sgarlato

Connecticut

Richard Cole, Executive Director, Connecticut Academy for
    Education
Douglas Rindone, Chief, Bureau of Research and Student
    Assessment, State Department of Education
Steve Leinwand, State Mathematics Consultant
Mari Muri, State Mathematics Consultant
Steve Weinberg, State Science Consultant
Bob Rosenbaum, PIMMS Department

Louisiana

Cecil Picard, State Superintendent
Kerry Davidson, Project Director, LaSIP
John Wallin, LaSIP
Carl Frantz, Coordinator for Evaluation, LaSIP and LaCept
Richard Anderson, LaSIP
Faimon Roberts, Assistant Director for Science, LaSIP
Barbara Andrepointe, Management Information Systems,
    Louisiana Department of Education

Columbus, Ohio

Rosa Smith, Superintendent, Columbus Public Schools
Camille Nasbe, Director, Columbus USI
Saundra Brennan, Project Evaluator, Columbus USI
Burt Wiser, Director of Assessment and Testing, Columbus
    Public Schools
Larry Sullivan, National Association of School Psychologists
Marc Foor, Columbus Public Schools
Maxine Smith, Site Coordinator

El Paso, Texas

Kenneth George, Interim Superintendent, El Paso Independent
    School District
Don Schulte, Superintendent, Socorro Independent School
    District

Irma Trujillo, Interim Superintendent, Ysleta Independent
    School District
Susana Navarro, Executive Director, El Paso Collaborative for
    Academic Excellence
Gabriel Della-Piana, Director of Evaluation, El Paso Collaborative
    for Academic Excellence
H. Susan Schneider, Evaluator
Anna Bone, Researcher
Ray Reynosa, District USI Director for El Paso ISD
Gary Ivory, Director of Research, Testing, and Evaluation
Maria Gutierrez, District USI Director for for Ysleta ISD
Joe Bob Shook, Director of Secondary Education
Joyce Zarowsk, District USI Director for Socorro ISD
Cathe Lester, Site Coordinator

We also wish to thank the hundreds of teachers, principals, and support staff who participated in the study and the thousands of students who completed our assessments, without whom this complex project could never have been possible.

Horizon Research, Inc., was responsible for the design, production, and scoring of the teacher surveys. We are grateful to Iris Weiss, Jon Supovitz, and the staff of Horizon for their careful and efficient work. CRB Associates provided data collection support in Connecticut, and Hugh and Connie Bruckerhoff deserve credit for their efforts on behalf of the Mosaic project.

Special thanks go to Janice Earle, NSF, for her encouragement, constant support, and timely assistance. There would be no Mosaic project without her foresight and guidance.

A project of this size and complexity requires substantial operational support, and we were fortunate to have the analytical skills of Tor Ormseth and the logistical assistance of Robert Reichardt and Peter Scott, all of RAND. Sharon Koga, Helen Rhodes, and Donna White contributed to the preparation of this report. Finally, the thoughtful, incisive reviews provided by Becky Kilburn and Larry Hanser improved the quality of this report.

Chapter One

INTRODUCTION

Many of the mathematics and science education reforms that are currently under way in the United States seek to improve achievement by fostering classroom practices designed to enhance the development of critical thinking and problem-solving skills, particularly among low-income and minority students. One approach being widely implemented today is called *systemic reform* because it attempts to align all parts of the educational system—curriculum, instruction, assessment, teacher preparation, and state and local policies such as graduation requirements—to promote change in the classroom and, ultimately, improve student performance (Smith and O'Day, 1991). Systemic reform efforts resulted in part from the observation that addressing one component of the educational system tended to be ineffective due to constraints imposed by other parts of the system (Hill, 1994; Knapp, 1997).

This report presents results from the first year of a study designed to investigate relationships between student achievement in mathematics and science and the use of instructional practices that are consistent with systemic reforms. We begin with background information on the reforms, particularly the initiatives currently being funded by the National Science Foundation (NSF). We summarize existing evidence on the effectiveness of these efforts and the difficulties researchers face in measuring relevant student outcomes. We then describe our approach to studying the problem, including our samples, measures, and methods of analysis. Following that, we present the results from the six sites at which we collected data during this phase of the project. The conclusion of the report summarizes our major findings, discusses the limitations of the analysis, and suggests directions for future research and evaluation.

THE SYSTEMIC INITIATIVES PROGRAMS

In 1990, NSF launched a series of initiatives designed to promote standards-based systemic reform of mathematics and science education. Through its Statewide Systemic Initiatives (SSI) program, NSF awarded grants to 25 states and the Commonwealth of Puerto Rico from 1991 to 1993. The state level was chosen as the initial target, in part because NSF viewed state policymakers as being uniquely able to influence all aspects of the educational system, including teacher training in institutions of higher education. Grants were awarded for a five-year period, but some states were able to renew their grants for additional years.

The Urban Systemic Initiatives (USI) program, established in 1993, targets cities where large numbers of children live in poverty. This program has funded 20 large urban districts with awards of up to $15 million over five years. The program is described as a "comprehensive and systemic effort to stimulate fundamental, sweeping, and sustained improvement in the quality and level of K–12 science, mathematics, and technology (SMT) education" (Williams, 1998, p. 7). The Local Systemic Change (LSC) program was created in 1995 to fund district-based teacher enhancement through curriculum implementation at more than 50 sites. These projects are also of five years' duration, but they are typically smaller in scope, with funding based on the number of teachers served. Most of the projects are receiving between $2 million and $6 million over the five-year funding period. A Rural Systemic Initiatives (RSI) program operating in several sites completes the set of NSF initiatives. Together, these Systemic Initiative (SI) programs have received approximately $100 million per year in NSF funding. In addition, most sites supplemented their NSF grants with additional local contributions—sites are currently using Title I funds, corporate donations, and grants from private foundations to support and expand their SIs (Williams, 1998).

Although these programs vary in scope and emphasis, all are relatively long-term (five years, with a small number of SSIs being extended for an additional five years), and all attempt coordinated reform, aligning various parts of the educational system with one another. These initiatives, in theory at least, generally involve the development of ambitious curriculum and performance standards and the mobilization of all components of the system to support and enable all students to reach those standards (Consortium for Policy Research in Education, 1995a).

To be effective, these reforms must ultimately be adopted by teachers and must take hold in the classroom (Tyack and Cuban, 1995). Thus, a primary emphasis of the SIs involves promotion of teaching practices that are assumed to facilitate student learning. Most initiatives offer professional development to teachers, and this component constitutes a fairly large proportion of the budget. For example, the SSI sites spent nearly one-third of their first-year budgets on inservice training for teachers, more than on any other category of spending (Shields, Corcoran, and Zucker, 1994). Most of this training is intended to increase teachers' use of classroom practices that are believed to improve achievement.

The kinds of practices being promoted by NSF, as well as by numerous other agencies and reformers, are consistent with curriculum standards and guidelines that have been published by the National Research Council (1996), the American Association for the Advancement of Science (1993), and the National Council of Teachers of Mathematics (1989). Common to all of these documents is an emphasis on instruction that engages students as active participants in their own learning and that enhances the development of complex cognitive skills and processes. Specific practices that are endorsed include cooperative learning groups, inquiry-based activities, use of materials and manipulatives, and open-ended assessment techniques. All of these practices are intended to support active rather than passive learning, to promote the application of critical thinking skills, and to provide opportunities to apply mathematics and science learning to real-world contexts.

EARLIER EVALUATIONS OF SYSTEMIC INITIATIVES

Numerous evaluations have been conducted by the individual SI sites and by outside organizations. Most of these evaluations have focused on the degree of implementation of the reforms (e.g., type and frequency of professional development offered to teachers, level of participation among teachers) rather than on student outcomes. However, NSF and the sites are becoming increasingly concerned about student achievement. Many of the SI sites have reported improvement in student test scores (Williams, 1998), but most offer little if any evidence that ties this improvement directly to SI participation.

A large-scale study conducted by SRI International revealed small but statistically significant differences in test scores that favored participating over nonparticipating schools at four of seven SSI sites (Laguarda, 1998). However, this study had a number of limitations. First, the analyses did not control for any preexisting differences in the teachers and students in SSI and non-SSI schools. We have observed that sites often implement large-scale reforms in phases, and those schools that participate in the earlier phases differ in important ways (e.g., in the experience of teachers and in the socioeconomic backgrounds of students) from those that participate in later phases. Second, the analyses did not examine the degree of implementation of the reforms within schools. The fact that a school is considered part of the reform effort does not guarantee that all the teachers in the school are responding in the intended manner. Other researchers have found that teachers' use of reform practices is influenced by many factors, including the nature and frequency of professional development participation (Cohen and Hill, 1998; Weiss et al., 1998) and the degree to which the teachers understand the subject matter (Cohen and Ball, 1990). Third, the data were collected and analyzed by site personnel rather than by the external evaluators, and no effort was made to address differences in the quality of these procedures across sites.

The absence of good evaluation data on SI programs has led some policymakers to express skepticism about the value of these programs (Fox, 1998). Others have called for more-rigorous evaluations that focus on student achievement and relate it to the degree of implementation of the reforms. There is some evidence of a positive relationship between the practices promoted by the SIs and student achievement in mathematics and science, and we review this evidence below.

EVIDENCE OF RELATIONSHIPS BETWEEN TEACHING PRACTICES AND ACHIEVEMENT

If the SIs do improve student achievement, it is undoubtedly due in large part to what occurs in the classroom. For this reason, professional development and the promotion of good instructional practices are critical to the success of the initiatives. Research provides some evidence of the effectiveness of some of the individual practices endorsed by the reforms. An experiment conducted by Ginsburg-Block and Fantuzzo (1998), for example, showed that low-achieving elementary students who were placed in problem-solving or peer-collaboration situations achieved higher mathematics scores and reported higher levels of motivation than did students who received neither of these interventions. Several other studies have also demonstrated the value of peer tutoring and collaboration (e.g., Fantuzzo, King, and Heller, 1992; Greenwood, Carta, and Hall, 1988; Webb and Palincsar, 1996), as well as the benefits of contextualizing instruction in real-world problems (Verschaffel and De Corte, 1997).

A few studies have focused on relationships between student achievement and teachers' use of combinations of these practices. Cohen and Hill (1998) studied teacher-reported use of several practices consistent with the 1992 California Mathematics Framework and found that frequency of use was positively related to scores on the California Learning Assessment System (CLAS) mathematics test at the school level, after controlling for demographic characteristics. The set of teaching practices examined in that study was similar to the sets being advocated and supported by the SIs. Mayer (1998) found small positive or null relationships between a similar set of practices and student scores on a standardized multiple-choice test. Thus, there is some evidence that, in certain contexts at least, use of reform practices is related to higher student achievement.

MEASURING STUDENT ACHIEVEMENT

One difficulty in evaluating ongoing programs in general, and the SIs in particular, is a lack of appropriate measures of student achievement. Most states do not currently administer tests that are well aligned with the systemic reforms (Consortium for Policy Research in Education, 1995b). Part of this misalignment may arise because many large-scale tests (whether developed by the state or by commercial publishers) rely on multiple-choice items, a format that does not always lend itself to measuring many of the scientific inquiry and mathematical problem-solving skills encouraged by the SIs. In addition, many state testing programs predate both the systemic reforms and the current national standards. As of 1995, 21 states did not test students in science at all (Bond, Braskamp, and van der Ploeg, 1996), although the number of states that test in science has increased in recent years.

An additional problem with state testing programs is that most do not provide data that can be used to track progress over time. In many states, students are tested only at selected grade levels (e.g., fourth, eighth, and tenth). Changes in scores of successive cohorts of students confound the effects of reforms with differences among the groups of students. In addition, improvements in scores over time, which are often cited as evidence of beneficial effects of reforms on student learning, may in many cases reflect inappropriate narrowing of the curriculum or teaching to the test (Koretz and Barron, 1998; Koretz et al., 1991). This problem is especially likely to occur when the tests are part of a high-stakes accountability system or when the same form of a test is administered multiple times. For all of these reasons, it is desirable to supplement existing state tests with additional measures whenever possible.

OVERVIEW OF THE MOSAIC PROJECT

The Mosaic project, described in this report, was designed to examine the relationship between teaching practices and student achievement in mathematics and science, a relationship that is at the heart of the SIs. We gathered data from a variety of SI sites using multiple measures of achievement to produce a "mosaic" of evidence about this relationship. Our approach is to model this relationship rather than to compare directly the performance of students whose teachers participated in different phases of the reform. One of the advantages of this approach is that we can include measures of student demographic characteristics as well as prior achievement in the model. This allows us to adjust our analyses for some of the major differences among students assigned to different classrooms and schools. Another advantage is that we measure directly the degree to which teachers actually use both traditional and reform practices, so we can focus on instruction at the classroom level rather than at the school level. Although at many sites the school is the unit of participation in the reform, we have found that there is substantial variation in teaching practices among teachers within a school, even though teachers may have been exposed to the same training. By collecting data on individual teachers, we can address these differences in our analysis. Finally, we measure student achievement using both multiple-choice and open-response tests, including some hands-on science tasks that we developed and administered ourselves. This provides greater sensitivity to potential gains in skills than would be provided by multiple-choice tests alone, and it gives us an opportunity to explore differences between the multiple-choice and open-response formats. The Mosaic study is being conducted at 11 sites, which will provide a strong test of the strength of the relationship across sites.

We adopted this modeling approach for a number of reasons. First, it was difficult to judge the effectiveness of the comprehensive SIs directly, because the reforms were already well under way when this study began. It was impossible to collect baseline data and other information that would be necessary to evaluate the cumulative impact of the reforms on student achievement. Second, the reforms were not implemented with an outcome analysis in mind, and in general, the sites did not address research design issues when they developed their programs. For example, some sites provided training to all teachers the first year, leaving no untreated classes to use for comparative analyses. Other sites that implemented reforms in phases defined those phases on the basis of geographic region. As a result, student demographic factors were not the same for each wave of the reform, and direct comparisons between phases would not be appropriate. In addition, few sites collected any measures of teaching, so it was impossible to know whether the training actually led to differences in classroom practices.

It is important to understand that the Mosaic project is not a comprehensive evaluation of the systemic reform initiatives. These initiatives are multifaceted, multiyear efforts to bring about changes in classroom practice and in other aspects of the educational system. The reform sites have adopted a wide range of strategies to recruit and train teachers in new methods, to implement new curricula, to provide appropriate materials, to encourage and sustain change at the school level, and to instill greater interest in mathematics and science. Their success at these tasks is the subject of a comprehensive evaluation being undertaken by SRI International (Corcoran, Shields, and Zucker, 1998; Shields, Marsh, and Adelman, 1998).

Chapter Two

METHODS

We collected data from six of 11 sites in year 1 (the focus of this report), and we recently completed data collection at six sites in year 2 (one of the sites is providing data in both years). Most of the data collection took place in elementary schools and middle schools because the bulk of the reform activities occurred at these grade levels. Our specific procedures for site selection, subject and grade-level selection, and data collection are described in this chapter.

SITE SELECTION

We knew that it would be difficult to study the relationship between reform instructional practices and achievement in the absence of a reasonable degree of reform, so we selected sites in a way that maximized the probability of encountering substantial numbers of teachers using reform practices. NSF proposed sites at which reforms in science and/or mathematics instruction appeared to be occurring, based on information drawn from their site visits and from progress reports submitted by the grantees.

Mosaic project staff visited each proposed site to discuss the goals of the study, data collection requirements, the availability of data, student achievement measures, requirements for linking teacher and student data, and local site coordination. On the basis of these visits, all of the proposed sites except three were included in the study. One proposed site declined to participate because its program was not yet advanced enough to study; the reforms at another site were so widespread in the district that the necessary variation in teaching practice was unlikely to be found, although this site was later incorporated into a statewide site; and the third site was excluded because the sample size was too small and testing was limited. The other proposed sites agreed to participate and to provide the necessary student, teacher, and demographic data. A local coordinator responsible for testing arrangements was designated by each site's administrators.

The six sites in our sample consisted of two states and four urban systems (three of which were single districts, and one of which was a group of three districts located in the same city). Data were collected from 324 mathematics teachers at 97 schools, and from 303 science teachers at 103 schools. At five of the sites, students received both multiple-choice and open-response and/or hands-on tests in the targeted subject(s). At the other site, multiple-choice assessments were administered, but we were unable to schedule any open-response assessments because of time constraints.

SCHOOL, SUBJECT, AND GRADE-LEVEL SELECTION

School district and program staff at each site specified the grade level(s) and subject(s) in which they believed reform practices were most pervasive, then nominated schools to participate in the study. The same basic research design was used at each site. We asked local staff to select approximately 10 schools in which there was good reason to believe mathematics and/or science instruction reforms had been implemented, and 10 demographically similar schools in which reforms had yet to be implemented. (All of the sites had been involved in the reform for more than one year, but some had not yet implemented the reforms in all of their schools.) We used the nominations only to ensure variation in teaching practices; we did not compare the high- and low-implementing schools with one another directly. Table 2.1 lists the grade(s) and subject(s) for which data were collected and the numbers of schools, teachers, and students participating at each site during year 1.

DATA COLLECTION

We collected three types of data at each site: student achievement test scores, teacher questionnaire responses, and student demographics. Data were collected in the spring of 1997.

Table 2.1

Details of Year 1 Participating Sites

Site	Grade	Subject	Number of Schools[a]	Number of Teachers	Number of Students (varied by test in some sites)
1	3rd	Math	17	46	804
2	5th	Math	20	100	1,651–1,686
2	5th	Science	20	99	1,639–1,662
3	5th	Math	18	73	1,366–1,451
3	5th	Science	20	74	1,367–1,438
4	5th	Science	19	45	909–932
5	7th	Math	17	48	2,937–3,018
5	7th	Science	19	33	2,047–2,079
6	7th	Math	25	57	3,237
6	7th	Science	25	52	3,279

[a]Some schools at each site are included in both the mathematics and science samples.

Student Achievement Data

We obtained student scores on the mathematics and science assessments regularly administered at each site and supplemented these with additional assessments, where feasible, to provide both multiple-choice and open-response scores. Supplementary tests were chosen in consultation with local staff, who were encouraged to select measures they believed were reasonably well aligned with their reform efforts. Hands-on science tasks developed by RAND were made available, and some sites opted to use them. Mosaic project staff trained exercise administrators to administer some of the supplementary measures, including RAND's hands-on tasks. All other tests were administered by the classroom teachers or by test administrators who worked at the local sites. Table 2.2 shows the types of tests administered at each site. Wherever possible, we used existing tests, including state-developed tests and commercially available standardized tests. The column headed *Added for Mosaic Study?* in-

Table 2.2

Sites, Subjects, and Assessment Instruments

Site	Grade	Subject(s)	Tests	Format[a]	Added for Mosaic Study?
1	3[b]	Math	State[c]	MC	No
			State	OR	No
			State	Grid-in	No
2	5	Math	State[c]	MC	No
			Stanford 9[d]	OR	Yes
		Science	Stanford 9[d]	MC	Yes
			RAND Levers and Friction[e]	OR (hands-on)	Yes
3	5	Math	CTBS[f]	MC	No
			Stanford 9[d]	OR	Yes
		Science	CSIAC[g]	MC	No
			CSIAC[g]	OR (hands-on)	No
4	5	Science	CSIAC[g]	MC	No
			CSIAC[g]	OR (hands-on)	No
5	7	Math	State[c]	MC	No
			Stanford 9[d]	OR	Yes
		Science	Stanford 9[d]	MC	Yes
			RAND Levers and Classification[e]	OR (hands-on)	Yes
6	7	Math	MAT7[h]	MC	No
		Science	MAT7[h]	MC	No

[a]MC = multiple-choice; OR = open-response.

[b]At this site, we studied teaching practices for third-grade teachers and measured the relationships with student test scores gathered during the following fall, when students had advanced to the fourth grade.

[c]Refers to tests developed by the state.

[d]Stanford Achievement Test Series, Ninth Edition, published by Harcourt-Brace Educational Measurement.

[e]See Stecher and Klein, 1996, for a description of tasks and scoring guides.

[f]Comprehensive Test of Basic Skills, published by CTB/McGraw-Hill.

[g]California Systemic Initiatives Assessment Collaborative. This test was developed by a consortium of educators and researchers and was designed to be aligned with NSF-supported reform efforts.

[h]Metropolitan Achievement Tests, Seventh Edition, published by Harcourt-Brace Educational Measurement. At this site, we were unable to schedule any open-response testing.

dicates whether we supplemented the district's or state's testing program with additional measures or relied only on those measures already used by the sites.

Teacher Questionnaires

Our primary measure of teaching practices at each site was a modified version of a questionnaire developed and used extensively by Horizon Research, Inc. (HRI) to evaluate the implementation of the Local Systemic Change (LSC) initiatives. Questionnaires were administered to all teachers in each school teaching the targeted subject and grade level. Typically, the site coordinator or assistant distributed the questionnaires either individually or at after-school meetings and then collected completed questionnaires in individual sealed envelopes for return to RAND.

We created separate questionnaires for mathematics and science teachers, but many of the items were identical across subjects. Teachers were asked to report the frequency of various instructional practices ranging from traditional (e.g., "Have students watch me [teacher] do a science demonstration") to reform ("[Students] conduct investigations where they develop their own procedures for addressing a question or problem"). General topics included the amount of time spent on science/mathematics, approach to introducing a new topic, typical teacher instructional practices, typical student activities, types of written assignments, teachers' use of students' written work, and methods of assessing student learning.

Although NSF did not mandate a particular curriculum or a specific set of teaching strategies for the SIs, there was an emerging consensus among mathematics and science educators about what should be taught and how it should be presented (National Council of Teachers of Mathematics, 1989; National Research Council, 1996). In light of this consensus, it is not surprising that the systemic reform programs adopted very similar content and instructional goals. An independent evaluation of the SSIs reported that "across the states there was remarkable similarity in the perceived shortcomings of current practices and the set of desirable reforms in curriculum content and instructional strategies" (Shields, Marsh, and Adelman, 1998, p. 2). The shared content goals included greater emphasis on the understanding of mathematics and science concepts, the application of this knowledge to everyday situations, and the integration of concepts across subjects. The instructional emphasis was equally distinct. The reforms sought to have instructors engage students actively in their own learning, to be sensitive to each student's learning style, to increase the use of technology, and to utilize new forms of assessment for instructional planning, rather than viewing students as passive learners who absorb unrelated facts and procedures. In mathematics, this meant more "data gathering and analysis, statistics, geometry and visualization, discovery learning, and 'constructivist' approaches"; in science, more "scientific processes, such as observation, comparison, experimentation, hypothesis generation, hypothesis-testing, and theory building" (New Jersey SSI Proposal, 1992, p. 7; quoted in Shields, Marsh, and Adelman, 1998, p. 3). Our measures of instructional strategies were designed to be consistent with this espoused commonality of purpose.

In addition, each teacher was asked to complete a brief demographic section, providing information about his or her college degree, teaching certification, coursework in mathematics and/or science, gender, ethnicity, and years of teaching experience. At sites where instruction was delivered by science or mathematics specialists instead of the regular classroom teacher, we administered surveys to the specialists and also asked the respondents to clarify their teaching situations.

HRI, acting as a subcontractor to RAND, developed the questionnaire, processed the data, and prepared analysis files. HRI also validated the instruments at one site in which RAND selected a sample of schools whose teachers were expected to have a wide range of implementation of the reforms. A local coordinator scheduled interviews with 40 teachers from these schools. Trained staff from HRI interviewed each teacher about a recent science or mathematics unit; the teachers were asked to discuss their goals for the unit, the extent to which students engaged in investigations and collaborations, and the types of assessment they used. Teachers were also asked to show associated artifacts (student work, journals, assignments, etc.). In some cases, the validator observed an actual lesson.

On the basis of the interviews, artifacts, and observations, the validator rated the instructional program of each teacher on a five-point scale on each of three dimensions: the use of student-centered strategies, the investigative culture of the classroom, and the use of reform-oriented strategies. The validator also made an overall judgment of the degree to which each teacher's instructional program reflected reform practice. These ratings were compared with the self-reported practice information from the teacher surveys. Reform-practices scales for science and mathematics were created by combining teachers' responses to items on the surveys that reflected standards-based instruction in each subject. We identified the items for these scales using factor analytic techniques and the judgment of recognized experts in science and mathematics instruction. A combined scale was computed by summing the results from the mathematics and science scales.

There was a statistically significant positive relationship between the validators' overall ratings and the combined survey scales: The Spearman-Rho correlation coefficient between these measures was 0.44. It is difficult to say what degree of correspondence we would expect to find between these two distinct measures of practice. The interviews and observations focus on one particular lesson, and they are probably sensitive in unknown ways to the dynamics of the interaction between teacher and interviewer. The surveys emphasize a longer span of time and a wider range of content, but they are subject to unknown self-report biases. In addition, the validators' ratings included their impressions of the quality of the instruction, whereas the questionnaires addressed only the frequency with which specific reform practices were used. Finally, the validators exhibited a tendency to assign scores near the middle of the five-point scale, resulting in low variability and restricted range among the ratings. In view of these considerations, an overall correspondence of 0.44 is reasonable.

Demographic Data

Information about student characteristics was obtained from the sites for three purposes: (1) to verify that comparison schools were similar to implementing schools in terms of student demographics, enrollment, and grade span; (2) to be included as covariates in the analysis of relationships between teaching practices and student achievement; and (3) to enable us to study whether these relationships varied as a function of student characteristics.

At most sites, we obtained data on students' race/ethnicity, gender, participation in free or reduced-price lunch programs, language background, participation in special education or gifted programs, and test scores from the previous year. We did not obtain the same set of covariates from all sites, partly because some of the covariates did not apply to particular student populations. For example, some sites have large numbers of students with limited English proficiency (LEP), whereas others have none; some sites exclude special education students from testing, and some include them. A few of the covariates, such as age and participation in a gifted program, were unavailable from some sites. Excluding these from the models had virtually no effect on relationships between student achievement and teaching practices.

PARTICIPATION RATES

Rates of participation in the study by schools, teachers, and students were quite high. It is difficult to summarize participation in a simple manner because of the multistage nomination and enrollment process, differences in procedures across sites, and partial participation by some schools, teachers, and students. Nevertheless, across the six sites, between 85 and 100 percent of the schools we initially contacted participated in the study, i.e., tests and teacher surveys were administered and completed by the majority of eligible individuals. Similarly, at the site level, between 71 and 98 percent of the teachers who received a survey completed it. Student participation rates were more difficult to compute because of partial participation and because of a variety of testing exclusions. In addition, we could not always link students and teachers. Nevertheless, across the six sites, between 65 and 94 percent of the students identified as being taught by the teachers in the study completed all the desired tests in mathematics or science. Detailed descriptions of school, teacher, and student participation at each of the sites are given in Appendix A.

ANALYSIS

We investigated the degree to which student achievement was associated with teachers' use of instructional practices consistent with the reforms, using linear regression analysis, which enabled us to control for student background characteristics and previous test scores. We found that teacher background variables did not provide any additional explanatory power, and therefore we do not include them in the results reported here. At each site, we conducted separate analyses for mathematics and science, for open-response and multiple-choice tests, and for reform and traditional practices. We fit these models using individual student data, with all students from the same classroom receiving the same values for the reform and traditional scales, and we used an adjusted standard-error estimate to account for possible correlation among responses from students with the same teacher (McCaffrey and Bell, 1997).

In addition, the use of data from multiple sites provided an opportunity to conduct a planned meta-analysis. We therefore also conducted pooled analyses, which combined data from all six sites to produce a single estimate of the coefficient relating teaching practices (reform or traditional) to student achievement. We conducted separate analyses by subject (mathematics or science), test format (multiple-choice or open-response), and teaching-practices scale (reform or traditional), for a total of eight pooled analyses.

Pooled analyses are appropriate when the coefficients from the various sites describe a single relationship, as was the case in this study. We examined the relationship between teaching practices and student test scores at all six sites, using the same study design and similar analyses. Specifically, we assumed that the coefficients from our models are homogeneous and that small differences in our site studies (e.g., differences in tests and the covariates in our models) can be modeled as small random variations among the coefficients. The homogeneity assumption was tested by examining the variability among the coefficients across the sites. Technical details on the pooled analyses and the estimates of variability are given in Appendix D.

For the pooled analyses, we used the estimated regression coefficients described earlier. We did not pool the individual student data, because we used different covariates in our site models, and thus we would have had to exclude some useful predictors from the model. However, the estimates we obtained by pooling the regression coefficients for instructional practices are similar to those we would have obtained by pooling individual scores and fitting a random-coefficients model with interactions between sites and the covariates (Goldstein, 1995). Thus, our approach enabled us to pool data across sites without requiring identical models for every site.

Chapter Three

FIRST-YEAR RESULTS

In this chapter, we present summaries of teachers' reported use of reform and traditional practices and our findings with regard to the relationships between use of these practices and student achievement at each site. Finally, we describe the results of an analysis of differences between open-response and multiple-choice achievement measures.

DISTRIBUTIONS OF TEACHING PRACTICES

On the basis of exploratory factor analyses of the questionnaire items, we identified two clusters of items and created scales from them by simply summing the scores on each item. The first scale measured the teachers' use of reform practices. Teachers were asked to report the frequency of use of 22 specific reform practices (e.g., co-operative groups, portfolios, and extended investigations). We also created a five-item traditional-practices scale based on items that measured the amount of time teachers spent on traditional teaching practices (e.g., textbook work, lectures, and short-answer tests). Appendix B lists the items in each scale. The distinction between reform-related practices and traditional practices that emerged from factor analyses conducted on each site's data is consistent with the kinds of definitions used in other research on mathematics and science instruction reform (e.g., Cohen and Hill, 1998). However, it is important to note that the two scales are not opposites of one another. A principal-components analysis of the questionnaire data identified these two separate scales at each site, suggesting that teachers may use both reform and traditional practices to different

19

degrees. Correlations between the two scales ranged across sites from moderately negative to moderately positive, with many close to zero. It is possible for teachers to be high on both scales, because the scale scores do not indicate the total amount of time spent on these practices, but rather the frequency with which they are used. Thus, a teacher who intersperses lecture-style teaching with opportunities for student discussion in every lesson might score high on both scales. In addition, there are other activities not addressed by either scale, so it is possible for teachers to receive low scores on both.

At each site we found a wide range of practices on both the reform and the traditional scales. The box-and-whiskers plots in Figure 3.1 show the distributions of mean scale scores for each combination of site and subject (mathematics or science). For these plots, the score for each teacher was simply the average item response across items. All items used a five-point Likert scale, so teachers' scores could range from 1 (rarely or never using any of the practices) to 5 (engaging in all practices daily or almost daily). The solid dots indicate the average score for all teachers. The lower end of the box is the 25th percentile of the distribution, and the upper end of the box is the 75th percentile; the whiskers show the extreme points, excluding outliers. Outlier values are shown as individual points in the plots.

Overall, the scores were similarly distributed across sites. Science teachers' average scores on the reform scale ranged from 3.27 at site 2 to 3.57 at site 4 (upper left quadrant of the figure). Site averages on the reform scale for mathematics teachers were somewhat more variable, ranging from 3.01 to 3.61 (lower left quadrant). On the traditional-practices scale, site averages for science were more variable than those for mathematics. The former ranged from 2.65 to 3.78 (upper right quadrant), whereas the latter ranged from 3.33 to 3.73 (lower right quadrant). Interestingly, sites at which teachers' average use of reform practices was quite similar showed fairly large discrepancies on the traditional-practices scale.

We also found substantial variation in teaching practices within schools (not shown in Figure 3.1), regardless of the degree of participation in the reform programs. Clearly, some teachers in participating schools had not adopted many of the reform practices emphasized by the SI, whereas some teachers in nonparticipating schools

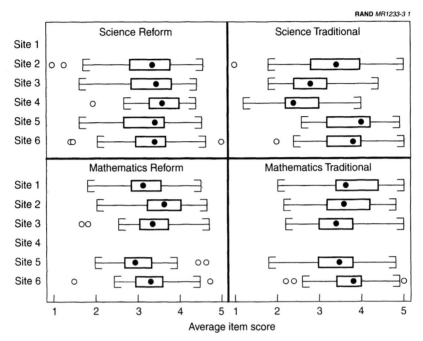

NOTE: Box-and-whiskers plots show mean score (dot), 25th to 75th percentile range (rectangle, or box), and extreme points (whiskers). Outliers appear as open circles.

**Figure 3.1—Distribution of Teacher Scores on Reform and
Traditional Scales by Site and Subject**

were using these practices even though they had not been exposed to SI-specific professional development. This underscores the importance of using classroom-level measures of teaching practices rather than studying differences at the school level.

RELATIONSHIPS BETWEEN TEACHING PRACTICES AND STUDENT ACHIEVEMENT

Our analyses relating teaching practices to student achievement showed that teachers' use of reform practices appeared to be positively related to student achievement at most sites, but the effects were quite small and rarely reached statistical significance. Use of traditional practices, by contrast, was often negatively related to student achievement, particularly in mathematics, but again the relationships were weak.

Figures 3.2 through 3.9 provide an overview of our findings in the six year 1 sites. The full regression models are given in Appendix C. The relationships reported in the figures are the estimated coefficients from our regression models for the reform- and traditional-practices scales. We standardized test scores and teaching-practices scales so that the reported coefficient is the expected difference in test score standard-deviation units for a one-standard-deviation unit increase in scores on the reform or traditional scale. The dark dot represents the point estimate for the coefficient, and the gray bar represents the 95 percent confidence interval for that point estimate. When the bar does not meet the zero line, the coefficient is statistically different from zero. The lowest bar in each figure shows the average coefficient from the pooled analysis, described later.

Figure 3.2 shows relationships between the use of reform practices and achievement on open-response mathematics tests. At four of the five sites that had open-response mathematics tests, higher scores were associated with greater use of reform practices. However, the coefficients were statistically significantly greater than zero at only two of these sites. Similarly, Figure 3.3 shows that for almost all of the participating sites, higher multiple-choice test scores in mathematics were associated with greater use of reform practices, but none of the estimates was statistically significantly different from zero. Figures 3.4 and 3.5 show that greater use of reform practices in science was associated with higher test scores on both open-response and multiple-choice measures. Again, most of the estimated coefficients were extremely small and were not statistically significantly different from zero, even though coefficients across sites show a consistent pattern of a weak positive relationship between the reform-practices scale and test scores.

In contrast, the majority of the relationships between the use of traditional practices and student achievement were negative. For example, Figure 3.6 indicates that at all of the participating sites, greater use of traditional teaching practices in mathematics was associated with lower scores on open-response mathematics tests. However, none of the estimated coefficients for traditional practices was statistically significantly different from zero.

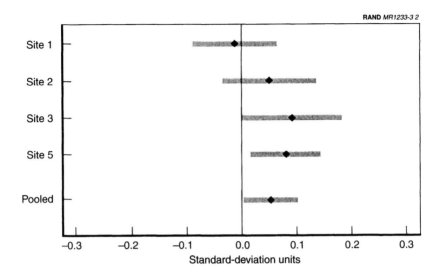

Figure 3.2—Estimated Coefficients by Site and Pooled Across Sites for
Mathematics: Reform Practices, Open-Ended Tests

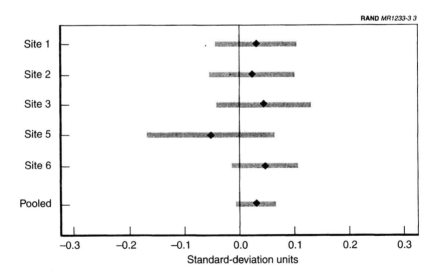

Figure 3.3—Estimated Coefficients by Site and Pooled Across Sites for
Mathematics: Reform Practices, Multiple-Choice Tests

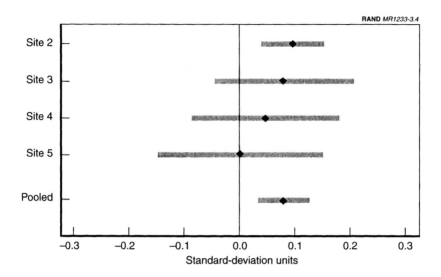

Figure 3.4—Estimated Coefficients by Site and Pooled Across Sites for
Science: Reform Practices, Open-Ended Tests

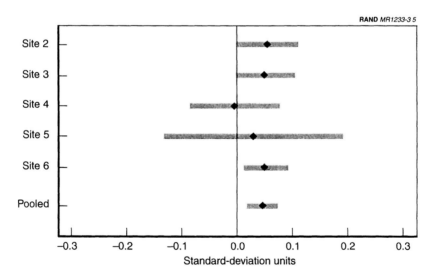

Figure 3.5—Estimated Coefficients by Site and Pooled Across Sites for
Science: Reform Practices, Multiple-Choice Tests

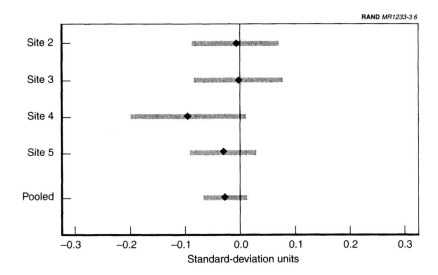

Figure 3.6—Estimated Coefficients by Site and Pooled Across Sites for.
Mathematics: Traditional Practices, Open-Ended Tests

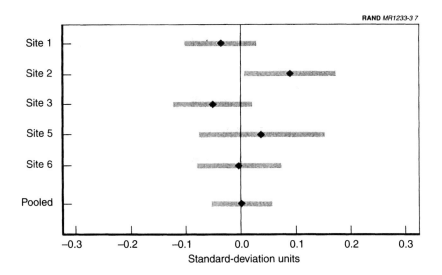

Figure 3.7—Estimated Coefficients by Site and Pooled Across Sites for
Mathematics: Traditional Practices, Multiple-Choice Tests

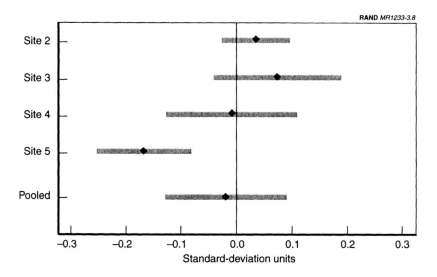

Figure 3.8—Estimated Coefficients by Site and Pooled Across Sites for
Science: Traditional Practices, Open-Ended Tests

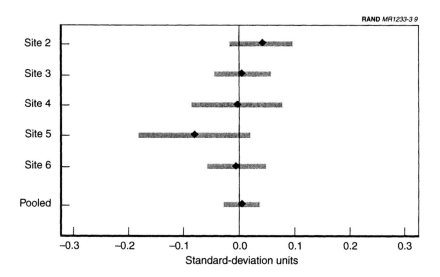

Figure 3.9—Estimated Coefficients by Site and Pooled Across Sites for
Science: Traditional Practices, Multiple-Choice Tests

The relationship between teaching practices and test scores is at most small in almost all our models. For example, the largest positive relationship was found between reform teaching practices and open-response science tests at site 2 (see Figure 3.4), where the standardized regression coefficient was 0.09. Our model suggests that with a teacher at this site using all of the reform practices monthly, the average student was predicted to score at about the 48th percentile on the test, while for a teacher using all of the reform practices weekly, we would predict that a similar student would score at about the 54th percentile on the test.[1] Smaller changes in percentiles would be expected at the other sites. Compared with the coefficients for most of the student background characteristics (e.g., an average coefficient of 0.54 across sites for participation in free and reduced-price lunch programs), all of the relationships we observed may be considered small.

We expected to see larger relationships between reform practices and open-response measures than between reform practices and multiple-choice measures because the former tend to be more closely aligned with the reforms. Inspection of the regression coefficients suggests that this is the case. Later we discuss a test of the statistical significance of this difference.

The bottom bars in Figures 3.2 through 3.9 show the pooled estimates of the standardized regression coefficients for each of the eight analyses. The coefficients and confidence-interval bounds are presented in Table 3.1, and additional detail is provided in Table D.1 in Appendix D. In most of the analyses, the variability of coefficients across sites was sufficiently small to be within the range expected as a result of sampling error within sites. In these cases, the pooled analysis is appropriate. In analyses where we did find variability (discussed below), the pooled estimate is difficult to interpret because it represents an average over a set of disparate coefficients.

---

[1]We used our model to predict the score for the "average" student (a student with all student background predictors set to the mean) with a teacher scoring 3 on each reform-practices item (monthly use of reform practices). We then found the percentile of this predicted score among the test scores from the site and repeated the process for the average student with a teacher scoring 4 on each item (daily use). The percentile is based on our sample and is not a percentile from a national norming group.

Table 3.1

Coefficients from Pooled Analyses of Relationships Between Instructional
Practices and Achievement

Subject	Test Format	Scale	Weighted Average Coefficient	Lower Bound of 95% Confidence Interval	Upper Bound of 95% Confidence Interval
Math	OR	Reform	0.053	0.008	0.098
Math	MC	Reform	0.030	−0.003	0.063
Science	OR	Reform	0.079	0.036	0.122
Science	MC	Reform	0.045	0.022	0.069
Math	OR	Traditional	−0.025	−0.061	0.012
Math	MC	Traditional	0.001	−0.049	0.052
Science	OR	Traditional	−0.018	−0.123	0.088
Science	MC	Traditional	0.006	−0.023	0.034

Note: OR = open-response; MC = multiple-choice.

One instance in which the variability of coefficients across sites was greater than zero was the relationship between reform practices and student achievement on open-response mathematics tests (Figure 3.2). The pooled coefficient was 0.053, but the test of variability indicated heterogeneity across sites. The variation was primarily a result of the negative relationship (−0.010) we observed for site 1; the other three coefficients ranged from 0.052 to 0.092. When we conducted the pooled analysis excluding site 1, the estimate was 0.075, with no indication of heterogeneity in the coefficients. This difference is probably due to the fact that at site 1 we used scores on a locally developed open-response mathematics test, whereas at the other three sites we administered the Stanford 9 test. The relationship between instructional practices and achievement may be sensitive to the particular instrument used or to the administration conditions. This problem is discussed further in Chapter Four.

Our pooled estimate of the relationship between reform teaching practices and student achievement on multiple-choice mathematics tests was 0.03, not statistically significantly different from zero. For traditional teaching practices, we obtained pooled estimates that were slightly less than zero for both multiple-choice and open-response tests in mathematics, but neither was significantly different from zero. The variability among coefficients was sufficiently small to permit pooling for all of these analyses except for that of traditional practices and multiple-choice tests; but again, this variability resulted primarily from a single outlier, the estimate of 0.09 from site 2. Although the pooled estimates for reform and traditional teaching practices are of different sign, the uncertainty in each estimate is substantial enough that the confidence intervals for the two estimates overlap. Thus we cannot rule out the possibility that the observed differences are only a result of sampling error.

We obtained pooled estimates of 0.045 for the relationship between reform teaching practices and multiple-choice test scores in science, and 0.079 for the relationship between reform teaching practices and open-response test scores. Both of these estimates were statistically significantly different from zero.

For traditional teaching practices in science, we obtained estimates of –0.018 for open-response scores and 0.005 for multiple-choice scores, neither of which differed significantly from zero. Both analyses revealed variability among coefficients relating science scores to traditional practices, suggesting that a pooled analysis might not be appropriate in these cases. Again, there is substantial uncertainty in the pooled estimates for both the traditional and reform scales for both types of science tests, and we cannot rule out the possibility that the observed differences are simply a result of sampling error.

To summarize, the pooled analyses revealed statistically significant positive relationships between teachers' use of reform practices and achievement on both kinds of tests and in both subjects. However, these relationships are much smaller than the relationships between test scores and other covariates, such as ethnicity and socioeconomic status (see Appendix C). Results for open-response mathematics scores appear somewhat sensitive to the particular test used, but for the other measures we detected no evidence of heterogeneity among sites in the strength of the relationships between reform practices and achievement.

In general, teachers' use of traditional practices was unrelated to student achievement. However, our measure of traditional practices is less reliable than our measure of reform practices. Across sites and subjects, the average alpha coefficient is 0.70 for traditional practices, while that for the reform-practices scale is 0.92. The lower reliability would tend to attenuate the relationship between the traditional practices and test scores and might contribute to the weakness of the estimated relationship between traditional practices and outcomes.

ALTERNATIVE FORMULATIONS FOR SITE MODELS

There are several alternative approaches we could have taken to model the relationship between instructional practices and student achievement. Because prior-year test scores were unavailable at sites 1 and 5, we used contemporaneous scores, but we could instead have omitted the achievement covariate altogether. We also chose to explore the reform and traditional scales in separate models, but we could have put them together in the same model. To explore the effects of our modeling decisions, we conducted some analyses using alternative model specifications. Appendix F discusses the results of our explorations of contemporaneous test scores, and Appendix G presents results of our analyses of the effects of combining the reform and traditional scales in a single model. The analyses revealed that including contemporaneous scores probably resulted in conservative estimates of the coefficients for instructional practices, but the effect is small. Including reform and traditional scales in the same model likewise had little effect on our results.

DIFFERENCES BETWEEN TEST FORMATS

Consistent with the individual site results, inspection of the coefficients from the pooled analyses suggested slightly larger relationships between open-response scores and reform teaching practices than between multiple-choice scores and reform teaching practices. This finding is consistent with the hypothesis that open-response tests tend to be more closely aligned with the reforms and therefore better able to indicate effects. To test the statistical significance of this difference, we calculated the difference in standard-deviation units between each student's score on the open-response test and his or her score on the multiple-choice test in the same subject. We then modeled these differences as a function of teaching practices and student background covariates. The analysis was repeated for both subjects and for all sites.

The coefficients for teaching practices obtained for each site are presented in Figures 3.10 through 3.13 and in Table E.1 in Appendix E. The coefficient for reform teaching practices was positive for three of the four sites where we collected data on mathematics achievement. However, only one of the differences, 0.113 for site 5, was statistically significant. Similarly, the coefficient for reform teaching practices was positive for three of the four sites where we collected data on science achievement, but none of these differences was statistically significant.

We again conducted a pooled analysis of coefficients across sites. Results are given in Table E.2 in Appendix E. For mathematics and the reform scale, the pooled estimate was 0.032. This implies that across the sites, the expected increase in student mathematics test scores for a unit increase in a teacher's score on the reform scale was 0.032 standard-deviation units higher for open-response tests than for multiple-choice tests. However, our estimate was not statistically significantly different from zero. In addition, we found a relatively large between-site variance in these estimated differences, even after controlling for sampling error within sites. In other words, we found that the difference in the sensitivity of open-response and multiple-choice tests varied from site to site. At the two fifth-grade sites where the open-response test was the Stanford 9, the differences were similar, 0.032 and 0.051. At site 5, we again administered the Stanford 9 open-response test, but this time to seventh graders, and the difference between open-response and multiple-choice tests was 0.113. At site 1, we used scores from a test developed by the state, and the difference was –0.041. Hence, the sensitivity of tests might depend on both the test form and the grade. Additional data are necessary to explore this hypothesis.

For science and the reform scale, the pooled estimate was 0.031. This implies that across the sites, the expected increase in student science test scores for a unit increase in a teacher's score on the reform scale was 0.031 standard-deviation units higher for open-response tests than for multiple-choice tests. Again, our estimate was not statistically significantly different from zero. For science, there was little variability in estimated differences across sites after we accounted for sampling error within sites.

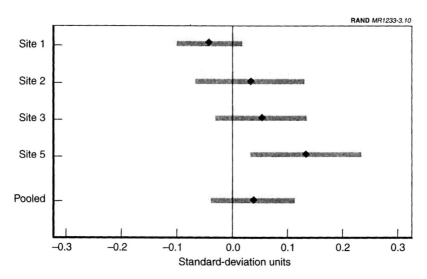

Figure 3.10—Estimated Coefficients by Site and Pooled Across Sites for Mathematics: Reform Practices, Difference Between Open-Ended and Multiple-Choice Tests

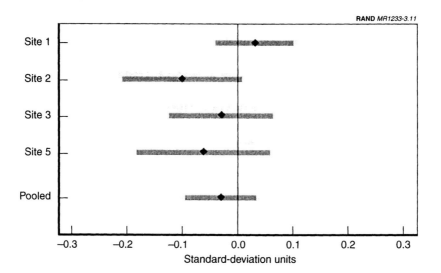

Figure 3.11—Estimated Coefficients by Site and Pooled Across Sites for Mathematics: Traditional Practices, Difference Between Open-Ended and Multiple-Choice Tests

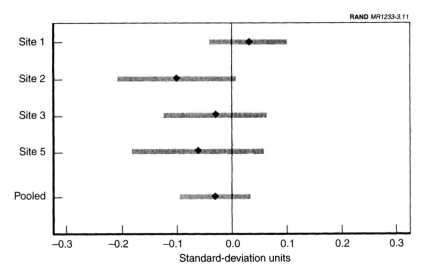

Figure 3.12—Estimated Coefficients by Site and Pooled Across Sites for Science: Reform Practices, Difference Between Open-Ended and Multiple-Choice Tests

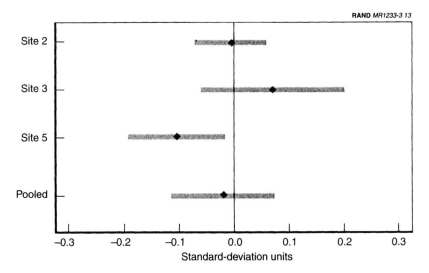

Figure 3.13—Estimated Coefficients by Site and Pooled Across Sites for Science: Traditional Practices, Difference Between Open-Ended and Multiple-Choice Tests

Thus, although inspection of regression coefficients suggests that open-response tests function differently from multiple-choice tests, our data do not provide sufficient evidence to support the claim that the formats differ in their sensitivity to the effects of the reform. Even so, the consistency in the patterns we observed and the fact that educators involved in these reforms believe that open-response tests are generally more closely aligned with their efforts suggest that further investigation is needed to explore format differences. As states continue to develop standards-based assessments, and as results from these assessments are increasingly used in evaluations of educational programs, it is critical that the validity of different test formats be examined.

STUDY LIMITATIONS

Several caveats must be considered when interpreting the results of this study. As in most educational research, our inability to investigate effects by using an experimental design places some limitations on the kinds of inferences that can be made from results. Perhaps the primary problem is that without random assignment of students and teachers to treatments, we cannot be certain that the relationships we observed can be attributed solely to classroom practices. There may be other differences in student characteristics across classrooms that contribute to differences in performance and that influence what teachers do. For example, teachers may tend to engage in more reform-based practices with higher-achieving students. Controlling for prior achievement is helpful, but it does not eliminate the problem completely.

A second limitation is the lack of information on what led teachers to use particular practices. Some may have adopted certain strategies as a result of participation in the professional development activities that are provided by the SI funds, but there are many other potential sources. The large variability in teaching practices within schools, which was observed for SI as well as non-SI schools, suggests that factors other than SI participation are influencing teachers' decisions about how to teach. Determining the reasons for teachers' use of practices was not the initial intent of our study, but information on those reasons would be helpful to people who are designing and implementing professional development programs.

A third weakness of our approach stems from the use of questionnaires to measure instructional practices. As on any questionnaire, our items are subject to inaccurate responses, particularly those items that reflect social desirability. Perhaps more important, our questions addressed only the frequency with which teachers used particular practices and did not address the way in which they were used or the overall quality of the instruction. Clearly, some approaches to using cooperative groups are more effective and more consistent with the intent of the reform than others are, but we cannot detect these differences on the basis of our questionnaires. Multiple classroom observations, interviews, and inspection of classroom materials would undoubtedly provide a better measure of instructional practice. This type of data, however, is considerably more expensive to collect and is usually collected only on a small scale.

Finally, as discussed earlier, our analyses focused on students' exposure to practices during a single academic year, and therefore we were not able to follow the development of teacher experience in reform practices or the impact of student exposure to these practices across several years. Many of the achievement tests used at our sites require students to apply knowledge and skills they have gained over a number of years, so performance on these tests is undoubtedly influenced by students' instructional experiences in prior years. Project directors at some of our sites reported that student exposure to reform practices is typically small, even at sites that have been grant recipients for several years, because programs generally need time to be fully implemented. It is widely believed that students must be exposed to reform practices for more than a single year before the effects of these practices on achievement can become clearly evident, but little information is currently available to support or refute this claim.

Chapter Four

DISCUSSION

In this chapter, we briefly summarize our findings from year 1 of the Mosaic study and discuss their implications. We also suggest possible explanations for the variability in findings across sites, and we then describe plans for future data collection and analysis.

SUMMARY OF YEAR 1 FINDINGS

As illustrated by Figures 3.2 through 3.9, the relationships between student achievement and teachers' use of instructional practices supported by the SI reforms tend to be positive but small, particularly in comparison with relationships between achievement and student background characteristics such as socioeconomic status and ethnicity. If, in fact, the observed relationships represent the effects of teaching practices on student achievement, their small magnitude may not be surprising, given the brief period of time (less than one academic year) captured by teachers' questionnaire responses. Use of particular instructional strategies in a single course during a single school year would not be expected to lead to effects as large as those associated with student background characteristics. Several years of exposure to instructional reforms may be needed to achieve a reasonably large effect. This suggests the need for longitudinal investigations, discussed below.

The direction of relationships was fairly consistent across sites, but there was some variation in magnitude. This variation may come from several potential sources. First, our models differed slightly across sites because we relied on locally available data to construct covariates. Second, various aspects of SI program implementation, such as the amount and quality of professional development activities, undoubtedly affected the kinds of teaching practices that were used. Even if two teachers report using reform practices with similar frequency, their approaches to those practices may differ substantially and may reflect specific features of the local reform program. Third, the achievement measures used at each site varied on a number of dimensions, including psychometric quality (e.g., reliability), content, and degree of alignment with the local curriculum.

This last source of differences has implications for future evaluations of SIs and other reforms. Most evaluations rely on locally available student achievement data, in large part because administering additional measures is expensive and often not feasible. Many principals and teachers believe that their students spend far too much time taking the tests that are required locally, and they are therefore reluctant to volunteer for supplementary testing. Locally developed and administered tests may also be preferred because they are presumed to be more closely aligned with local reform efforts than a measure chosen and administered by outside evaluators would be. Although many districts and states are working to develop tests that reflect local standards and curricula, at the sites we studied, most test development lagged far behind reform implementation, leaving local personnel to rely on tests they did not necessarily believe were appropriate.

Our analyses revealed that in most cases, tests that we added specifically for the Mosaic study functioned better than the locally administered tests. Local tests often had lower reliability than our tests. In addition, local tests exhibited unexpected relationships with other measures of student achievement and with student background characteristics that raise questions about the validity of scores. For example, at two sites, there was an extremely high correlation between the percentage of students in a school receiving free or reduced-price lunch and the school's average score on our supplementary multiple-choice and open-ended tests (which is consistent with nearly all prior research on this topic), but the correlation with the local test, measuring similar content, was close to zero. This unexpected result suggests that caution is warranted in interpreting the results of the locally administered tests.

Although the overall differences we observed between achievement on multiple-choice and open-response tests were not significant, the general pattern suggests that format effects should be investigated further. In particular, it raises questions concerning whether the two types of tests measure different constructs. Most advocates of systemic reform believe that traditional multiple-choice tests do not adequately reflect the range of competencies the reforms are expected to develop, and that tests requiring students to construct their answers and to engage in complex problem-solving are more appropriate. Our results do not indicate that this is necessarily the case, but the question deserves further investigation, particularly given the resources that many states and districts are devoting to open-ended testing.

PLANS FOR FUTURE DATA COLLECTION AND ANALYSIS

During the second year of the Mosaic project, data were collected from one of the sites that participated during the first year and five additional sites. The data-collection design was essentially the same as that of the first year and will provide us with additional estimates of the relationships between teaching practices and student outcomes. At the site that was also used in year 1, the same grade level was used, so we will not be able to track students over time. However, results from this site will enable us to explore changes in teaching practices by individual teachers and to examine what happens to student achievement as schools and teachers are involved in the reform for longer periods of time.

We have also planned a longitudinal study using one of the sites that participated during year 2. At this site, we hope to follow students over three years, collecting data on the instructional practices used by their teachers during each year. This will enable us to conduct a multiyear "dose-response" study in which degree of exposure to the practices can be related to student growth in achievement over a longer period of time.

PARTICIPATION AT YEAR 1 SITES

SITE 1

Our sample at site 1 consists of fourth-grade students from 17 schools. Our original sample consisted of 20 schools, but two schools refused to participate, one nominated as highly involved and one nominated as a control. We also excluded a school where no third-grade teachers responded. This school was also nominated as highly involved in the reform. From the remaining 17 schools, we obtained survey responses from 46 of the 60 third-grade teachers we surveyed.

We linked 1,012 fourth-grade students to the responding teachers. For our analyses, we eliminated students who were missing scores on the fourth-grade test, as well as a handful who were missing data on other covariates. This left 804 students for our analyses.

SITE 2

Our site 2 sample contains students from 20 schools—10 schools nominated as highly engaged in the reform and 10 matched control schools. The site's systemic reform was implemented for both mathematics and science, and schools involved in one reform were expected to be involved in the other. Hence, we used the same schools to study the effects of both mathematics and science teaching practices.

We surveyed 115 fifth-grade teachers in these 20 schools. We asked every teacher about teaching practices for both mathematics and science and obtained responses for 100 mathematics and 99 science teachers.

There were 2,345 fifth graders in these 20 schools.[1] However, we could not accurately link 45 students from one school to their science teacher, because teachers at this school shared teaching responsibility in an informal manner that was not documented. We excluded these students and their teachers from our analyses. In addition, we excluded 444 students who did not complete the fifth-grade state multiple-choice tests. We also excluded 21 students for whom we had incomplete data on background characteristics. Of the remaining 1,835 students, 1,639 completed both of the hands-on science tasks and 1,662 completed the multiple-choice science test.

Our two outcome measures for mathematics achievement were the state's fifth-grade multiple-choice mathematics test and a RAND-administered open-ended mathematics test. Of the 2,345 students in our sample, we eliminated 45 students whose links to teachers could not be verified. We also excluded 444 students who did not complete fifth-grade state testing. An additional 19 students had incomplete data on background characteristics. Of the remaining 1,837 students, 1,651 completed the SAT-9 open-ended tests. We excluded 151 students who completed the state's multiple-choice mathematics test but received a score of zero, because they appear to be outliers in a number of respects (although including them has no substantial impact on results). Therefore, the sample for our analyses of the state's multiple-choice mathematics tests contains 1,681 students.

We imputed values for missing prior-year test-score data. For the mathematics multiple-choice sample, we imputed 210 prior-year mathematics and reading scores. For the open-ended mathematics sample, we imputed 202 prior-year mathematics and reading scores. For the hands-on science sample, we imputed 200 prior-year mathematics and reading scores. For the multiple-choice science sample, we imputed 203 prior-year mathematics and reading scores. We used hierarchical Bayesian models (Schafer, 1997) to impute mul-

---

[1] Fifth-grade classrooms are any classrooms that contain fifth-grade students. Because several schools in our site 2 sample use multigrade classes, some of our fifth-grade classrooms include fourth- or sixth-grade students as well as fifth graders. However, only fifth-grade students are included in our study.

tiple values for each missing value. The imputation models included all variables used in our regression models and contemporaneous reading and mathematics scores. The models also accounted for the hierarchical structure of the data for students nested within classrooms.

SITE 3

Our site 3 mathematics sample consists of students from 18 schools throughout the school district—10 schools nominated as highly engaged in the reform and eight matched control schools. Our original sample consisted of 20 schools, 11 nominated as highly engaged and nine matched controls. However, we obtained no teacher survey responses from two schools, so data from these schools were excluded from our analyses. Our science sample from site 3 consists of 20 schools from the district—10 nominated as highly engaged and 10 matched controls. Five schools are included in both the mathematics and science samples.

We obtained survey responses from 73 of the 87 mathematics teachers in our sample and 74 of the 85 science teachers. Only students whose teachers responded were included in our study.

There were 1,498 eligible fifth graders in our mathematics sample. We excluded students whose teacher did not complete a survey; students exempted from district testing because of LEP or special education status; and students not in fifth grade, even if they were in mixed grade-level classrooms. We included all students identified as LEP or special education but not exempted from district testing. We believe that if the district uses these students' scores to measure school outcomes, the scores are appropriate for measuring the effects of teaching practices. Of the 1,498 eligible students, 1,366 completed the open-ended mathematics test and 1,451 completed both the general mathematics and the computation subtests of the district's multiple-choice mathematics test. An additional 16 students completed only the general mathematics portion, and six students completed only the computation portion of the test.

We used identical criteria to create the science sample, leaving us with 1,652 eligible fifth graders. Of these 1,652 students, 1,438 were administered the multiple-choice science test and 1,367 were administered a hands-on science test.

We imputed values for missing prior-year test-score data. For the mathematics multiple-choice sample, we imputed 390 prior-year mathematics scores and 412 prior-year reading scores. For the open-ended mathematics sample, we imputed 380 prior-year mathematics scores and 401 prior-year reading scores. For the hands-on science sample, we imputed 334 prior-year mathematics scores and 353 prior-year reading scores. For the multiple-choice science sample, we imputed 346 prior-year mathematics scores and 366 prior-year reading scores. We used hierarchical Bayesian models (Schafer, 1997) to impute multiple values for each missing value. The imputation models included all variables used in our regression models and contemporaneous reading and mathematics scores. The models also accounted for the hierarchical structure of the data for students nested within classrooms.

SITE 4

Our original site 4 sample included 25 schools, 11 nominated as high implementing and 14 as controls. There were 74 eligible teachers teaching 1,566 eligible students in these 25 schools. Four schools in the original sample did not conduct science testing, and no teachers responded from an additional two schools in the sample. Thus, our final sample included 19 schools, 62 eligible teachers, and 1,314 eligible students. From this sample, a total of 49 teachers responded to our survey.

Only 45 of the 49 teachers who completed the survey also conducted science testing, and those teachers make up our final sample. This sample contains 1,012 students, of whom only 954 completed any science tests: 932 completed the multiple-choice test and 909 completed the hands-on tasks.

We imputed values for missing prior-year test-score data. For the multiple-choice sample, we imputed 41 prior-year mathematics and reading scores. For the hands-on science sample, we imputed 38 prior-year mathematics and reading scores. We used hierarchical Bayesian models (Schafer, 1997) to impute multiple values for each missing value. The imputation models included all variables used in our regression models and contemporaneous reading and mathematics scores. The models also accounted for the hierarchical structure of the data for students nested within classrooms.

SITE 5

At site 5, we started with a sample of 20 schools in which we evaluated mathematics instruction (10 nominated as engaged in the reform and 10 nominated as yet to be involved) and a separate sample of 20 schools (10 engaged and 10 yet to be involved) for science instruction. Two schools were in both the mathematics and science samples. Three schools refused to participate in our mathematics study, and one refused to be in our science study.

We obtained survey responses from 48 of the 49 mathematics teachers in our mathematics sample and 33 of the 46 science teachers in our science sample. Only students whose teachers responded were eligible for our study.

Our mathematics sample consisted of 3,199 students in the participating schools, 2,940 of whom completed the open-ended mathematics test and 3,028 of whom completed the state's multiple-choice mathematics test. Some students were not tested because of absence from school or because they are exempted from testing (e.g., some special education students). For our analyses of the open-response test scores, we excluded 48 students who received a score of zero on the open-ended test.[2] Hence, our final analysis samples included 2,937 students with open-ended mathematics test scores and 3,018 students with multiple-choice mathematics scores.

Our science sample included 2,436 students in the participating schools. We excluded two students who received a score of zero on the multiple-choice science test. Of the eligible students, 2,047 completed both of the hands-on science tasks and 2,079 completed the multiple-choice science test.

For the multiple-choice mathematics sample, we imputed free or reduced-price lunch status for 60 students, age for 26 students, and contemporaneous language test scores for 10 students. For the open-response mathematics sample, we imputed free or reduced-price lunch status for 136 students, age for 11 students, and contemporaneous language test scores for 95 students. For the multiple-

---

[2]Students who scored zero on the open-ended math test were outliers and influential in our results. However, we did not want our conclusions to be sensitive to a handful of unrepresentative students, so we excluded these students from our analysis.

choice science sample, we imputed free or reduced-price lunch status for 53 students, age for one student, and contemporaneous language test scores for 34 students. For the hands-on science sample, we imputed free or reduced-price lunch status for 54 students, age for 17 students, and contemporaneous language test scores for 36 students. For the science multiple-choice sample, we imputed free or reduced-price lunch status for 53 students, age for one student, and contemporaneous language test scores for 34 students. For the hands-on science sample, we imputed free or reduced-price lunch status for 54 students, age for 17 students, and contemporaneous language test scores for 36 students. We used hierarchical Bayesian models (Schafer, 1997) to impute multiple values for each missing value. The imputation models included all variables used in our regression models. The models also accounted for the hierarchical structure of the data for students nested within classrooms.

SITE 6

Our site 6 sample included all 25 middle schools in the district. Twelve schools had been involved in the Urban Systemic Initiative (USI) for one or more years, and 13 had not yet been involved. All 58 seventh-grade mathematics and 57 seventh-grade science teachers identified by the district completed surveys. However, only 57 of the responding mathematics teachers linked to seventh-grade students, and only 52 of the science teachers linked to students. The remaining respondents appeared to be incorrectly identified as seventh-grade teachers. The science sample included 3,812 students, and 3,279 of these had scores on the multiple-choice science test. The mathematics sample included 3,682 students, of whom 3,237 had scores on the multiple-choice mathematics test.

For the science sample, we imputed prior-year science test scores for 445 students. For the mathematics sample, we imputed prior-year mathematics test scores for 407 students. We used hierarchical Bayesian models (Schafer, 1997) to impute multiple values for each missing value. The imputation models included all variables used in our regression models. We also included sixth- and seventh-grade reading scores in the imputation models, and all models included both sixth- and seventh-grade science and mathematics scores. The models also accounted for the hierarchical structure of the data for students nested within classrooms.

ITEMS ON TEACHING-PRACTICES SCALES

The wording of items on the teaching-practices scales is identical across sites. The reform-practices score for mathematics is the sum of scores on the 22 items listed in Table B.1, and the traditional-practices score for mathematics is the sum of scores on the five items listed in Table B.2.

The reform-practices score for science is the sum of scores on the 22 items listed in Table B.3, and the traditional-practices score for science is the sum of scores on the five items listed in Table B.4.

Table B.1

Items on Reform-Practices Scale for Mathematics

About how often do you typically do each of the following in your *mathematics* instruction in this class?

Arrange seating to facilitate student discussion

Use open-ended questions

Require students to explain their reasoning when giving an answer

Encourage students to communicate mathematically

Encourage students to explore alternative methods for solutions

Allow students to work at their own pace

Read and comment on the reflections students have written in their notebooks or journals

About how often do students in this class typically take part in each of the following activities as part of their *mathematics* instruction?

Participate in student-led discussions

Work in cooperative learning groups

Make formal presentations to the class

Work on solving a real-world problem

Share ideas or solve problems with each other in small groups

Engage in hands-on mathematical activities

Design or implement their *own* investigations

Work on extended mathematics investigations (a week or more in duration)

Participate in fieldwork

Record, represent, and/or analyze data

Write a description of a plan, procedure, or problem-solving process

Write reflections in a notebook or journal

Work on portfolios

Take tests requiring open-ended responses (e.g., descriptions, justifications of solutions)

Engage in performance tasks for assessment purposes

Table B.2

Items on Traditional-Practices Scale for Mathematics

About how often do you typically do each of the following in your *mathematics* instruction in this class?

Lecture/introduce content through formal presentations

About how often do students in this class typically take part in each of the following activities as part of their *mathematics* instruction?

Read from a mathematics textbook in class

Practice computational skills

Memorize mathematics facts, rules, or formulas

Take short-answer tests (e.g., multiple-choice, true/false, fill-in-the-blank)

Table B.3

Items on Reform-Practices Scale for Science

About how often do you typically do each of the following in your *science* instruction in this class?

Arrange seating to facilitate student discussion

Use open-ended questions

Require students to supply evidence to support their claims

Encourage students to explain concepts to one another

Encourage students to consider alternative explanations

Allow students to work at their own pace

Read and comment on the reflections students have written in their notebooks or journals

About how often do students in this class typically take part in each of the following activities as part of their *science* instruction?

Participate in student-led discussions

Work in cooperative learning groups

Make formal presentations to the class

Work on solving a real-world problem

Share ideas or solve problems with each other in small groups

Engage in hands-on science activities

Design or implement their *own* investigations

Design objects within constraints (e.g., egg drop, toothpick bridge, aluminum boats)

Work on extended science investigations or projects (a week or more in duration)

Participate in fieldwork

Record, represent, and/or analyze data

Write reflections in a notebook or journal

Work on portfolios

Take tests requiring open-ended responses (e.g., descriptions, justifications of solutions)

Engage in performance tasks for assessment purposes

Table B.4

Items on Traditional-Practices Scale for Science

About how often do you typically do each of the following in your *science* instruction in this class?

Lecture/introduce content through formal presentations

About how often do students in this class typically take part in each of the following activities as part of their *science* instruction?

Read from a science textbook in class

Answer textbook/worksheet questions

Learn science vocabulary

Take short-answer tests (e.g., multiple-choice, true/false, fill-in-the-blank)

FULL REGRESSION MODELS

FULL REGRESSION MODELS FOR SITE 1

Table C.1

Site 1 Regression Models for Mathematics Tests (Grade 4)

State Open-Response Mathematics Test, N = 804

Predictor Variable	Coefficient	T-statistic[c]	p-value
Model Including Reform-Practices Scale			
Intercept	0.289	3.130	0.002
Free or reduced-price lunches	−0.189	−2.856	0.004
African-American[a]	−0.140	−1.770	0.077
Hispanic	−0.252	−2.345	0.019
Other race	−0.144	−1.267	0.205
Female	−0.023	−0.339	0.735
Reading score	0.487	12.927	0.000
Reform scale[b]	−0.010	−0.261	0.794
Model Including Traditional-Practices Scale			
Intercept	0.294	3.266	0.001
Free or reduced-price lunches	−0.192	−2.957	0.003
African-American[a]	−0.141	−1.806	0.071
Hispanic	−0.252	−2.378	0.017
Other race	−0.144	−1.268	0.205
Female	−0.022	−0.332	0.740
Reading score	0.486	12.832	0.000
Traditional scale[b]	−0.006	−0.156	0.876

[a]Reference group for ethnicity is white, non-Hispanic.

[b]Standardized to mean = 0, standard deviation = 1.

[c]T-statistics are adjusted for clustering (McCaffrey and Bell, 1997).

Table C.1 (continued)

State Grid-In Mathematics Test, N = 804

Predictor Variable	Coefficient	T-statistic[c]	p-value
Model Including Reform-Practices Scale			
Intercept	0.328	4.863	0.000
Free or reduced-price lunches	−0.159	−1.914	0.056
African-American[a]	−0.253	−3.730	0.000
Hispanic	−0.152	−1.423	0.155
Other race	−0.090	−0.834	0.404
Female	−0.071	−1.098	0.272
Reading score	0.516	16.964	0.000
Reform scale[b]	0.050	1.941	0.052
Model Including Traditional-Practices Scale			
Intercept	0.324	4.749	0.000
Free or reduced-price lunches	−0.157	−1.872	0.061
African-American[a]	−0.252	−3.726	0.000
Hispanic	−0.166	−1.521	0.128
Other race	−0.093	−0.870	0.385
Female	−0.072	−1.113	0.266
Reading score	0.514	16.832	0.000
Traditional scale[b]	−0.040	−1.792	0.073

State Multiple-Choice Mathematics Test, N = 804

Predictor Variable	Coefficient	T-statistic[c]	p-value
Model Including Reform-Practices Scale			
Intercept	0.462	8.821	0.000
Free or reduced-price lunches	−0.206	−3.387	0.001
African-American[a]	−0.264	−3.709	0.000
Hispanic	−0.160	−1.986	0.047
Other race	−0.218	−1.852	0.064
Female	−0.224	−4.099	0.000
Reading score	0.631	19.294	0.000
Reform scale[b]	0.031	0.870	0.385
Model Including Traditional-Practices Scale			
Intercept	0.463	9.206	0.000
Free or reduced-price lunches	−0.207	−3.303	0.001
African-American[a]	−0.265	−3.864	0.000
Hispanic	−0.172	−2.053	0.040
Other race	−0.221	−1.872	0.061
Female	−0.224	−4.129	0.000
Reading score	0.628	19.014	0.000
Traditional scale[b]	−0.037	−1.223	0.221

[a]Reference group for ethnicity is white, non-Hispanic.

[b]Standardized to mean = 0, standard deviation = 1.

[c]T-statistics are adjusted for clustering (McCaffrey and Bell, 1997).

FULL REGRESSION MODELS FOR SITE 2

Table C.2

Site 2 Regression Models for Science and Mathematics Tests (Grade 5)

RAND Hands-On Science Tasks, N = 1,639

Predictor Variable	Coefficient	T-statistic[d]	p-value
Model Including Reform-Practices Scale			
Intercept	0.183	2.361	0.018
Free or reduced-price lunches	−0.195	−3.818	0.000
LEP	0.025	0.380	0.704
Special education	−0.422	−4.975	0.000
Gifted	0.373	6.108	0.000
Minority[a]	−0.081	−1.143	0.253
Female	0.099	2.217	0.027
Grade 4 state MC math[b]	0.279	9.231	0.000
Grade 4 state MC reading[b]	0.291	10.207	0.000
Reform scale[c]	0.094	3.511	0.000
Model Including Traditional-Practices Scale			
Intercept	0.195	2.561	0.010
Free or reduced-price lunches	−0.198	−3.712	0.000
LEP	0.009	0.125	0.900
Special education	−0.409	−4.925	0.000
Gifted	0.376	5.984	0.000
Minority[a]	−0.098	−1.335	0.182
Female	0.101	2.247	0.025
Grade 4 state MC math[b]	0.276	9.165	0.000
Grade 4 state MC reading[b]	0.291	10.345	0.000
Traditional scale[c]	0.035	1.192	0.233

[a]Includes all students not identified as white, non-Hispanic.
[b]NCE standardized to mean = 0, standard deviation = 1.
[c]Standardized to mean = 0, standard deviation = 1.
[d]T-statistics are adjusted for clustering (McCaffrey and Bell, 1997).

Table C.2 (continued)

Stanford 9 Multiple-Choice Science Test, N = 1,662

Predictor Variable	Coefficient	T-statistic[d]	p-value
Model Including Reform-Practices Scale			
Intercept	0.392	5.499	0.000
Free or reduced-price lunches	-0.107	-1.914	0.056
LEP	-0.029	-0.467	0.641
Special education	-0.550	-4.752	0.000
Gifted	0.309	5.480	0.000
Minority[a]	-0.208	-2.813	0.005
Female	-0.188	-4.018	0.000
Grade 4 state MC math[b]	0.161	4.936	0.000
Grade 4 state MC reading[b]	0.325	11.103	0.000
Reform scale[c]	0.054	2.043	0.041
Model Including Traditional-Practices Scale			
Intercept	0.394	5.411	0.000
Free or reduced-price lunches	-0.106	-1.819	0.069
LEP	-0.044	-0.694	0.488
Special education	-0.550	-4.753	0.000
Gifted	0.306	5.526	0.000
Minority[a]	-0.214	-2.793	0.005
Female	-0.187	-3.976	0.000
Grade 4 state MC math[b]	0.159	4.994	0.000
Grade 4 state MC reading[b]	0.326	11.398	0.000
Traditional scale[c]	0.041	1.522	0.128

Stanford 9 Open-Response Mathematics Test, N = 1,651

Predictor Variable	Coefficient	T-statistic[d]	p-value
Model Including Reform-Practices Scale			
Intercept	0.180	1.705	0.088
Free or reduced-price lunches	-0.078	-1.587	0.113
LEP	-0.036	-0.459	0.646
Special education	-0.385	-3.996	0.000
Gifted	0.426	6.960	0.000
Minority[a]	-0.074	-0.810	0.418
Female	-0.103	-2.334	0.020
Grade 4 state MC math[b]	0.302	7.540	0.000
Grade 4 state MC reading[b]	0.146	3.995	0.000
Reform scale[c]	0.052	1.244	0.214
Model Including Traditional-Practices Scale			
Intercept	0.181	1.779	0.075
Free or reduced-price lunches	-0.081	-1.702	0.089
LEP	-0.035	-0.469	0.639
Special education	-0.391	-4.158	0.000
Gifted	0.425	7.149	0.000
Minority[a]	-0.074	-0.811	0.417
Female	-0.103	-2.340	0.019
Grade 4 state MC math[b]	0.304	7.667	0.000
Grade 4 state MC reading[b]	0.141	3.828	0.000
Traditional scale[c]	0.000	-0.012	0.991

[a]Includes all students not identified as white, non-Hispanic.
[b]NCE standardized to mean = 0, standard deviation = 1.
[c]Standardized to mean = 0, standard deviation = 1.
[d]T-statistics are adjusted for clustering (McCaffrey and Bell, 1997).

Table C.2 (continued)

State Multiple-Choice Mathematics Test, N = 1,686

Predictor Variable	Coefficient	T-statistic[d]	p-value
Model Including Reform-Practices Scale			
Intercept	0.028	0.303	0.762
Free or reduced-price lunches	0.008	0.147	0.883
LEP	0.075	0.956	0.339
Special education	−0.527	−4.199	0.000
Gifted	0.170	3.156	0.002
Minority[a]	−0.030	−0.478	0.633
Female	0.026	0.652	0.514
Grade 4 state MC math[b]	0.543	13.136	0.000
Grade 4 state MC reading[b]	0.116	3.679	0.000
Reform scale[c]	0.023	0.618	0.536
Model Including Traditional-Practices Scale			
Intercept	0.037	0.432	0.666
Free or reduced-price lunches	−0.001	−0.009	0.993
LEP	0.045	0.603	0.546
Special education	−0.514	−4.197	0.000
Gifted	0.157	2.867	0.004
Minority[a]	−0.021	−0.354	0.723
Female	0.028	0.700	0.484
Grade 4 state MC math[b]	0.539	13.157	0.000
Grade 4 state MC reading[b]	0.119	3.701	0.000
Traditional scale[c]	0.088	2.195	0.028

[a]Includes all students not identified as white, non-Hispanic.
[b]NCE standardized to mean = 0, standard deviation = 1.
[c]Standardized to mean = 0, standard deviation = 1.
[d]T-statistics are adjusted for clustering (McCaffrey and Bell, 1997).

FULL REGRESSION MODELS FOR SITE 3

Table C.3

Site 3 Regression Models for Science and Mathematics Tests (Grade 5)

CSIAC Hands-On Science Test, N = 1,367

Predictor Variable	Coefficient	T-statistic[c]	p-value
Model Including Reform-Practices Scale			
Intercept	0.139	1.797	0.072
Free or reduced-price lunches	−0.106	−1.305	0.192
English proficiency 1	0.062	0.289	0.774
English proficiency 2	0.041	0.492	0.623
Special education	−0.146	−1.435	0.151
African-American[a]	−0.074	−0.865	0.387
Hispanic	−0.155	−2.818	0.005
Asian	0.028	0.237	0.813
Female	0.205	4.376	0.000
Grade 4 math	0.172	4.232	0.000
Grade 4 reading	0.352	7.731	0.000
Missing grade 4 scores	−0.160	−2.104	0.035
Reform scale[b]	0.079	1.281	0.200
Model Including Traditional-Practices Scale			
Intercept	0.140	1.737	0.082
Free or reduced-price lunches	−0.113	−1.319	0.187
English proficiency 1	0.069	0.320	0.751
English proficiency 2	0.043	0.519	0.604
Special education	−0.136	−1.350	0.177
African-American[a]	−0.065	−0.736	0.462
Hispanic	−0.145	−2.650	0.008
Asian	0.028	0.242	0.808
Female	0.209	4.394	0.000
Grade 4 math	0.175	4.273	0.000
Grade 4 reading	0.358	7.684	0.000
Missing grade 4 scores	−0.153	−2.014	0.044
Traditional scale[b]	0.075	1.328	0.184

[a]Reference group for ethnicity is white, non-Hispanic.
[b]Standardized to mean = 0, standard deviation = 1.
[c]T-statistics are adjusted for clustering (McCaffrey and Bell, 1997).

Table C.3 (continued)
CSIAC Multiple-Choice Science Test, N = 1,438

Predictor Variable	Coefficient	T-statistic[c]	p-value
Model Including Reform-Practices Scale			
Intercept	0.473	8.291	0.000
Free or reduced-price lunches	−0.190	−3.388	0.001
English proficiency 1	−0.199	−0.855	0.405
English proficiency 2	−0.057	−0.804	0.421
Special education	0.022	0.336	0.737
African-American[a]	−0.248	−3.336	0.001
Hispanic	−0.193	−3.549	0.000
Asian	−0.239	−2.756	0.006
Female	−0.078	−1.714	0.087
Grade 4 math	0.135	3.813	0.000
Grade 4 reading	0.521	16.222	0.000
Missing grade 4 scores	−0.128	−2.389	0.017
Reform scale[b]	0.049	1.951	0.051
Model Including Traditional-Practices Scale			
Intercept	0.480	8.247	0.000
Free or reduced-price lunches	−0.202	−3.568	0.000
English proficiency 1	−0.192	−0.821	0.423
English proficiency 2	−0.057	−0.806	0.420
Special education	0.024	0.377	0.706
African-American[a]	−0.242	−3.286	0.001
Hispanic	−0.193	−3.470	0.001
Asian	−0.241	−2.746	0.006
Female	−0.078	−1.709	0.088
Grade 4 math	0.136	3.806	0.000
Grade 4 reading	0.526	16.461	0.000
Missing grade 4 scores	−0.124	−2.321	0.021
Traditional scale[b]	0.007	0.280	0.779

[a]Reference group for ethnicity is white, non-Hispanic.

[b]Standardized to mean = 0, standard deviation = 1.

[c]T-statistics are adjusted for clustering (McCaffrey and Bell, 1997).

Table C.3 (continued)

Stanford 9 Open-Response Mathematics Test, N = 1,366

Predictor Variable	Coefficient	T-statistic[c]	p-value
Model Including Reform-Practices Scale			
Intercept	0.356	3.454	0.001
Free or reduced-price lunches	−0.106	−1.171	0.242
English proficiency 1	0.005	0.037	0.970
English proficiency 2	0.134	2.121	0.034
Special education	−0.204	−2.510	0.012
African-American[a]	−0.331	−4.526	0.000
Hispanic	−0.183	−2.915	0.004
Asian	0.026	0.262	0.794
Female	−0.168	−3.407	0.001
Grade 4 math	0.277	5.531	0.000
Grade 4 reading	0.275	6.424	0.000
Missing grade 4 scores	−0.137	−2.296	0.022
Reform scale[b]	0.092	2.055	0.040
Model Including Traditional-Practices Scale			
Intercept	0.374	3.606	0.000
Free or reduced-price lunches	−0.125	−1.386	0.166
English proficiency 1	0.010	0.070	0.944
English proficiency 2	0.135	2.104	0.035
Special education	−0.219	−2.683	0.008
African-American[a]	−0.336	−4.328	0.000
Hispanic	−0.192	−2.914	0.004
Asian	0.043	0.412	0.680
Female	−0.175	−3.560	0.000
Grade 4 math	0.281	5.183	0.000
Grade 4 reading	0.287	6.619	0.000
Missing grade 4 scores	−0.157	−2.489	0.013
Traditional scale[b]	−0.091	−1.760	0.078

[a]Reference group for ethnicity is white, non-Hispanic.

[b]Standardized to mean = 0, standard deviation = 1.

[c]T-statistics are adjusted for clustering (McCaffrey and Bell, 1997).

Table C.3 (continued)

CTBS Multiple-Choice Mathematics Test, N = 1,451

Predictor Variable	Coefficient	T-statistic[c]	p-value
Model Including Reform-Practices Scale			
Intercept	0.360	4.491	0.000
Free or reduced-price lunches	−0.176	−2.436	0.015
English proficiency 1	−0.036	−0.240	0.812
English proficiency 2	0.102	1.850	0.064
Special education	−0.228	−3.149	0.002
African-American[a]	−0.080	−1.323	0.186
Hispanic	−0.120	−2.318	0.021
Asian	0.044	0.532	0.595
Female	−0.089	−2.059	0.040
Grade 4 math	0.365	9.004	0.000
Grade 4 reading	0.380	13.073	0.000
Missing grade 4 scores	−0.132	−2.377	0.018
Reform scale[b]	0.044	1.047	0.295
Model Including Traditional-Practices Scale			
Intercept	0.366	4.798	0.000
Free or reduced-price lunches	−0.182	−2.464	0.014
English proficiency 1	−0.037	−0.252	0.803
English proficiency 2	0.102	1.868	0.062
Special education	−0.233	−3.195	0.002
African-American[a]	−0.080	−1.288	0.198
Hispanic	−0.121	−2.245	0.025
Asian	0.055	0.640	0.522
Female	−0.093	−2.219	0.027
Grade 4 math	0.368	8.828	0.000
Grade 4 reading	0.386	13.142	0.000
Missing grade 4 scores	−0.143	−2.487	0.014
Traditional scale[b]	−0.050	−1.460	0.144

[a]Reference group for ethnicity is white, non-Hispanic.
[b]Standardized to mean = 0, standard deviation = 1.
[c]T-statistics are adjusted for clustering (McCaffrey and Bell, 1997).

FULL REGRESSION MODELS FOR SITE 4

Table C.4

Site 4 Regression Models for Science Tests (Grade 5)

CSIAC Hands-On Science Test, N = 909

Predictor Variable	Coefficient	T-statistic[c]	p-value
Model Including Reform-Practices Scale			
Intercept	0.196	2.150	0.032
Free or reduced-price lunches	−0.087	−0.819	0.413
English proficiency 1	−0.401	−2.659	0.008
English proficiency 2	0.438	2.496	0.013
Gifted	0.205	3.044	0.002
Special education	−0.001	−0.011	0.991
African-American[a]	−0.872	−6.630	0.000
Chinese	−0.035	−0.400	0.689
Filipino	−0.316	−1.829	0.067
Hispanic	−0.099	−0.794	0.427
Japanese	−0.084	−0.443	0.658
Korean	0.169	1.085	0.278
Other race/ethnicity	−0.187	−1.529	0.126
Female	0.066	1.016	0.309
Grade 4 math	0.149	1.709	0.088
Grade 4 reading	0.183	1.988	0.047
Reform scale[b]	0.046	0.698	0.485
Model Including Traditional-Practices Scale			
Intercept	0.195	2.102	0.036
Free or reduced-price lunches	−0.080	−0.761	0.446
English proficiency 1	−0.400	−2.610	0.009
English proficiency 2	0.452	2.595	0.009
Gifted	0.203	2.979	0.003
Special education	−0.009	−0.070	0.944
African-American[a]	−0.857	−6.296	0.000
Chinese	−0.028	−0.309	0.757
Filipino	−0.298	−1.694	0.090
Hispanic	−0.100	−0.810	0.418
Japanese	−0.049	−0.260	0.795
Korean	0.182	1.155	0.248
Other race/ethnicity	−0.172	−1.357	0.175
Female	0.064	1.013	0.311
Grade 4 math	0.149	1.728	0.084
Grade 4 reading	0.182	2.008	0.045
Traditional scale[b]	−0.008	−0.138	0.891

[a]Reference group for ethnicity is white, non-Hispanic.
[b]Standardized to mean = 0, standard deviation = 1.
[c]T-statistics are adjusted for clustering (McCaffrey and Bell, 1997).

Table C.4 (continued)

CSIAC Multiple-Choice Science Test, N = 932

Predictor Variable	Coefficient	T-statistic[c]	p-value
Model Including Reform-Practices Scale			
Intercept	0.219	2.793	0.005
Free or reduced-price lunches	−0.155	−2.519	0.012
English proficiency 1	−0.483	−5.645	0.000
English proficiency 2	0.216	1.247	0.212
Gifted	0.347	5.633	0.000
Special education	0.214	1.898	0.058
African-American[a]	−0.661	−7.437	0.000
Chinese	0.002	0.024	0.981
Filipino	−0.244	−2.193	0.028
Hispanic	−0.037	−0.368	0.713
Japanese	0.010	0.049	0.961
Korean	0.317	3.232	0.001
Other race/ethnicity	−0.110	−1.607	0.108
Female	−0.232	−5.162	0.000
Grade 4 math	0.114	2.050	0.041
Grade 4 reading	0.407	8.041	0.000
Reform scale[b]	−0.003	−0.094	0.925
Model Including Traditional-Practices Scale			
Intercept	0.144	1.817	0.069
Free or reduced-price lunches	−0.156	−2.771	0.006
English proficiency 1	−0.479	−5.387	0.000
English proficiency 2	0.241	1.349	0.177
Gifted	0.338	5.343	0.000
Special education	0.217	1.892	0.059
African-American[a]	−0.682	−7.143	0.000
Chinese	0.006	0.097	0.923
Filipino	−0.244	−2.090	0.037
Hispanic	−0.056	−0.532	0.595
Japanese	0.049	0.193	0.847
Korean	0.312	3.078	0.002
Other race/ethnicity	−0.108	−1.540	0.123
Female	−0.218	−4.610	0.000
Grade 4 math	0.120	2.202	0.028
Grade 4 reading	0.397	7.962	0.000
Traditional scale[b]: linear	−0.052	−1.171	0.242
Traditional scale[b]: quadratic	0.077	1.985	0.047

[a]Reference group for ethnicity is white, non-Hispanic.
[b]Standardized to mean = 0, standard deviation = 1.
[c]T-statistics are adjusted for clustering (McCaffrey and Bell, 1997).

FULL REGRESSION MODELS FOR SITE 5

Table C.5
Site 5 Regression Models for Science and Mathematics Tests (Grade 7)

RAND Hands-On Science Tasks, N = 2,047

Predictor Variable	Coefficient	T-statistic[c]	p-value
Model Including Reform-Practices Scale			
Intercept	1.338	2.721	0.007
Free or reduced-price lunches	−0.180	3.505	0.000
Age	−0.088	2.285	0.022
Minority[a]	−0.549	5.666	0.000
Female	0.038	0.995	0.320
Grade 7 language	0.392	24.769	0.000
Special education	−0.040	0.309	0.757
Reform scale[b]	0.001	0.015	0.988
Model Including Traditional-Practices Scale			
Intercept	1.321	3.264	0.001
Free or reduced-price lunches	−0.122	2.485	0.013
Age	−0.092	2.877	0.004
Minority[a]	−0.529	7.820	0.000
Female	−0.024	0.731	0.464
Grade 7 language	0.390	24.221	0.000
Special education	−0.038	0.333	0.739
Traditional scale[b]	−0.166	3.966	0.000

Stanford 9 Multiple-Choice Science Test, N = 2,079

Predictor Variable	Coefficient	T-statistic[c]	p-value
Model Including Reform-Practices Scale			
Intercept	0.733	1.285	0.199
Free or reduced-price lunches	−0.135	2.987	0.003
Age	−0.032	0.737	0.461
Minority[a]	−0.518	4.088	0.000
Female	−0.176	3.358	0.001
Grade 7 language	0.526	24.101	0.000
Special education	−0.240	2.144	0.032
Reform scale[b]	0.030	0.377	0.707
Model Including Traditional-Practices Scale			
Intercept	0.688	1.154	0.249
Free or reduced-price lunches	−0.114	2.483	0.013
Age	−0.031	0.674	0.501
Minority[a]	−0.510	4.246	0.000
Female	−0.179	3.393	0.001
Grade 7 language	0.527	22.569	0.000
Special education	−0.216	1.896	0.058
Traditional scale[b]	−0.080	1.622	0.105

[a]Includes all students not identified as white, non-Hispanic.
[b]Standardized to mean = 0, standard deviation = 1.
[c]T-statistics are adjusted for clustering (McCaffrey and Bell, 1997).

Table C.5 (continued)

Stanford 9 Open-Response Mathematics Tests, N=2,937

Predictor Variable	Coefficient	T-statistic[c]	p-value
Model Including Reform-Practices Scale			
Intercept	1.902	5.984	0.000
Free or reduced-price lunches	−0.056	1.712	0.087
Age	−0.130	5.233	0.000
Minority[a]	−0.365	9.719	0.000
Female	−0.128	4.610	0.000
Grade 7 language	0.361	15.145	0.000
Special education	−0.004	0.030	0.976
Reform scale[b]	0.080	2.691	0.007
Model Including Traditional-Practices Scale			
Intercept	1.977	5.868	0.000
Free or reduced-price lunches	−0.064	2.010	0.044
Age	−0.136	5.075	0.000
Minority[a]	−0.377	10.226	0.000
Female	−0.130	4.655	0.000
Grade 7 language	0.364	15.216	0.000
Special education	−0.028	0.190	0.849
Traditional scale[b]	−0.028	0.943	0.346

State Multiple-Choice Mathematics Tests, N=3,018

Predictor Variable	Coefficient	T-statistic[c]	p-value
Model Including Reform-Practices Scale			
Intercept	1.230	3.214	0.001
Free or reduced-price lunches	−0.047	1.654	0.098
Age	−0.084	3.030	0.002
Minority[a]	−0.106	3.036	0.002
Female	−0.165	6.975	0.000
Grade 7 language	0.674	28.019	0.000
Special education	0.176	2.068	0.039
Reform scale[b]	−0.052	0.897	0.369
Model Including Traditional-Practices Scale			
Intercept	1.173	3.085	0.002
Free or reduced-price lunches	−0.045	1.634	0.102
Age	−0.079	2.913	0.004
Minority[a]	−0.102	2.833	0.005
Female	−0.164	7.086	0.000
Grade 7 language	0.673	28.193	0.000
Special education	0.193	2.205	0.027
Traditional scale[b]	0.037	0.660	0.510

[a]Includes all students not identified as white, non-Hispanic.
[b]Standardized to mean = 0, standard deviation = 1.
[c]T-statistics are adjusted for clustering (McCaffrey and Bell, 1997).

FULL REGRESSION MODELS FOR SITE 6

Table C.6

Site 6 Regression Models for Science and Mathematics Tests (Grade 7)

MAT-7 Multiple-Choice Science Test, N=3,279

Predictor Variable	Coefficient	T-statistic[d]	p-value
Model Including Reform-Practices Scale			
Intercept	0.146	3.472	0.001
Free or reduced-price lunches	−0.188	−5.729	0.000
Minority[a]	−0.062	−1.948	0.051
Female	−0.053	−1.758	0.079
Grade 6 science[b]	0.620	26.376	0.000
Reform scale[c]	0.051	2.750	0.006
Model Including Traditional-Practices Scale			
Intercept	0.149	3.351	0.001
Free or reduced-price lunches	−0.198	−6.071	0.000
Minority[a]	−0.051	−1.620	0.105
Female	−0.053	−1.775	0.076
Grade 6 science[b]	0.624	26.640	0.000
Traditional scale[c]	−0.004	−0.149	0.881

MAT-7 Multiple-Choice Mathematics Test, N=3,237

Predictor Variable	Coefficient	T-statistic[d]	p-value
Model Including Reform-Practices Scale			
Intercept	0.097	1.867	0.062
Free or reduced-price lunches	−0.076	−1.917	0.055
Minority[a]	−0.048	−1.185	0.236
Female	−0.031	−1.308	0.191
Grade 6 math[b]	0.755	24.564	0.000
Missing grade 6 math	−0.148	−3.598	0.000
Reform scale[c]	0.046	1.589	0.112
Model Including Traditional-Practices Scale			
Intercept	0.105	1.963	0.050
Free or reduced-price lunches	−0.071	−1.695	0.090
Minority[a]	−0.058	−1.389	0.165
Female	−0.033	−1.393	0.164
Grade 6 math[b]	0.752	23.682	0.000
Missing grade 6 math	−0.154	−3.724	0.000
Traditional scale[c]	−0.004	−0.096	0.923

[a]Includes all students not identified as white, non-Hispanic.
[b]Scale score standardized to mean = 0, standard deviation = 1.
[c]Standardized to mean = 0, standard deviation = 1.
[d]T-statistics are adjusted for clustering (McCaffrey and Bell, 1997).

DETAILS OF POOLED ANALYSIS OF
REGRESSION COEFFICIENTS

We used the following model to obtain our pooled estimates and to determine whether sites were comparable and pooled analyses appropriate. For a given subject, test type, and scale, we assumed that our sample is a random sample of all possible sites and that

$$b_i = \beta + \eta_i + \varepsilon_i ,$$

where b_i denotes the estimated coefficient from the ith site, β denotes the average coefficient across all sites, η_i denotes the deviation of site i from the average, and ε_i denotes sampling error in our estimate b_i as an estimate of $\beta + \eta_i$. The deviations, η_i, are assumed to be normally distributed with mean zero and variance τ^2. The errors, ε_i, are assumed to be normally distributed with mean zero and variance σ_i^2. Error variability differs from site to site depending on the distribution of teacher responses and other covariates, and depending on the residual variance from the regression model fit for each site.

We used the square of the standard error estimates from the individual site analyses as our estimates of the σ_i^2 parameters. Treating these estimates as fixed, we then estimated τ^2 using restricted maximum likelihood (Searle, Cassella, and McCullogh, 1992). This method also provides a confidence interval for our estimate of τ^2. We then estimated the average coefficient, β, as a weighted average of the b_is, where the weight for the ith site is

$$w_i = \frac{1}{\hat{\tau}^2 + \hat{\sigma}_i^2} \bigg/ \sum \frac{1}{\hat{\tau}^2 + \hat{\sigma}_j^2}$$

The weighted averages, their standard errors, and lower and upper 95 percent confidence bounds are provided in Table D.1. Estimates and confidence intervals of τ^2 are also given for each set of pooled analyses.

Table D.1

Results from Pooled Analyses of Relationships Between
Practices and Achievement

Subject	Test Format	Scale	Weighted Average Coefficient	Standard Error	CI for Coefficient	τ^2	CI for τ^2
Math	OR	Reform	0.053	0.023	(0.008, 0.098)	0.001	(0.000, 0.017)
Math	MC	Reform	0.030	0.017	(−0.003, 0.063)	0.000	(0.000, 0.004)
Science	OR	Reform	0.079	0.022	(0.036, 0.122)	0.000	(0.000, 0.015)
Science	MC	Reform	0.045	0.012	(0.022, 0.069)	0.000	(0.000, 0.003)
Math	OR	Trad.	−0.025	0.019	(−0.061, 0.012)	0.000	(0.000, 0.009)
Math	MC	Trad.	0.001	0.026	(−0.049, 0.052)	0.002	(0.000, 0.018)
Science	OR	Trad.	−0.018	0.054	(−0.123, 0.088)	0.009	(0.001, 0.098)
Science	MC	Trad.	0.006	0.015	(−0.023, 0.034)	0.000	(0.000, 0.013)

RESULTS FROM ANALYSIS OF FORMAT DIFFERENCES

Table E.1

Standardized Coefficients for Models Predicting Differences Between Formats

Site	Subject	Scale	Beta	T-statistic	p-value
1	Math	Reform	−0.041	−1.364	0.179
1	Math	Traditional	0.032	0.906	0.370
2	Math	Reform	0.032	0.664	0.507
2	Math	Traditional	−0.098	−1.862	0.063
2	Science	Reform	0.036	1.291	0.197
2	Science	Traditional	−0.005	−0.174	0.862
3	Math	Reform	0.051	1.266	0.205
3	Math	Traditional	−0.028	−0.599	0.549
3	Science	Reform	0.045	0.646	0.518
3	Science	Traditional	0.071	1.107	0.268
4	Science	Reform	0.048	0.805	0.421
4	Science	Traditional	(a)	(a)	(a)
5	Math	Reform	0.132	2.683	0.010
5	Math	Traditional	−0.060	−1.008	0.319
5	Science	Reform	−0.030	−0.457	0.651
5	Science	Traditional	−0.102	−2.385	0.023

[a]No estimate is available; model for scores and the traditional scale is not linear.

Table E.2

Results from Pooled Analyses of Differences Between Formats

Subject	Scale	Weighted Average	Standard Error	CI Lower Bound	CI Upper Bound	τ^2	CI for τ^2
Math	Reform	0.037	0.037	−0.035	0.109	0.004	(0.000, 0.044)
Science	Reform	0.031	0.022	−0.013	0.075	0.000	(0.000, 0.011)
Math	Trad.	−0.028	0.031	−0.088	0.032	0.002	(0.000, 0.028)
Science	Trad.	−0.019	0.046	−0.109	0.070	0.004	(0.000, 0.119)

SENSITIVITY ANALYSES: USE OF CONTEMPORANEOUS TEST SCORES

The results presented in this report use contemporaneous reading and language scores as covariates in the models for student outcomes at sites 2 and 5 because prior-year test scores were unavailable for these sites. Both prior-year scores and contemporaneous scores serve as measures of student achievement. However, unlike prior-year scores, contemporaneous test scores are not necessarily independent of the teaching practices measured by the survey. If reform teaching in mathematics or science involves activities that promote the use of verbal skills, it is conceivable that students' reading or language scores will be higher when their teachers use greater amounts of reform teaching practices. Including contemporaneous scores in the model might absorb some of the effect of reform (or traditional) practices and could lead to under- or over-estimation of the relationship between teaching practices and scores in science or mathematics.

On the other hand, models that exclude contemporaneous scores are probably liberal in the sense that the spurious correlation between student background characteristics that are not included in the model and teacher practices is attributed to the effect of teaching practices. Lacking good independent measures of students' achievement, we chose to present the possibly conservative models that include contemporaneous scores. However, when we use models without contemporaneous scores for sites 1 and 5, the pooled results are similar to the estimates presented in the text, although the estimates without contemporaneous scores tend to be larger (in absolute value). Without contemporaneous scores for sites 1 and 5, we still estimate a small positive relationship between the reform-practices scale and the mathematics and science multiple-choice and open-response test scores. These estimates are statistically significant except those for multiple-choice mathematics scores.

The results for the traditional scale are similar. For both science multiple-choice and science open-response scores, the pooled results for models without contemporaneous scores are of the same sign and same magnitude as the results from models that include contemporaneous scores. For mathematics, the pooled results for the traditional scale are somewhat different when we exclude the contemporaneous scores. Without contemporaneous scores, the pooled estimate for open-response scores is -0.045 and is statistically significant. With contemporaneous scores, the pooled estimate is -0.025 and is not statistically significant. For both site 1 and site 5, controlling for contemporaneous scores attenuates the negative relationship between the traditional scale and the open-response mathematics scores, although the attenuation is greater for site 1. Similarly, controlling for contemporaneous scores attenuates the negative relationship between the traditional scale and the multiple-choice mathematics scores for sites 1 and 5. The result is that the pooled analysis with estimates from models that include contemporaneous scores yields a very small positive relationship, while the pooled analysis with estimates from models that exclude contemporaneous scores yields a small negative estimate. Neither estimate is statistically significant, and we might conclude that the difference primarily reflects the very weak relationship between the traditional scale and the multiple-choice mathematics scores.

We are uncertain about how the two sets of estimates would compare with estimates that use prior-year scores. Using scores from sites 2, 3, 4, and 6, we found that models with contemporaneous scores often result in attenuated relationships between scores and teaching-practices scales (16 out of 23 models) when compared with models that include prior-year scores. We also found that for these sites, models that include neither prior-year nor contemporaneous scores tend to exaggerate the relationship between the reform scale and the test scores when compared with models that include prior-year scores. However, models that include neither prior-year nor contemporaneous scores tend to attenuate the relationship between the traditional scale and the test scores when compared with models that include prior-year scores. The difference between traditional and reform scales is due in part to the fact that at some sites, students of teachers who report greater use of traditional practices are somewhat more likely to have lower prior-year scores. Similarly, at some sites, students whose teachers report greater use of reform practices tend to have higher prior-year test scores, although this is less common and the relationship is weaker than the relationship between traditional practices and lower prior-year scores.

Figure F.1 summarizes the results of using prior-year, contemporaneous, or no test scores in our models for mathematics and science for sites 2, 3, 4, and 6. The x-axis is the absolute value of the estimated coefficients from the models that include prior-year test scores. These scores are also plotted as the solid line. The empty squares denote the absolute values for the coefficients for the reform scale in models that do not control for student achievement. The solid squares denote the absolute values for the coefficients for the reform scale in models that use contemporaneous test scores to control for achievement. The empty and solid circles denote the

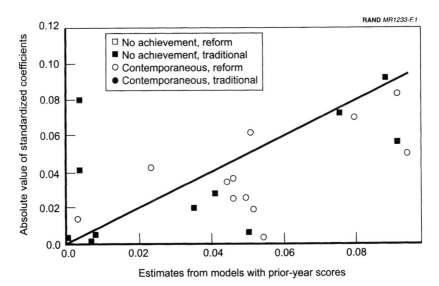

Figure F.1—Estimated Coefficients for Mathematics and Science Tests, Sites 2, 3, 4, and 6: Models Include Prior-Year, Contemporaneous, or No Test Scores

analogous estimates for the traditional scale. Points above the solid line indicate that the estimate was exaggerated compared with the estimate from a model that included prior-year scores. Points below the line indicate that the estimate was attenuated toward zero compared with the estimate from a model that contained the prior-year scores. For example, nine of the 12 empty circles are below the line, indicating that for nine of the 12 models that include the reform scale, including the contemporaneous tests scores attenuates the estimated coefficient for reform compared with including prior-year scores.

SENSITIVITY ANALYSES: COMBINING REFORM AND TRADITIONAL SCALES IN A SINGLE MODEL

Our analyses involved fitting separate models for the reform and traditional scales to estimate the full "effect" of either the reform or the traditional scale. The coefficient for the reform scale estimates the change in the average test score associated with a one-standard-deviation unit increase in the scale, adjusted for differences in student backgrounds. No adjustment is made to account for differences in the use of traditional practices when traditional and reform practices are correlated. In this case, any "effect" due to changes in the traditional scale is attributed to changes in the reform scale. Similarly, the estimated coefficient for the traditional scale is not adjusted for differences in the reform scale. We feel that estimation of the full effect is most interesting because reform practices might encompass both using teaching techniques that are advocated by the reform *and* using fewer traditional practices, or the reform might encompass simply using more of the techniques advocated by the reform. We wanted our estimates to reflect either approach to reform.

Alternatively, we could have included both the reform and traditional scales in our model and estimated the relationship between the reform (traditional) scale and scores, conditional on the level of use of traditional (reform) practices. As discussed above, for most sites the reform and traditional scales are weakly correlated, so including both scales in the same models yields estimates that are very similar to the estimates from fitting separate models. Figure G.1 compares the two sets of estimated coefficients. The standardized coefficients from the separate models are plotted on the x-axis and the solid line. The standardized coefficients from models that include both the tradi-

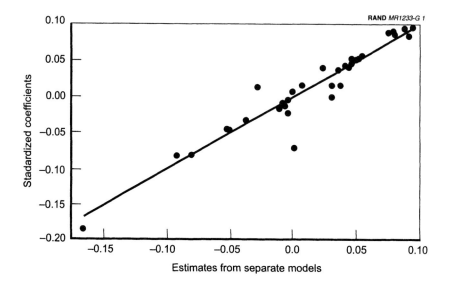

Figure G.1—Estimated Coefficients for Mathematics and Science Tests

tional and reform scales are plotted as the solid circles. The circles closely follow the line, indicating that the estimates from the separate models are very similar to estimates from models that include both the reform scale and the traditional scale. The correlation is 0.958. Only one point deviates from the line: (0.001, –0.070), the estimates for the reform scale and the open-response science test scores for site 5. For this site, the weak positive relationship that we estimate in the model without the traditional scale changes to a moderate negative effect after we control for the traditional scale. The relationship between the traditional scale and the open-response science scores is large and negative for site 5. In addition, teachers who score higher on the reform scale tend to score lower on the traditional scale. Hence, in the model that includes both the traditional and the reform scales, the estimate for the reform scale turns from slightly positive to negative. However, overall, our analyses are not greatly affected by fitting separate models or fitting models that include both scales, although the pooled estimates for the relationship between open-response science scores and the reform scale are somewhat smaller and no longer statistically significant. Figures G.2 through G.9 and Table G.1 provide a summary and pooled results from models that include both scales.

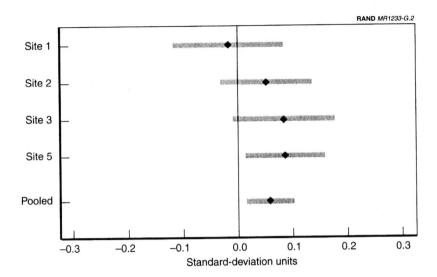

Figure G.2—Estimated Coefficients by Site and Pooled Across Sites for Mathematics: Reform Practices, Open-Ended Tests

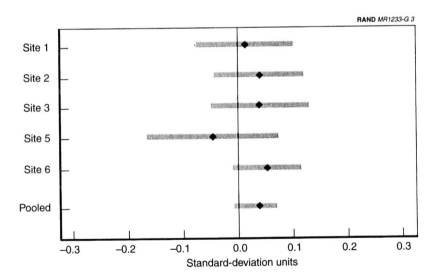

Figure G.3—Estimated Coefficients by Site and Pooled Across Sites for Mathematics: Reform Practices, Multiple-Choice Tests

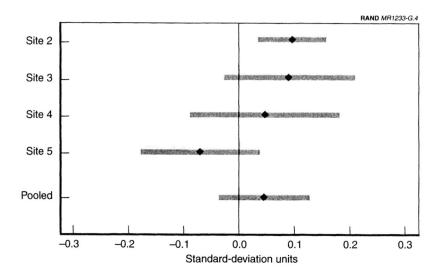

Figure G.4—Estimated Coefficients by Site and Pooled Across Sites for Science: Reform Practices, Open-Ended Tests

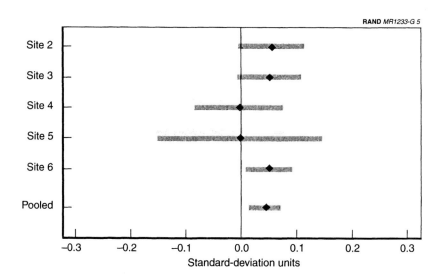

Figure G.5—Estimated Coefficients by Site and Pooled Across Sites for Science: Reform Practices, Multiple-Choice Tests

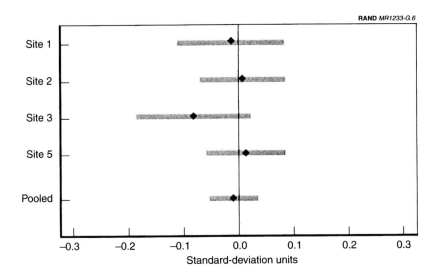

Figure G.6—Estimated Coefficients by Site and Pooled Across Sites for
Mathematics: Traditional Practices, Open-Ended Tests

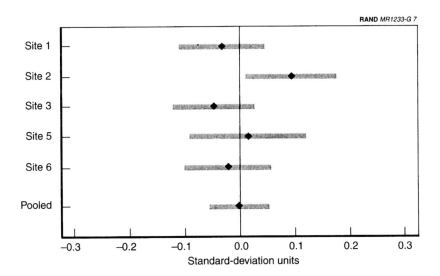

Figure G.7—Estimated Coefficients by Site and Pooled Across Sites for
Mathematics: Traditional Practices, Multiple-Choice Tests

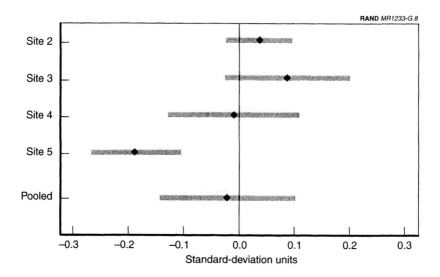

**Figure G.8—Estimated Coefficients by Site and Pooled Across Sites for
Science: Traditional Practices, Open-Ended Tests**

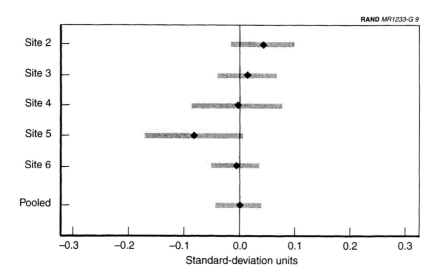

**Figure G.9—Estimated Coefficients by Site and Pooled Across Sites for
Science: Traditional Practices, Multiple-Choice Tests**

Table G.1

Results from Pooled Analyses of Relationships Between Practices and Achievement

Subject	Test Format	Scale	Weighted Average	Standard Error	CI Lower Bound	CI Upper Bound	τ^2	CI for τ^2
Math	OR	Reform	0.059	0.021	0.018	0.099	0.000	(0.000, 0.015)
Math	MC	Reform	0.033	0.018	−0.002	0.068	0.000	(0.000, 0.005)
Science	OR	Reform	0.045	0.040	−0.033	0.123	0.004	(0.000, 0.051)
Science	MC	Reform	0.045	0.013	0.019	0.070	0.000	(0.000, 0.003)
Math	OR	Trad.	−0.009	0.021	−0.049	0.032	0.000	(0.000, 0.012)
Math	MC	Trad.	0.000	0.026	−0.051	0.051	0.002	(0.000, 0.018)
Science	OR	Trad.	−0.020	0.060	−0.138	0.099	0.012	(0.002, 0.123)
Science	MC	Trad.	0.001	0.019	−0.036	0.039	0.001	(0.000, 0.018)

American Association for the Advancement of Science (1993). *Benchmarks for science literacy: Project 2061.* New York: Oxford University Press.

Bond, L. A., Braskamp, D., and van der Ploeg, A. (1996). *State student assessment programs data base.* Oak Brook, IL: North Central Regional Educational Laboratory.

Cohen, D. K., and Ball, D. L. (1990). Relations between policy and practice: A commentary. *Educational Evaluation and Policy Analysis, 12,* 331–338.

Cohen, D. K., and Hill, H. C. (1998). *State policy and classroom performance: Mathematics reform in California* (CPRE Policy Brief). Philadelphia: Consortium for Policy Research in Education.

Consortium for Policy Research in Education (1995a). *Reforming science, mathematics, and technology education: NSF's State Systemic Initiatives* (CPRE Policy Brief). New Brunswick, NJ: Author.

Consortium for Policy Research in Education (1995b). *Tracking student achievement in science and math: The promise of state assessment programs* (CPRE Policy Brief). New Brunswick, NJ: Author.

Corcoran, T. B., Shields, P. M., and Zucker, A. A. (1998). Evaluation of the National Science Foundation's Statewide Systemic Initiatives (SSI) Program: The SSI's and professional development for teachers. Menlo Park: SRI International.

Fantuzzo, J. W., King, J. A., and Heller, L. R. (1992). Effects of reciprocal peer tutoring on mathematics and school adjustment: A component analysis. *Journal of Educational Psychology, 84,* 331–339.

Fox, J. (1998). NSF programs attacked as weak, unclear. *Education Daily,* July 24, 1–2.

Ginsburg-Block, M. D., and Fantuzzo, J. W. (1998). An evaluation of the relative effectiveness of NCTM standards-based interventions for low-achieving urban elementary students. *Journal of Educational Psychology, 90,* 560–569.

Goldstein, H. (1995). Multilevel statistical models, second edition. London: Arnold.

Greenwood, C. R., Carta, J. J., and Hall, R. V. (1988). The use of peer tutoring strategies in classroom management and educational instruction. *School Psychology Review, 17,* 258–275.

Hill, P. T. (1994). *Reinventing public education* (MR-312-LE/GGF). Santa Monica, CA: RAND.

Knapp, M. S. (1997). Between systemic reforms and the mathematics and science classroom: The dynamics of innovation, implementation, and professional learning. *Review of Educational Research, 67,* 227–266.

Koretz, D., and Barron, S. I. (1998). *The validity of gains in scores on the Kentucky Instructional Results Information System (KIRIS)* (MR-1014-EDU). Santa Monica, CA: RAND.

Koretz, D., Linn, R. L., Dunbar, S. B., and Shepard, L. A. (1991). The effects of high-stakes testing: Preliminary evidence about generalization across tests, in R. L. Linn (chair), *The effects of high stakes testing,* symposium presented at the annual meetings of the American Educational Research Association and the National Council on Measurement in Education, Chicago.

Laguarda, K. G. (1998). *Assessing the SSIs' impacts on student achievement: An imperfect science.* Menlo Park, CA: SRI International.

Mayer, D. P. (1998). Do new teaching standards undermine performance on old tests? *Educational Evaluation and Policy Analysis, 20,* 53–73.

McCaffrey, D., and Bell, R. (1997). "Bias reduction in standard error estimates for regression analyses from multi-stage designs with few primary sampling units." Paper presented at the Joint Statistical Meetings, Anaheim CA.

National Council of Teachers of Mathematics (1989). *Curriculum and evaluation standards for school mathematics.* Reston, VA: Author.

National Research Council (1996). *National science education standards.* Washington, DC: National Academy Press.

New Jersey SSI Proposal (1992). *Achieving excellence in mathematics, science and technology education. Statewide systemic initiative: New Jersey proposal to the National Science Foundation.*

Schafer, J. L. (1997). *Imputation of missing covariates under a general linear mixed model.* Technical report available at http://www.stat.psu.edu/~jls/.

Searle, S. R., Cassella, G., and McCullogh, C. E. (1992). *Variance components.* New York: John Wiley and Sons, Inc.

Shields, P. M., Corcoran, T. B., and Zucker, A. A. (1994). *Evaluation of NSF's Statewide Systemic Initiatives (SSI) program: First-year report.* Menlo Park, CA: SRI International.

Shields, P. M., Marsh, J. A., and Adelman, N. E. (1998). *Evaluation of the National Science Foundation's Statewide Systemic Initiatives (SSI) Program: The SSI's impacts on classroom practice.* Menlo Park: SRI International.

Smith, M., and O'Day, J. (1991). Systemic school reform. In S. H. Fuhrman and B. Malen (Eds.), *The politics of curriculum and testing* (pp. 233–268). Bristol, PA: The Falmer Press.

Stecher, B. M., and Klein, S. P. (Eds.) (1996). *Performance assessments in science: Hands-on tasks and scoring guides* (MR-660-NSF). Santa Monica, CA: RAND.

Tyack, D., and Cuban, L. (1995). *Tinkering toward utopia.* Cambridge, MA: Harvard University Press.

Verschaffel, L., and De Corte, E. (1997). Teaching realistic mathematical modeling in the elementary school: A teaching experiment with fifth-graders. *Journal for Research in Mathematics Education, 28,* 577–601.

Webb, N. M., and Palincsar, A. S. (1996). Group processes in the classroom. In D. C. Berliner and R. C. Calfee (Eds.), *Handbook of educational psychology* (pp. 841–873). New York: Macmillan.

Weiss, I. R., Montgomery, D. L., Ridgway, C. J., and Bond, S. L. (1998). *Local Systemic Change through teacher enhancement: Year three cross-site report.* Chapel Hill, NC: Horizon Research, Inc.

Williams, L. (1998). *The Urban Systemic Initiatives (USI) program of the National Science Foundation: Summary update.* Washington, DC: NSF.